Blood Sweat

&

Tiaras

Dare To Dream!

[signature]

Blood Sweat & Tiaras

Adrienne Rosel Bulinski

William V. Anderson

be known

2016

Contact Adrienne

To book Adrienne for corporate events,
school assemblies, or conferences:

ab@adriennebulinski.com
adriennebulinski.com

Edited with William V. Anderson
Photography by Chris McLaughlin (www.cmpdenver.com)
Photo location courtesy of Ralston Valley High School
Formatting and cover design by Adrienne Rosel Bulinski

First Printing: 2016

ISBN-10: 0-9978990-0-X
ISBN-13: 978-0-9978990-0-9
B

Library of Congress Control Number: 2016914355

Published by Be Known LLC
Arvada, CO, 80007
U.S.A.

Special discounts are available on quantity purchases by corporations, associations,
educators, and others. For details, contact the publisher at ab@adriennebulinski.com

U.S. trade bookstores and wholesalers: please contact Be Known LLC at
ab@adriennebulinski.com

To my parents who have never left my side. Thank you for being my legs when mine were out of commission and my sounding board as I navigated some of the darkest times in my life.

I love you.

Acknowledgements

To my wonderful husband, Mr. Salsa. Thank you for providing the opportunity and encouragement to sit down and make this book happen. We are definitely "in it together". I love you *so much.* I am proud to share the Bulinski name with such an amazing man.

To my mentor and dear friend Bill Anderson. Without your encouragement this book would still be in my head and heart. Now it's on paper and in a book. Thank you! Thank you for being such an incredible friend to me and your constant encouragement, *"Just right, now just write."*

To Dr. Rev. Bradley Stoltenow who helped me understand my situation and spent hours counseling me through one of my greatest challenges. I cherish our friendship and your spiritual guidance.

To my team of seven readers: Mom, Dad, Michelle, Eric, Dr. S, "P", and Danita. Thank you for graciously offering to read the manuscript version of this book. I have applied your edits throughout! It should make for an interesting second read!

To all my doctors: Thank you! Dr. Bjork, it is because of you I have a foot. Dr. Nelson, it is because of you I learned there is always "more than one way to skin a cat". Dr. Carlisle, because of you I overcame infection and kept my foot! Dr. Conklin, it is because of you I walk without pain.

To my brothers and sisters (in laws too!). I'm proud to be your "bright and colorful" sibling. I love you and appreciate your support throughout the years. I took notice when you came to all the dance recitals, musicals, and pageants (especially when you had a lot better things to do other than sit in the audience).

To the reader. I wrote this for you. For with *hope* there is always a path to a solution.

Forward

I do not remember the exact day I first met Adrienne. I do remember the exact moment we became lifelong friends. After you read this book, I hope you recognize the value of such people in your own lives.

It was a labor of love for Adrienne to write this book for you. I know she wants you to not only hear her story, but to tell your own as well. It is through each other we continue to grow and understand our own place in this world. Maybe, through her trials and tribulations you can see your own growth and successes. Maybe you will even see how your failures (we all have them) shaped you to be a more resilient person today.

Many of the stories you are about to read will make you laugh, but some will make you cry. That's okay. Sometime during this book you may even wonder about this young woman. She had so many successes early in her life, how could she have possibly had any failures? Through her successes, you will be able to better understand some of the setbacks she endured. You will understand, through her own words, how she never gave up. I saw her at the lowest possible point in her life. Angry. Frustrated. Determined. At times, I could hardly tell the difference between those three emotions with Adrienne. They blended together into a Texas Panhandle whirlwind of action. She persevered through it all and you will be amazed at what she accomplished.

You are going to meet some truly amazing people in these next few pages. Many of these people helped mold Adrienne into the wonderful person she is today. Along the way, she has touched the lives of many from around the world. I can say, first hand, she always tries to find the good in everybody. I can also say, first hand, that some of the people she (and I) had to deal with presented a great challenge to the previous statement, but Adrienne never lost her faith in her fellow human being. Yes, sometimes she had to turn the other cheek.

Many times in our lives we miss opportunities. We do not realize what is given to us. I will pat myself on the back for not missing the chance to know Adrienne. In some ways, I hardly had the chance to make that decision one fateful afternoon you will soon read about. Since that Sunday in 2007, the two of us have worked very hard to keep our friendship and creative spirit between us alive and nurtured. I remember being very frustrated with her a number of years ago. I wanted her to write part of this story. She would not. I didn't understand why, but she had her reasons. So she challenged me to write it myself. It should be noted she was working for me at the time and I signed her paycheck. That is Adrienne Rosel Bulinski. I wrote the article. I like to think that short piece allowed her to write this book.

This book will give you a glimpse of how one person chose to live her life. I truly believe if you will apply some of her thoughts and ideas to your own situation, it will change your life. In an upcoming chapter, Adrienne will challenge you to take five minutes each day to change your life. I will make that challenge to you as well by asking you to take just five minutes to read the first few pages and follow that up with another five minutes. It can, *and will*, change you for the better.

Happy reading.

Sincerely,
William V. Anderson

Author's Note

A communications coach once taught me: as a speaker all you can offer is your story. It is up to the individual to apply the story to his or her own life situations to make a positive difference.

Many of the names of the characters you are about to meet have been changed to protect the not-so-innocent.

There are always two sides to every story, *this is my side...*

Act I

Scene One

Palo Duro Canyon State Park, Pioneer Amphitheatre, Texas, July 2007
(Thirteen days *before* the accident)

"Make each day your masterpiece." *–Coach John Wooden*

I stood at the back of the stage waiting for my entrance. The only thing separating me from the audience was a row of trees. I could hear the audience laughing at one of the characters on stage, but from where I stood I could not see the crowd nor could they see me. I could feel their presence sensing their attitude toward the show. There was a light-heartedness in their laughter that comes from the leisure of a Saturday night versus the stress of a work week. It was a good crowd which meant I could breathe easy.

Just like a child has moods so does a live audience. It would vary from night to night, but I suppose that was one of the many reasons I loved live theatre.

The Pioneer Amphitheatre was the only theatre in the world I knew of that was so grand and yet so natural. It was majestic. The rocks had years of history carved into them from the wind, rain, and occasional snow. Like any canyon, you could see how a river had cut through the rocks grinding it away year after year, grit by tiny grit.

I glanced out across the canyon floor and over at the 600 foot canyon wall that was our natural back drop. What the audience didn't know and couldn't see was the 600 foot detonator cord that ran from the top of the canyon to a lone tree. Right before intermission the stage manager would fire the cord and it would explode, causing it to look and sound like a lightning strike that struck the tree. The tree would catch fire and then split in half causing a dramatic Texas-sized prelude to intermission.

That majesty was my playground. I was playing a character from the 1800s. When I heard my cue from stage I would enter and meet my "stage love" for the first time. By the end of Act One we would fall in love in the midst of a Texas lightning storm that was reproduced by our designers. The act would end with a kiss and that infamous lightning bolt.

I heard my cue. I snapped open my white lace parasol and placed the cane of the umbrella over my left shoulder. I gracefully floated out and onto the stage gently kicking up the hem of my custom-made long green dress that was a replica of the 1800s high-end fashion.

I walked up to Calvin, the character I was starring opposite, and began our first on-stage conversation. I felt all 1,492 sets of eyes studying me, my look, and making a first impression on my acting ability. I stood a little taller, which wasn't because of my cinched corset, it was because I knew I was a great actress. I knew my role well. I had put in the years of rehearsals and hard work. The performance was the payoff.

As I joined Calvin on stage I batted my eyes at the character and the man. He paced from my right to my left, obviously flirting with me but acting as though he wasn't. I twirled my parasol returning the tease.

Our first scene together was quick, but it established our characters and our quirky 1800s love affair in its infancy. We said our good-byes at the end of the scene and I exited the stage heading straight for the dressing room. I had a limited amount of time to change from one costume to the next.

Within a few scenes I would be waltzing center stage in the grand "party scene". Calvin and I would try to kiss for the first time, but predictably we would be interrupted.

I was fulfilling a contract for fifty-seven shows, and a fun contract at that. Every night I got to meet a handsome man, fall in love, make-out on stage (and get paid for it), get married, and live happily ever after. Even if only on stage it was every girl's dream come true.

Scene Two

Texas Panhandle, Sunday, 6 p.m., August 12, 2007, 95 degrees, a pasture, a horse, three women
(The day of the accident)

"It is impossible to live without failing at something unless you live so cautiously that you might as well not have lived at all – in which case you fail by default." –J.K. Rowling

"I think I'm done. I'm getting tired," I said to my two friends who stood in the field encouraging my acrobatics. It was my last day off from the musical. While I was having fun, I didn't want my body to be too fatigued for my final week of performances.

I had been in the Texas heat for an hour learning how to mount and dismount a horse bareback. Scout was a beautiful black quarter horse with a tail so long it brushed the ground. He stood good-naturedly in the pasture as I charged him, like I had charged the bar when high-jumping in high school track. I would run, jump, grab his mane, and pull myself up onto his back. With my athleticism it was quite easy. Scout's laziness made the three of us – Shelly, Paula, and me - think he was the perfect horse to learn my equestrian skills. Scout cared more about being next to the barn than he did about going for a ride which meant no one was concerned about standing next to him to calm his nerves. We all assumed he would stand still. So there he stood while I, the crazy human, jumped onto his swayback and then back off so I could do it again.

"Give it one last try," Shelly encouraged from about thirty feet away, while Paula sat on the metal corral fence taking pictures.

Earlier that day Shelly and I had been watching celebrities on TV learn how to ride bucking bulls while eating cherry pie and potato chips.

5

We were gorging ourselves on sweet and salty being two typical girls spending their last few days together before I packed up my belongings and said my good-byes. I had five more performances of the musical "Texas" before I was scheduled to return to New York.

I would only be in New York for three months before I reported to Florida for my next contract as a triple threat (singer, dancer, actor) aboard a cruise ship. Destination: the Mediterranean. I had auditioned for that particular contract six months prior to the actual offer. So when I got the call it was out of the blue and I was ecstatic. A performance gig on a cruise was a dream-come-true as one of my goals was to work my way around the world on a ship. I wanted to see the seven continents and the best way I knew how was to utilize my skills and talents in order to make it happen.

The cruise line had originally asked me to start a contract on August 3rd, but I told them I wanted to honor my "Texas" contract. The production staff was very understanding and simply moved me to a different ship with a different contract and a different start date.

Shelly and I weren't sure when our paths would cross again so we were enjoying each other, junk food, and junk TV. A sort of last hurrah.

On the TV show, professional cowboys were teaching celebrities how to dismount a bareback horse before they transitioned those celebrities to bucking bulls. I was impressed. Shelly, a seasoned cowgirl, said it wasn't that difficult and offered to show me how to do it. The only horse we had access to that afternoon was Scout.

"Besides," Shelly said, "when you get your first movie contract that includes horses they won't have to hire a double for you because you know how to ride, and ride well."

I had never considered all the movies with horses in them, but as we started going through a laundry list of cinema I was convinced when we got to Jennifer Lopez riding a horse in *The Wedding Planner*. I asked Shelly to teach me how to become a better rider, and it was then or never because it was my last Sunday in the Lone Star State.

"Okay," I said to my friends as I stood in the field preparing to jump on Scout one last time. "Kevin Costner is going to be impressed when I show up on a movie set and can ride my own horse. Bareback no less," I laughed. "Here I go," I was tired, but I was also not one to quit until I hit pure exhaustion. "This is the last time," I reminded them, more a reminder to myself.

6

Without much thought I looked at Scout, charged him, jumped, grabbed his mane, and I tried to pull myself up on the horse's back. I had done the same thing at least a dozen times that late-afternoon and Scout had patiently stood still, not moving. But that time, the last time, something went wrong, terribly wrong.

Scene Three

Liberal, Kansas. Saturday, September 17, 1994, sunset, a fishing pond and a
neighborhood block party
(Thirteen years *before* the accident)

"Be yourself. Everyone else is already taken." –Oscar Wilde

"I got one," I yelled at the top of my eleven-year-old lungs to anyone and everyone within earshot, including the neighbors across the pond. They cheered as I lifted my home-made contraption over my head. I stuck my chest out and smiled with the same pride an athlete has when displaying a coveted trophy overhead. I lowered my minnow-catcher from the sky so I could take a closer look at my one-inch captive. I smiled. "You're a keeper," I told him in a whisper as I didn't want to damage his ear drums with my powerful voice.

I turned and walked through the weeds, which were as tall as my waist, and made my way over to the dock where I could deposit my *catch-of-the-day* into the big blue plastic bin. The bin was specifically designated for prizes reeled in throughout the evening. It was full of water and had one lonely catfish in it, a fish my brother had caught earlier that day. *Mr. Whiskers* was swimming short laps around his tiny new home. He was obviously lonely, but not for long.

I took my minnow-catcher and tipped it upside down. I smiled as I watched the water and the minnow dump into the blue tub with a *cur-plunk*. My new captive swam in circles next to his new bin-mate and I turned to run back to my new lucky spot.

I was staying with my Aunt Janny and Uncle Wes - my favorite place to stay when my parents were out of town. My aunt and uncle lived near a pond, had paddle boats, fishing poles, a huntin' dog, and a trampoline. Most importantly they were carefree which meant they let me run wild. It was a tomboy's heaven-on-earth.

On that particular evening I had been walking up and down the pond's shoreline for hours dipping my minnow-catcher in and out of the water trying my dangdist to catch a coveted, slimy minnow. Why? Because that is what you do on a Saturday evening in southwest Kansas.

I had made my minnow-catcher contraption myself. It was constructed out of a wire hanger and a red Solo cup. I had stuck the wire through the cup and *v-wa-la* I had a minnow-catcher.

I bobbed my cup up and down in the water once again. I had wanted to catch my new minnow a friend as I didn't want him to be lonely. Yes, he had *Mr. Whiskers*, but there was room for another tiny minnow. I would come up with names for my minnows later, but first I wanted to catch my little *Mr.* a little *Miss.*

There was a neighborhood block party commencing in my aunt and uncle's backyard. The party took place most weekends. But that was the norm. There was always plenty of food, good laughs, and a flow of cold beverages. It was a great gathering place for fishing, BBQ, mosquitoes, and good 'ol small town fun. Everyone smelled like bug spray *and* smoke from the chimenea that was roaring with a fire. It was the picture perfect small town summer setting. That party, however, was particularly important as it would end with everyone gathered around the basement TV for *the big event.*

"Adrienne, its 7:40," my aunt hollered from the deck. She knew I didn't want to miss a moment of the broadcast.

I jumped off the dock and tossed my minnow-catcher in the yard. I ran up to the house, through the living room, and into the kitchen. There was an array of beautifully displayed food spread throughout the kitchen. I grabbed a plate followed by a bun and the most-burnt looking hotdog I could find in the batch. I squirted my dog with ketchup before I grabbed the large ladle in the crock pot and scooped baked beans onto my plate.

When my plate looked satisfactory, I skipped out of the kitchen, through the living room, and opened the back door to holler at everyone scattered through the yard, on the dock, and on the deck, "Its getting ready to start!" I yelled in my excited high-pitched girly voice. I dismissed the fact my aunt had already made the announcement.

I slammed the door and the pictures on the wall bounced. I hustled back through the living room and over to the basement door. I was careful not to brush against the floral sofa or designer leopard-print pillows as I passed through the "no-no" room that looked like a picture straight from *Better Homes And Gardens* magazine. I skipped down the carpeted stairs managing to keep all my food on my plate even in my hurried excitement.

The basement had been renovated into an entertainment room and would serve as the gathering spot for the "big event". There was a newly built wrap-around bar on one side of the basement and a circular shaped sofa on the other side. The sofa could easily hold fifteen people and there were already ten people scattered across the cushions.

On the far wall was a fireplace and three feet away was a big screen TV that took up a large footprint in the overall layout. I took my place on the floor in front of the TV. I sat crossed legged on the carpet directly in front of the screen. I was as close as I could get without my eyeballs going cross eyed.

Laughter, excitement, and the aroma of BBQ filled the room. The ten people who sat behind me were engrossed in their dogs, burgers, and conversations. Everyone was excitedly talking about how *she* would fare on the national stage.

My stomach growled from my long day of outdoor play and the delicious smell that filled the room. I took an oversized bite of my hot dog and dripped ketchup all over my lap. *Oops* I thought as I scooped up the red goo with my fingers and stuck my fingers in my mouth. I could smell the scent of fish on my hands, but it didn't bother me in the slightest. I licked my fingers making sure I didn't miss any of my favorite condiment.

My parents were in Atlantic City and it was possible we might see them on TV. Our local girl, Trisha Schaffer, was Miss Kansas and she was competing for the Miss America crown at Boardwalk Hall. My dad and Trisha's dad were good friends, which is why my parents were at the Miss America Competition.

Mr. Schaffer had been cutting my dad's hair for years. In a small town that meant they were tight. Mr. Schaffer knew most of Liberal, Kansas. So along with Trisha's parents and my parents, many of our community members were in Atlantic City cheering for Trisha while the rest of us were at home glued to our TV sets.

Trisha's chances of winning the Miss America crown were better than great. Mom and Dad had already called home reporting her successes. She had received the Preliminary Talent Award and the buzz was around Miss Kansas and how well she would finish.

Trisha was beautiful, talented, and one of the kindest soul's I had met in my eleven years. Although that didn't mean she knew who I was. The few times I had seen her I was star struck.

But the pageant didn't come without controversy and it wasn't even Donald Trump's Miss USA pageant. The Miss America controversy of the year was revolving around the infamous swimsuit competition. *Surprise, surprise!* That year the girls had to look like they were *really* going to the beach/pool, which meant they had to kick off their four inch heels and walk barefoot across the stage. As an eleven-year-old I completely agreed with the new protocol. I never went to the pool in high heels, and when I saw Trisha at the pool I never saw her in heels either – she would be fine, I had seen the proof.

"They should wear flip flops," I remember telling my mom when she informed me about the controversy. At my age, swimsuits and stilettos were as silly as fishing and make-up. I wasn't sure how going barefoot canceled out the pageant hair, massive amounts of make-up, and glitzy jewelry, but that was the controversy and it was what it was.

How a rambunctious little tomboy loved pageants surprised most of my family, but I never missed the Miss America broadcast.

I had spent most of my childhood running around barefoot, scabs on my knees, and challenging boys my age to wrestling matches. My challenge went something like this, "I bet I can throw you on the ground before you can throw me on the ground." Yes, sometimes I ended up in tears, but only when the boys would gang up on me. I'm proud to report I was often a top pick when it came to dividing into teams for a neighborhood game of "war".

In the midst of my rambunctiousness my dad would often tell me, "If you don't start wearing pants you will never be Miss America." At that time in my life I didn't really care. I knew I would be Miss America if I wanted to be Miss America, scabs on my knees and all. I wouldn't need a pair of heels to make it happen either.

I think my parents were hopeful pageants would encourage a feminine side of their tomboy daughter which would counter balance my daring personality. They enrolled me in a few pageants when I was in elementary school. I loved getting all dolled up and acting like a lady on stage. Little did I know I would become obsessed with beautiful heels and would one day grow a collection larger than a closet could hold.

As the broadcast began our group of basement dwellers cheered. The girls went through their introductions during the opening number and then they transitioned into their lineup that scattered them across the stage. The rest of the neighbors were piling into the basement for the announcement of the top ten. Regis and Kathy Lee would do the honors.

"The 1994 semi-finalists are," there was a pause, "Trisha Schaffer, Miss Kansas."

We cheered along with the crowd on TV. Trisha was the first one called and she took her spot on the stage. I was ecstatic. Some of the neighbors high-fived behind me.

Kathy Lee quickly finished announcing the top ten and the competition was set to begin. They cut away to a commercial while the girls changed into their swimsuits *without shoes*.

The competition unfolded and Trisha rocked the stage even barefoot, as I expected. But none of us were surprised.

At one point the camera cut away to the crowd and zoomed in on the Kansas section of cheerleaders – and there were my parents cheering along with the rest of us.

Trisha didn't win the crown that year, Heather Whitestone did. Both women, nonetheless, made a lasting impact on the goals I set for myself that evening sitting in my aunt and uncle's basement covered in dried ketchup, mosquito spray, and an overwhelming perfume of fish.

Scene Four

Liberal, Kansas. High school senior enrollment, August 2000
(Seven years *before* the accident)

"If you really want to do something you will find a way. If you don't, you'll find an excuse." –Jim Rohn

It was a hot August day in Southwest Kansas and unless you were up with the sun you would melt in the furnace blast. My alarm had gone off at 5:50 a.m. and I stumbled through my normal morning routine of sleepwalking to the bathroom followed by brushing my teeth and giving myself a pep talk in the mirror. Once I had dressed it was a mad-dash to the track for 6:30 a.m. cheerleading practice. I was a cheerleader because my small town didn't have a dance team. It was odd for a girl who stood at 5'9" (barefoot) to be a cheerleader, but half the cheerleading squad also made up the competitive dance team at my local dance studio. We didn't think twice about our dancers who were posing as cheerleaders. After practice and run-throughs of our dance routines several of us would hustle over to the weight room for off-season basketball and track training. In a small Kansas town teenagers are involved in everything or there isn't a team. Besides, I loved my cross training and so did everyone else. It's what kept *all* the sports fun.

I was still in my work-out gear when I walked through the front glass doors of the high school. I was headed inside for my senior enrollment. School was scheduled to start ten days later.

When I stepped inside I immediately felt the hair on my legs grow a quarter of an inch. The air conditioner was working at full blast and it felt like it was a chilly 65 degrees inside the building, while temperatures outside were soaring at 98 degrees - and it was only 11 a.m.

I immediately saw a flood of faces I hadn't seen in three months. We made our pleasantries as we stepped in the enrollment line together. As we wound our way through the lines we traded summer stories to pass the time. We were signing up for yearbooks, getting our new locker assignments and class schedules, and buying lunch passes. It was a typical school enrollment. Not much had changed in the 12 years I had been going through the process.

As I came to my last stop there was a lady behind a table I didn't recognize. I had everything I needed for the year so I wasn't sure what she wanted. She had her eye on me and I could tell she was going to make a sales pitch.

"Hi. Are you interested in competing for Miss Liberal, a preliminary to the Miss Kansas Pageant?" Lu Haynes, the executive director to the Miss Liberal Pageant, asked with a smile.

"No," I responded rather shortly and quickly.

"You would be perfect," Lu encouraged.

I looked at the dates for the competition. She was pointing at a Saturday and Sunday in February. February was also basketball season and there was no way I could play "pageant" and basketball.

"No, that won't work," I responded politely. "It's smack dab in the middle of basketball season. I'll have to pass, but thanks for asking."

Yes, I was *a little* interested but I didn't want to admit it. My high school career was focused on basketball, cheerleading, track, and dance. I didn't have time for pageants. Besides, how would that go over with my coach if I crammed a pageant into basketball season? He already cringed at the thought of one of his star players as a part-time cheerleader and dancer covered in lycra three evenings a week.

"It is a great way to earn scholarships," Lu continued.

I kept saying no. I was quickly realizing the only way I was going to end the conversation was to either walk away or say yes. Being the polite mid-west young lady my parents raised me to be I responded, "I'll think about it."

Apparently my response was code for *please, please continue to bug me about competing until I agree.* Because that is exactly what she did. Lu continued her recruitment for the next five months. Between my childhood obsession with the Miss America Pageant and her consistent encouragement, I couldn't keep saying no. Not to mention, my competitive spirit wanted to take on the challenge.

I weighed my credentials: I was in shape (swimsuit competition: check), I had a dance routine (talent competition: check), I had a beautiful prom dress (evening gown competition: check), and I knew how to talk to people (interview competition: check). How hard could a pageant be anyway?

I finally agreed.

By the time I had made the commitment I had drug my heels long enough. I only had two months left to prepare. I knew I needed to polish my overall presentation. And so, I utilized any free time I could find - between classes, sports, and dance - to gather my wardrobe, pick a platform, and fill out the reams of paperwork. I also started sneaking into the auditorium to practice my talent and walk around stage in my high heels, practicing my modeling technique. I knew I needed to ditch my "jock walk" and walk like a lady, which was going to take some work.

For two months I hid my boom box in my locker, along with dance shoes and high heels. I used a typical athletic bag, as a disguise, so it looked as though I was carrying around an extra pair of basketball high tops. When the coast was clear, I would grab the bag and head for the auditorium. The auditorium was conveniently located across the hall from the gymnasium so no one asked questions.-

Above the auditorium entrance was one of my favorite inspirations within the entire school. It was the *Wall of Fame*. The wall was a row of framed autographed pictures of LHS graduates that had gone on to do something outstanding with their life.

The pictures were in one long line that spanned ten yards. My small town in Southwest Kansas had contributed many assets to society – U.S. Congressmen, NFL players, a Dallas Cowboys Cheerleader, and Miss Kansas 1994 Trisha Schaffer, to name a few. Miss USA used to be up there too until she become a porn star (and the administration quickly removed her picture and never spoke of her again).

Every time I passed by the *Wall of Fame* I would look up at the pictures and wonder which side of the row my own picture would be added. I knew I had it in me to accomplish something worthy of that wall, for what purpose I wasn't quite sure, but I would get it up there some way, somehow.

Under the pictures the auditorium doors were always locked. But I knew better. There was a stage door always *unlocked* and no one ever

15

reported it. I would slip into the darkness and tip toe across the stage and over to the light-switch-board behind the curtains.

I would push the "on" button and glide the slider-switch into its brightest position. The lights would come to life and my heart would naturally pound with excitement as I could hear the buzz of the bulbs glowing with life. I often wondered how long I would get away with my "breaking and entering" before someone shooed me away or gave me detention. But I took my chances.

With the lights at their brightest setting I silently walked out to the middle of the stage. I stood in the silence and stared out across the 700 empty red seats.

The two story tall ceiling and deep stage was the home to stage-sets some dreamer had yet to create or even imagine. I loved the feeling of possibility within an empty auditorium. It was as though magic was always waiting to be created. And when the magic did come to life the acoustics sang. Even for a bad performance it was *still* a performance and a stage welcomed anyone who was willing to face their insecurities. The stage was a drug only an entertainer understood. As I became an entertainer I also became addicted to that drug. Once I tasted the high it had to offer I found myself desperate to feed that craving. And the more I fed the craving the more I craved the drug.

I felt the warmth of the lights on my skin. I closed my eyes. My heart slowed to a steady thump - a happy rhythm in my chest. This was my all-time favorite place to be: center stage, audience or no audience. The mixed feelings of *freedom* and *coming home* were the underlying current to my obsession with where I was standing.

I could smell the dust as the lights heated the particles in the air. The auditorium was quickly taking on a musty smell. It was a smell of dreams and sweat and hard work, and for some it was the smell of the future in the making. I wondered what the stages of my life would look like? Would I perform for five, 500, 5,000 or more? Where would my dream take me? I knew I would chase my dream around the world if necessary. My dream was to be a dancer on Broadway.

I opened my eyes and walked from center stage to the front of the stage. I only had forty-five minutes on that particular day and I needed to get started. I listened to the stage creek under my feet as I walked. The theatre was eerily silent yet unnervingly comforting.

I bent at my waist for a long hamstring stretch as I set my bag on the black painted wood. I unloaded my bag: boom box, dance shoes, and high heels. I bent my knees and sat down to put on my tan dance shoes. As I buckled my strap I admired the hole I had worn into the toe of my right shoe.

I put a CD with a collection of my favorite songs into the player. I clicked to track three and hit the rewind button. I rewound the CD ten seconds into the end of track two. I needed time to get into my position before the music started. I released my finger and ran over to my starting spot.

Track two came to a close and track three started with a *Wham-Bam-Ala-Ka-Zam!*

The big band sound led by a group of trumpets was enough to make anyone want to get up and dance. It was a happy sound. A sound of celebration.

The blaring song was originally written in 1933 for an unsuccessful musical, but later became a hit toward the end of World War II. My favorite rendition of the song was recorded in 1991 and was on the album "Unforgettable... With Love" which also received the coveted "Album of the Year" award at the Grammys.

An entire orchestra backed up the blast of horns while the tipity-tap of the drum-sticks on the cymbals gave any listener the natural urge to tap their toes. Even decades later the song was loved by a girl preparing for a pageant. I was dancing to Natalie Cole's *It's Only A Paper Moon.*

I pranced around the stage flicking my heels up to my bum and turning circles around the stage. I was celebrating the gift of dance and preparing my talent for my hometown audience. I made two split leaps across the stage and gracefully transitioned into a series of turns to get me back to my starting point. I was dancing in a girly style that was fitting for the music and the occasion. The lyrics were happy and my movement followed suit... *"and it wouldn't be make believe, if you believed in me..."*

There was a freedom I only experienced through dancing. It was self-expression, self-determination, and self-discipline. I didn't need an audience to love dancing. It was just that: a love. Through music and movement I could work through frustration or celebrate the gift of life. I could be girly or I could be fierce. I could be light on my feet and floating across the stage like a graceful ballerina, or I could get down into my legs and tap it out with the fiercest "stomp" master. Did I need to dance in the style of Fred Astaire or Dick Van Dyke? No problem. I could do that too. The expression and the sound were of my choosing and my mood.

I had so much more I wanted to learn about dance. I had not reached my full potential and I knew it. I planned on studying dance in college along with all my other formal studies. Yes, I was a die-hard athlete in my small town and I was starting to receive track and basketball scholarship letters from junior colleges, but my heart wasn't in those sports. Those sports were not my dream. My dream was to be a dancer and to be on the stage. I wanted to break free of the chains of a small town. I had wings and I knew I was preparing to use them.

I hit my final pose as the music came to a close. I was breathing hard. I bent at the waist and grabbed the back of my calves to pull myself closer for a deep hamstring stretch. My nose was on my shins and I took three deep breaths to slow my breathing.

I stood and walked one lap around the stage, ending back at the front next to my boom box. I skipped the CD back to track three and rewound it ten seconds into track two. I walked to my starting position and struck my pose.

Wham-Bam-Ala-Ka-Zam! I was off once again. *Dance like no one is watching.* I was good at that.

When I was done dancing I skipped my CD over to some slower music and slipped on my heels. I didn't have a lot of practice modeling in a swimsuit or an evening gown, but I was determined to look like I had the experience of a pro. And a pro knew how to walk in a pair of heels.

Some women never take the time to learn how to walk in the beautiful shoes they purchase. Why? Shoes are your foundation. You have to spend time building a solid foundation to make the rest of a structure steady. I saw modeling as no different.

The only way I would sell my ease and confidence was to practice, practice, practice. So that is what I did: I practiced. I tried all sorts of different walks and styles. I also practiced turning and posing all while my feet were in 3 ½ inch heels.

I spent hours walking back and forth across that stage in that empty auditorium. Had anyone walked in on me I would have felt beyond silly, but it was the risk I took. I would have rather felt silly in front of one person than an entire audience.

When I had circled back to the front of the stage I stopped at my bag and dug out my watch. Basketball practice was starting in ten minutes. My rehearsal time was up.

I kicked off my heels and stuffed all my belongings into my athletic bag. I hustled over to stage right and turned the lights off before I slipped back out the unlocked door.

I walked across the corridor to the gym. I had just enough time to replace my high heels with my high-tops out of the locker room, change into my knee length shorts, and hustle out to the court for practice.

Scene Five

Basketball locker room, girls' varsity team, February 2001
(Six years and six months *before* the accident)

"Stop looking for permission to pursue your dreams! They are your dreams and you don't need a co-signer to chase them." –Eric Thomas

I was lacing up my sneakers as I asked nonchalantly, "Is anyone going to the pageant next weekend?"

I could feel the beat of my heart as it began to increase. It was competition week and still no one except my family, my dance instructor, and Lu, the executive director of the pageant, knew I was competing for the Miss Liberal crown. I wasn't sure how my friends were going to respond to my girly decision that fell during the week of a basketball tournament, a tournament *our* school was hosting. I didn't want my teammates to think I was compromising the integrity of our efforts to win. I knew I could win both. But would they be mad? Would they feel I wasn't focused on the team? I had less than five days before they would find out. I knew I had to tell them.

"I don't know," Josi responded. "Are you?"

"Yes." I said trying to hide my grin.

"Maybe we can all go together," Karrisa chimed in.

I suddenly realized I didn't want someone to say something negative before they knew I was part of the competition. *That* would have been even *more* awkward.

"Actually," I said and braced myself for their response, "I'm one of the contestants."

There was a pause as the girls glanced at each other before turning their eyes on me.

"Seriously?" Sara asked with raised eyebrows and a disapproving look.

Then awkward silence.

"That's great!" Karrisa said breaking the hush, clearly trying to silence Sara.

"You will totally win!" Josi added, also silencing Sara's sarcasm.

"Oh my goodness, we will be there in full support," Heather, beamed. "We will make posters and be your fan section! The judges will have to pick you or they'll have to deal with us afterwards," she said matter-of-factly and then spun around to go recruit more soon-to-be fans.

"Please don't tell coach," I pleaded with those still standing there. "I don't want him to know."

"He's going to find out," Sara said while she rolled her eyes.

"I know," I sighed. "I suppose I should tell him."

"Just tell him and get it over with," Josi encouraged. "What's he going to do about it anyway? Besides, he can't dog on the next Miss Liberal."

I shot Josi an appreciative smile and she shrugged her shoulders sending me the body language of "no problem". Then she punched me in the arm as she walked past me and out of the locker room door. I guess I wasn't surprised how supportive my friends were. I was relieved.

My anxiety almost immediately switched from how my friends would react to how I was going to tell my coach about my latest endeavor. Coach and I hadn't exactly hit it off during his first year as the Head Coach for the Women's Varsity Basketball Team. A headstrong teenager and a know-it-all coach blend like oil and water: I was the oil, he was the water. We had our conflicts both in games and at practices. I had once challenged him during a game and he didn't bat an eye when he benched me. But that only lasted a few minutes as I was a fierce player. He needed me. I knew it. He hated it.

But how was he going to react to the news I was competing in a pageant the same week as our biggest basketball tournament, hosted on our home court no less?

My nerves sent heat through my limbs. I needed to let him in on the secret and I knew there was no time like the present. My feet lead me to his office. His door was closed. I knocked.

"Come in," I heard from the other side of the door.

I opened the door and walked in. My legs felt like lead, my heart was racing. Coach looked up and said, "What's up?"

"We are going to have a great tournament this week," I started. "I'm really looking forward to playing."

"What's up?" he asked annoyed, shifting his gaze back to his paperwork.

I jumped to business. "I'm competing in the Miss Liberal Pageant on Sunday," I blurted and then braced myself for his response.

He stopped writing and looked up. "That explains the nails," he said with a smirk. I looked down at my hands and admired my nails. No, the acrylic claws weren't exactly appropriate for the basketball court, but they were pretty.

Before he could say anything else I spun on my heel and exited as quickly as I had entered. I didn't want his opinion on the matter. I had, at the very least, done my part by telling him. What was he going to do, bench me?

I am going to rule my life and not let anyone else dictate my story.

On Tuesday we won our first tournament game. We also won our games on Thursday and Saturday. I want to say we won our tournament, but it really didn't matter. I didn't get benched and scored my share of points. By Sunday I was covered in jewels with make-up caked on my face.

I had the rowdiest cheering section at the pageant, posters and all. Sneakers or swimsuits my basketball team knew how to cheer on a teammate.

I won the interview competition and the crown. I received $1500 in scholarships and $500 in gift certificates. With the tiara on my head also came the "you may pass go" and proceed to the Miss Kansas Competition in June. The cherry on top: my winnings amounted to enough money to pay for a portion of my first semester at the University of Kansas. Furthermore, in June I had the opportunity to add to my winnings, which I did.

At the Miss Kansas Competition I placed in the top ten adding to my ego and scholarship money. Not bad for an 18-year-old rookie if you had asked me.

At 18-years-old I just knew Miss Kansas was *written in my stars*. Obviously I was made for the job and I would return the next year and win.

Humility keeps us honest with ourselves.

Ego check. During my freshman year of college I competed in two preliminary pageants and I didn't win, which meant I didn't qualify to compete for the Miss Kansas crown. I was crushed. With my ego bruised I decided to audition for two different summer jobs as a performer. I had two companies on my radar: 1) the musical "Texas" in the Palo Duro Canyon State Park outside of Canyon, Texas and 2) *Worlds of Fun* in Kansas City.

Each company was holding auditions in several places around the country and I picked the most convenient locations for me. For the *"Texas"* audition I would travel to Oklahoma. For the *Worlds of Fun* audition it was less of a commitment as they were holding auditions on my university's campus.

Scene Six

University of Oklahoma, March 2002
(Five years and five months *before* the accident)

"Greatness begins beyond your comfort zone." –Robin Sharma

In March of 2002, on a quiet Saturday morning, I walked through a set of double doors and into a theatre on the University of Oklahoma's campus. The theatre was in the round which meant the auditorium was built on risers *surrounding* the stage. There was no "backstage" so *everything* was on display and part of a performance at all times.

The stage floor was painted black and the seats were a deep shade of maroon that absorbed the stage lights. The overhead lights were on, but it was still dark. There were no windows and no natural light filling the space. It wanted to feel like a gloomy space except it couldn't because it was a space were stories came to life.

I stepped up on the stage, which was raised six inches off the ground, and quickly walked over to the registration table on the other side. The table was a long, portable plastic table with three folding chairs behind it. There were papers organized into scattered piles. Most of the piles were of auditionee's resumes and headshots. I noticed the resume on top of one of the piles. That particular resume had a lot more experience listed than the one I held in my hands.

I looked down at the paper I was holding. My resume was barren. I had very little experience and I didn't want to share that knowledge with anyone. Part of me wanted to run, but the other part made my legs stand still. I really wanted to be cast in that particular show and I knew the only way I would gain experience was by doing what I was doing at that very moment. So I silently stood there, frightened, waiting for someone to notice I was ready to check in.

24

Two of the folding chairs were occupied by an older couple who looked like they were in charge. After they finished discussing business and organizing a couple of details, one of them looked over at me with a warm smile.

"Good mornin," she said in a southern twang. "I'll take your resume and you can sign in here," she said as she pointed at a clip board. She also handed me a name tag that had "25" written in black permanent marker. "We'll be startin' in a few minutes."

All I could mutter was a quiet and shy "thank you."

I scribbled my name on the sign-in sheet next to line number 25. I turned to find a place to set my bag and change into my dance shoes.

There were approximately thirty other dancers filling the space. They were scattered around the room doing warm-ups and stretches. Some were on the floor rolling around and stretching while others were quietly moving around the stage. You could feel the nervousness that engulfed the air.

The room remained silent except for the wooden stage creaking under the dancers' weight, and the older couple chatting quietly. They were welcoming another auditionee.

The dance instructor – or choreographer – entered the room. Without an introduction you could tell immediately she would be the dancer in charge. Her hair was tucked up in a bun and she was covered from head to toe in black – black leotard, black pants over her black leotard, black jazz shoes. She had black mascara on her lashes but no other make-up. She walked with a confidence that aired on the side of arrogance, yet her expression made her appear warm and friendly.

I watched her walk across the stage as she carried her personal sound system. She walked like a dancer – feet slightly turned out and her pelvis leading the way. She stopped at the edge of the registration table and set her boom box on the corner.

As I leaned into my center splits I watched her take a CD off the table and place it in the player. She pushed play and turned a lever. The sound grew louder. She was adjusting the volume levels. The twang of the music filled the quiet space. It was a bright and lively sound. Kind of hokey, but it sounded like the musical *"Texas"*.

I took a deep breath and stretched further into my splits. My muscles were tighter than I wanted them to be and I didn't feel relaxed. The audition was scheduled to begin in three minutes so I closed my eyes, stretched deeper, and tried to get my nerves under control.

I had arrived for the audition later than I wanted. My mom, doubling as my encourager and traveling companion, helped me navigate the University of Oklahoma's campus on that quiet Saturday morning. I had traveled the five hours from the University of Kansas to the University of Oklahoma the day before. My mom met me along the way, parked her car in a random parking lot, and jumped in my car to ride with me.

We stayed at a hotel the night before, which she insisted on paying for. We went out for dinner, which was also on her. After the audition we had plans to hang out for a mother/daughter day in Oklahoma City. Again at her expense.

I was in college and had no money. I was chasing a dream, and since I was excelling in my book studies, she was being supportive. This was my first audition for a professional show. I was excited and nervous, as was she. To add to the excitement of the weekend that morning we couldn't find the theatre. I had the theatre name written down on a sheet of paper, but failed to write down the name of the building that housed the theatre. This was an age before the Internet was accessible on our phones, so we drove around the giant campus tugging on locked doors and looking for someone to point us in the right direction. My anxiety coupled with my disorientation sent me into a frenzy.

I stretched further into the splits and took another deep breath.

"Ok," the choreographer said as she walked to the self-appointed "front" of the room. "Let's get started."

Everyone quickly and quietly stood and scattered across the stage. I took a spot slightly in the middle and close to the front.

"Hi. I'm the choreographer for the show and I'll be teaching you a section from the opening number," she said as she sized up her auditionees. Her eyes connected with mine and I felt my heart thump. She kept talking, "Then we will divide into groups of three and perform the piece. Ready?"

There were scattered responses that came from the group of dancers. Others shook their heads. I made no sound and no movement. I was ready and waiting.

Wasting no time, she turned around and began teaching. She stepped on her left leg – *count one* – and kicked her right foot out to the side, heel resting on the ground and toe pointing to the sky. She swung her arms across her body and over to the other side – *count two*. She

26

took a two-step turn - *counts three and four*. She repeated the heel kick to the opposite side - *counts five and six*. She finished the musical phrase with another two-step turn - *counts seven and eight*. That was the first 8-count and she didn't repeat it.

The next phrase started with bell-kicks to the left and then to the right (clanking our heels in mid-air). Next we took three more steps, one of which was on the half-beat, before we kicked our right leg to our nose. We untwisted our bodies to kick our nose with our left leg.

She continued with an 8-count of detailed footwork. I shuffled around my space trying to see her feet, but I only caught her last four steps before she glanced over her shoulder and said, "Let's do that again." She showed us the eight counts of steps and without a breath she said, "From the top. 5-6-7-8."

We all started again. Some followed along, while others tried to follow along. The girl next to me bumped into me and said, "Sorry," in a whispered voice. I hardly noticed her as I was focused on the choreographer's feet. She was moving through the steps at a professional pace.

She had a friendly demeanor as she taught, but she also expected us to pick up the steps on her first demonstration. Everyone was focused. It was quiet in the room except for feet pounding and the choreographer counting off the steps.

She glanced over her shoulder, "One more time or can I move on?"

I silently willed her to go over the steps another time. I wasn't sure I had them. As I opened my mouth to make the suggestion nothing came out. The smart-ass standing front and center that could see her every movement said "Move on."

I wasn't sure I had the first three 8-counts, but I was stunned speechless. I simply did my best. She taught us two more 8-counts and repeated the entire series five more times.

I didn't have room for another thought to enter my mind nor a smile. I was focused on the steps. My heart was pumping blood through my veins at a healthy rate and the ten *battements* (kicks) I had just demonstrated in the first five minutes of the audition had my hamstrings warm and flexible. I hardly noticed the sweat dotting my forehead.

She pushed play on the boom box and counted us in. The music was upbeat and faster than she had counted it. It was definitely an energetic opening to the two-hour musical.

She led us through the sequence with the music. I missed a few steps the first time but I nailed it the second time. She advised all of us to be light on our feet as it would help us keep in step with the music. I was not the dancer she was, but I was keeping up. She was obviously a trained ballerina. I obviously was not.

She pushed pause and asked, "Are we ready to continue?"

I decided to join in with the others that said "yes," but I wasn't convincing myself.

She taught four more 8-counts. The girl standing next to me bumped into me again and I ignored her and her apology.

As we continued dancing I was committing the steps to memory. I was getting the footwork, but I was also fighting my own self-imposed insecurities. I started comparing myself to the other people in the room. I compared my outfit, my body, my feet – anything I could physically compare, I did. I was entering into a danger zone of self-destruction.

My chest felt restricted as I started to pull my shoulders inward. I tried to push the comparisons out of my mind, but as we were separated into groups of three it got worse. I was number 25, which meant I had to stand off to the side and watch eight sets of dancers dance the combo before I got my chance. And in true audition form I judged the others. I judged them based on my own skills. I watched some nail the piece and others completely butcher it. When it was my turn I did all the steps correctly but I wasn't sure I managed a genuine smile throughout the entire process.

And just as quickly as the audition started, it ended. The kind people behind the folding table stood and told us we would hear from them in the next couple of weeks, "But please don't call us, we will contact you."

I changed my shoes and walked out into the hall. My mom gave me a big hug and asked, "How did it go?"

"Okay, I think," I said with a shrug of my shoulders. "We'll find out in a few weeks."

We walked back to the car and headed to lunch. I was starving and she was buying.

I was also digesting the fact that while I wanted to be a "dancer on Broadway" I had a long way to go and years of work to get comfortable with my craft.

"Every time I thought I was being rejected from something good, I was actually being re-directed to something better." –Dr. Steve Maraboli

------

Three weeks later I hadn't heard from *"Texas"* so I went to the *World's of Fun* audition. It followed in much the same format; however, they had an added component. I had to stand next to a piano and sight read sheet music. The problem: I didn't know how to read music, which made the entire audition rather embarrassing.

That evening when I got back to my dorm room, before I even had time to change out of my leotard, my mom called. She had excitement in her voice. "A letter from *"Texas"* just arrived," she said. They had mailed the letter to my permanent address which was six hours away in my small hometown in Kansas.

"Did you open it?" I asked.

"No. Do you want me to?"

"Yes," I said.

We were silent while she opened the letter. I could hear her ripping the edges while I waited on the phone. I held my breath and crossed my fingers.

She began reading, "Dear Adrienne: Thank you for auditioning to be a member of the *"Texas"* company. As always, there were many more auditioning then we have positions for in the cast. Due to the fact we had a very large turnout of very talented people this year, casting and hiring decisions have been very difficult. We are very sorry that we don't have a position to offer you at this time."

My heart sank. She read a couple more sentences that said "thanks but no thanks" but I had quit listening. Tears were forming in the corners of my eyes.

My first rejection letter.

Two weeks later my mom called again. This time she was holding a letter that had *World's of Fun* written in the return address.

My second rejection letter. Deep down I knew there would be more.

I was mortified by my lack of accomplishment. My mom even started a "rejection" file for me. I asked her not to but she insisted. She told me the letters would be valuable someday when I was a star on Broadway.

I loved her encouragement, but I felt so discouraged I had a hard time believing her. Over the course of the year I was two pageants and two auditions into my "career" and I wasn't good enough for any of them. I quickly realized it was time to shut-up and get my butt in gear.

29

Just because I had a dream didn't mean I was going to automatically obtain it. I had to work for it. I had to work *hard* for it. I had to stay focused. I had to commit to it. I also realized I needed a back-up plan, or a Plan B. What happens when life doesn't go according to *our* plans?

Scene Seven

Pioneer Amphitheatre, August 2, 2007
(Ten days *before* the accident)

"God is the only one who can make the valley of trouble a door of hope."
–Hosea 2:15

It wasn't my first time on a horse. I had actually ridden a handful of times in Kansas and in Texas. Before my accident I had even ridden professionally, sort of...

You see, there is a scene in the show where Elsie (my character) goes storming off the stage having had a fight with her romantic counterpart and in the very next scene the audience sees her riding across the back of the stage area out near the canyon wall. But she doesn't exactly "ride" she more or less flies.

Since I was the star of the show the production team had hired a "double" to ride in my place. They put a real cowgirl on the horse to ride in the distance, but to make the cowgirl look like me she wore a replica of my dress and a brown wig to match my hair. Since it was in the distance no one could recognize if it was me or the cowgirl.

All that summer I had begged the cowgirl to let me ride in her spot. And during show number 45 we switched places, secretly of course. There were only three of us that knew we were trading places because if we had told more people it would have gotten back to the director and he would have told me "no".

But I wanted to ride that scene. And so I did... *successfully.*

I had practiced riding the path, at a full gallop, when the rest of the cast was getting ready for the show. It was also during a time I knew the stage manager was busy and the director was out mingling with the guests.

31

The stagehand had shown me where I would wait for my cue and he warned me the horse would get antsy as he waited to take off. I practiced the ride in daylight. I rode the horse at a full gallop back and forth across the "high road" that stretched almost a half mile.

That night during the show when I mounted the horse in the dark, we walked to our starting line. The stagehand greeted us. He looked at me and smiled.

As the three of us waited together my four legged friend danced in place underneath me. Those horses loved to run and they loved the audience as much as we, the humans, did.

The stagehand was quiet as he stood next to us listening to his headset that was connected to the stage manager in the sound booth. He looked at me and said, "Ten seconds."

I leaned forward – up and over the saddle horn – to prepare myself for the zero to thirty take off. My feet were secure in the stirrups. The cue lights turned from red to yellow. The horse let out a big sigh as he kept his enthusiasm at bay.

The stagehand counted down, "Three. Two. One." The light turned green as the horse took off on his own cue. It was pitch black as we raced toward the lights that lit up the high road. I held on for dear life.

I couldn't see the road beneath us and I instantly realized I had to trust the horse. He was in full control. I was merely along for the high speed ride.

When we raced through the lights I heard a character on stage recite his line, "Look there she goes."

A smile spread across my face and I wasn't sure which was racing faster: the horse or my heart.

My eyes had quickly adjusted to the bright stage lights so when we disappeared into the darkness once again I couldn't see anything. And so I did what I could: I held the reins and trusted the horse.

Scene: Back in the horse pasture, August 12, 2007
(The accident)

As I felt Scout spook between my legs I also felt his mane slip from my hand. He bucked and I didn't have a hold of anything.

I launched into the air.

Oh no! I thought. I had no control. It was not good.

32

I went up and gravity brought me down.

I hit the ground. Hard. And when I did I felt my right ankle snap. My body jarred. I took another step, on what I'm not sure, and I collapsed to the ground.

I didn't hear my ankle break, nor did I initially feel the pain. I didn't know I had more-or-less severed my foot from my leg.

My stomach did a loop like I was on a roller coaster. And then the pain raced in like a rush of frantic water. The pain sped up my leg and into my chest, bursting through my consciousness. I was overwhelmed with pain in a way I couldn't imagine, nor can I ever explain.

Oh my God! I thought.

The pain grew with instant intensity. And then more. And more.

Oh my God it hurts!

It was my ankle.

I can't breathe!

The pain was flooding over me as my mouth went dry.

It hurts!

I was drowning in pain. My mind was racing.

The pain! I'm hot! Oh my God what just happened?!

Shelly was at my side in seconds. My mind began to whirl out of control. I began to silently scream, *"Oh my God! Please help me! I'm so hot! It hurts! God where are you?"*

"Mom get dad," Shelly screamed as I started to hyperventilate. "Adrienne breathe," Shelly begged as she grabbed a hold of my shoulders, careful not to move the lower half of my body. She looked me in the eyes, her dark brown eyes meeting my own. "Breathe!" She forcefully said to me.

I was trying, but the air wasn't helping.

Shelly leaned her forehead to mine, "Dear Jesus, be with us," Shelly prayed over me. "We need You now! We know You are here. Please be with Adrienne."

Not knowing what else to do Shelly continued to pray...

Scene Eight

A girl in her college dorm, frustrated, April 2002
(Five years and four months *before* the accident)

"Success is going from failure to failure without losing your enthusiasm."
-Abraham Lincoln

What did I enjoy besides dance? I had no idea. I had ruled out a Plan B career in medicine or law and I was leaning toward something such as journalism or business.

I racked my brain for ideas. What could I possibly do? I was headed home for my first college summer and I didn't have a whole lot of growth opportunities in my hometown, *or so I thought*.

I was 19-years-old and had no job prospects and no money. I was going home to live with my mom and dad, but I wasn't allowed back in the house without a job. I was quickly becoming less concerned with impressing people and more concerned with finding an income and bettering myself.

After a lot of thought and endless lists of things I could try, an idea finally sparked. I picked up the phone and made a call.

"Jeans Beans and BBQ," A man's voice answered on the other end. It was Jay, Grandma's third husband.

"Hi Jay, is Grandma there?" I asked laughing. Jay was a kind man with a sense of humor.

"Yes, hang on a second." I heard him holler for her to pick up the phone. Grandma didn't run a BBQ joint per say, but she was always in the kitchen, usually cooking for a church function.

"Hello," her voice answered.

"Hi Grandma. It's me. Adrienne. How are you?"

34

"Oh it's so nice to hear from you," she responded. I could hear her smile through the phone.

"I'm great, but I sure do miss you," I said.

"I miss you too. I'm going to put you are speaker phone so I can keep rolling out my noodles."

"Ok. Who are you cooking for this time?" I asked.

"Church. I'm making butterball soup and noodles."

I could almost smell her kitchen through the phone. When Grandma said "and noodles" there was no such thing as store bought noodles. Grandma's noodles were made from scratch – egg yolks, flour, and salt. I know this because I have memories of making pounds of those scrumptious noodles with her throughout my childhood.

We gabbed for thirty minutes about college life, who I *wasn't* dating, and what I thought about my new sorority. We talked about school and what classes I liked and disliked.

"So why are you calling?" she finally asked.

"Well, I have an idea for a summer job but it will only work if you are interested," I explained.

"I'm listening."

"I would like to start a swimming lesson school and use your pool if you will let me," I kept going, "No one would ever come in the house. We can use the side gate and I would pay for the chlorine and pool maintenance if you agreed that I could use the pool."

"What days and hours are you considering?" she asked.

"Monday thru Friday from 8 until 3ish."

"Hmmm, that sounds like a pretty good idea but I need to talk to Jay first," she responded. "But I bet he says yes," she lowered her voice to a whisper, "and I doubt you will need to pay for the chlorine."

"Oh grandma that would be so awesome!" I said with excitement, almost screaming into the phone.

Grandma was always supportive of my ideas and aspirations, and while I *thought* she would say yes I wasn't sure.

"We would be so happy to see you every day anyway."

"You ask Jay and I am going to get signed up for all my appropriate certifications!" I responded with enthusiasm.

We finished chatting and working out some of the details: what kind of certifications I needed, when I was going to be home for the summer, and how many months I was planning on using the pool.

It was going to be my first business venture and I was as nervous as I was excited! I wasn't sure how it was going to play into my "dance dream" but I was okay with that. **It was experience and experience is a successful person's greatest asset.**

"Out of difficulties grow miracles." –Jean de La Bruyére

I blew my whistle and the six girls and four boys lined up in the driveway each of them at full attention. You would have thought I was running a military school instead of a swimming school. But that particular group of swimming students needed the organized fun. That group arrived after lunch and typically juiced on sugar from a summer snow cone. My goal was to wear them out in the forty-five minutes I had them, and teach them a thing or two in the process. Their parents were always appreciative of my successful efforts.

"Is everyone ready?" I hollered.

"Yes!" they all yelled in unison.

"Follow-me," I said with a dramatic gesture of my arm.

I walked to the front of the line and started marching as I sang *"Left. Left. Left, right, left."* I marched in place as my minions followed suit.

I led our march from the front driveway, around the house, and into the backyard. My students followed and chanted with me, drowning out the sound of my own voice, *"Left. Left. Left, right, left."*

The whole neighborhood had taken notice of my small, yet successful business I was conducting out of grandma's backyard. Four times a day, five days a week I started class in much the same fashion. I disrupted the peacefulness of the neighborhood, but the neighbors laughed at the control I had over my class-after-class of students. Only a kid teaching kids knew how to have *that* much fun on the job.

I had ten students per class and my favorite was my fourth class of the day. They were between the ages of nine and eleven. They all knew how to *not drown*, but they *didn't* know how to properly swim. My job was to teach them. On their first day of class I assessed their dog-paddles and realized my work was cut out for me. My personal goal was for everyone to have fun yet learn something in the process. And that's what we did.

"Left. Left. Left, right, left."

When we reached the backyard I blew my whistle and stopped abruptly. The students followed suit and fell silent.

36

"Okay," I started very matter-of-factly as I began to pace back and forth in front of my row of soldiers. "Today's warm-up will be a full sprint to the fence," I pointed to the fence at the back of the yard. It was 50 feet from where we stood. "Then you must run back to the center of the yard and run three laps around any one of the inner tubes," I had spaced three inner tubes across the yard. "Next, I must hear you count off ten jumping jacks." I looked at my row of swimmers "and I want to hear you!" I instructed at them as though I was a drill instructor.

They were all smiling.

"Then you must touch the fence again before you sprint to the pool and jump in the deep end. You must swim to the shallow end as fast as you can, using the *stroke* of your choice. No dog paddling," I yelled as loud as I could. "The last person to the shallow end of the pool has to do ten *bobs* on the class's count."

One of the over excited boys took off and I yelled "I didn't say go!" He walked back laughing.

"On your mark... get set..." the same boy took off again. "I didn't say go!" I said laughing. He walked back and this time I made him take three penalty steps backwards.

"Ahh, Miss Adrienne."

"Don't *ahh* me," I said. "I didn't jump the gun, you did!" I said with a chuckle. "On your mark, get set, go!" I yelled. They were off and the race was on.

They sped across the artificial grass that circled the pool and onto the real grass of the yard. The boys made it to the fence first, but the girls' agility gave them the edge when it came to the coordination of running circles around the tubes. They speed-demoned through their jumping jacks - all starting at different times, but miraculously finishing together. They sprinted back to the fence, slapped the white paint, and raced to the pool jumping in the deep end.

Grass scattered through the water as they hit the surface. They swam to the shallow end as I monitored the pool making sure no one drowned.

As they reached the three foot area, one by one they stood huffing and puffing as they wiped water from their eyes. They were all silent except for their heavy breathing. My laughter floated up into the summer sky.

"I didn't see one proper swim stroke!" I yelled. "Only dog paddles. Everyone, ten bobs!" And without argument they dipped under the water and sprung up again. "One!" I yelled as they bobbed again, "Two!"

The bobbing continued. When I hit *"Ten!"*, again they stood, all breathing heavily and wiped water from their eyes.

I had ten, quiet, half-drown kids.

Class could officially begin.

"A truly happy person is one who can enjoy the scenery while on a detour."
–unknown

That summer of 2002 I ran a successful business. I taught approximately 100+ kids how to swim. I had fun in the process. What I didn't realize at the time was the hands-on business experience I was learning as it pertained to money management, marketing, and organization that I would later put into action as an entertainer (and even now as an author).

My older students, age seven to thirteen, knew their swim strokes and could swim back and forth from the deep end to the shallow end *with confidence*. They came to me as dog paddlers and they left as competent swimmers. For my students younger than seven, and those who were terrified of the water, I had them swimming the short length of the pool at the five foot deep line.

All my students graduated my program confident and strong. The parents were equally happy as they were already inquiring about a spot in one of my classes for their children the following summer. I took their names and guaranteed them a space if I opened my business again in 2003. If my performance dream fell on its face for a second year, I would indeed return to teach another summer of outstanding swimming lessons, but I didn't.

In an eight week time frame I worked from 9 a.m. to 2 p.m. and made good money. I made more than most of my friends that summer and because I didn't have a clue I was supposed to report my earnings to the IRS I didn't. I didn't know I had to. I guess if the government wants their money they should teach students about filing taxes. After all I graduated from a public high school and I was enrolled in a public university. But they didn't teach it so I didn't know to do it.

Funny how that summer, and paying my taxes late, would forever leave a lasting impact on my journey and my future work with kids.

Scene Nine

"If you want something you've never had, you've got to do something you've never done." –unknown

During that summer of teaching kids to swim I also thought about competing in another Miss Kansas preliminary. If I was going to be a strong contender I needed a "platform" to run on. A platform would guide me to be more than a pageant contestant. It would give me a purpose to wear the crown. It would allow me the opportunity to champion a cause that was bigger than myself.

Choosing a platform was one thing, but going out into the community and making a difference was completely different. I needed to do something big. I needed to stand out. I needed to make a difference.

I tossed around ideas by making lists of "causes" in which I could get involved. But I needed more than a "cause". I needed an organization in which I could get excited about volunteering.

In months of investigation I kept circling back around to the word "cancer". I knew too many people who knew the word first hand, including my immediate family.

I turned to the place you go for research: the Internet. Every time I typed the word "cancer" in a search bar *The American Cancer Society (ACS)* was always at the top.

I dug deeper: The ACS web site states they help people with cancer "stay well and get well, by finding cures, and by fighting back."

I came across ACS's signature fundraising event called *Relay For Life*. I had heard of it in my community, but I didn't know what the event was about. I researched it further.

Relay for Life is an event held in communities around the world. The *Relay* honors cancer survivors, loved ones lost, and recognizes the caregivers who have lived through the hardships. All *Relays* raise funds for cancer research. Community members form teams and those teams raise money. The *Relays* are six to twenty-four hours in length. They usually take place on a high school or college track. Most events take place over night, which makes it that much more challenging. Just as cancer never takes a break neither do the participants during the event.

It was a good cause *and* it sounded fun.

I continued to research. I wanted to know where in the country all the *Relays* were taking place. As I surfed the Net I discovered universities were starting *Relays* for their student communities, but not many universities had *Relays* as the idea of it was in its infancy. Not surprisingly, I discovered the University of Kansas didn't have a *Relay For Life*.

The more I researched, the more I wanted to volunteer.

I decided I wanted to found a *Relay for Life* at the University of Kansas. So I picked up the phone and dialed the number. In less than five minutes I had an appointment scheduled with the woman in charge.

"I am only one, but still I am one. I cannot do everything, but still I can do something. And because I cannot do everything, I will not refuse to do something that I can do." –Helen Keller

------

I walked into the American Cancer Society's state headquarters in Topeka, Kansas. I was dressed like a typical college student that didn't know how to dress for a professional appointment. I had on a spaghetti strap floral tank top and black unfitted capri pants (that doubled as hiking pants in the summertime), flip flops, and my hair tied back in a pony-tail.

I had an appointment with a lady named Melinda. When I had scheduled my appointment all I told her was I was interested in more info about starting a *Relay for Life*. That was code for "free labor" and so she graciously accepted my appointment request.

"Hi. My name is Adrienne. I have an appointment with Melinda," I said to the receptionist at the front counter.

"I'll let her know you are here."

The receptionist picked up the phone as I walked around the lobby anxiously waiting to meet the woman in charge of the university *Relays*.

"Adrienne?" a lady asked as I turned around. She was shorter than I was, and older, but she had energy in her voice and seemed pleasant enough.

"Yes. Are you Melinda?" I asked in response.

"Yes." We shook hands. "It's nice to meet you. Shall we have a seat?" She gestured to a small waiting area with a few chairs.

We sat and I suddenly felt nervous. I wanted to start a *Relay for Life*, but I had never actually *attended* a *Relay for Life*. Was that thought just then dawning on me? Two weeks prior to our meeting was the first time I researched what *Relay for Life* even was. And in a split second I realized I needed to avoid the part of the conversation that had anything to do with my experience.

Fake it 'til you make it, I told myself.

I dodged my own thoughts, "I'm starting my sophomore year at KU and I was doing some research over the summer. I noticed we don't have a *Relay for Life* on campus. Did I miss it my freshman year or was my research correct?"

"Unfortunately, you are correct," Melinda said. "We would like to start one, but we haven't found anyone to spearhead the event."

"Hmmm," I pondered. "That's too bad."

"Do you know someone who might be interested?" Melinda asked as she looked at me with her head tilted.

"Well…" I paused for a few seconds, adding a dramatic effect. "Today is your lucky day!" I said with a smile. "I would like to start the first ever *Relay for Life* at the University of Kansas."

"Serious?" Melinda responded with raised eyebrows and hint of shock.

"Completely," I said more confidently than I felt.

Melinda was shocked into silence so I continued, "Whether or not you want to help me, I plan on doing it," I said boldly.

"Wow. We have been looking for someone to start this for a couple of years now. I can't believe you just walked through the door." I smiled as she continued. "We would love to have you start a *Relay*. And you don't have to be completely on your own. We can help you. We provide support, but it will ultimately be *your* event." She paused. "Do you think you are up to the challenge?"

"Absolutely."

"What time of year would you like to have it?"

"In the spring. Perhaps April. Maybe May. I want it to be at least two weeks before finals."

"That sounds good. Any idea where you would like to hold it?"

"Memorial Stadium." (Memorial Stadium was the official stadium of the university. It is the stadium where they play Division One college football games. But more impressively, it is a stadium that holds over 50,000 people.)

Slightly shocked at my cockiness, Melinda asked, "Do you think you can get the university to agree to that?"

"Sure. I'll pester them until they do."

We both laughed.

"I like your attitude," Melinda said with a smile. "This is going to be fun. First, let's exchange info and then once you get settled into the new school year let's schedule a committee meeting date. But first you will need to recruit a committee. "

"No problem," I said. "Let's plan on a meeting in late September. That will give me time to post flyers and recruit a team. "

We exchanged info. We shook hands once again and I turned to walk out of the building.

My heart thumped in my chest and I couldn't' wipe the smile off my face. I had no idea what I was doing, but that wasn't going to stop me. (Never has.)

I was taking my first step in the journey of a thousand miles. My heart and my mind knew I could do it. I felt passion in my belly and I could taste the excitement I had about my future.

My mom was waiting for me in the parking lot and I ran to greet her. "They agreed!" I screamed as I gave her a bear hug. She hugged me back and told me how proud she was.

"Go stand in front of the building," she said. "I want to take your picture."

Scene Ten

Lawrence, Kansas. a copy-store on Massachusetts Street, August 2002
(Five years *before* the accident)

*"I may only be one person but I can be one person who makes a
difference." –unknown*

I grabbed the stack of flyers off the printer and walked up to the
counter and paid for them. I had two hundred flyers, a stapler, tape, and
a load of enthusiasm. The flyers were advertising a Wednesday night
Relay For Life Committee Formation Meeting.

I had two hours to walk the university campus and hang the freshly
printed announcements; my only marketing plan to recruit my *Relay*
committee. I canvassed the campus on a one-woman mission of
determination.

In the meantime, I was harassing the university to give me full reign
of Memorial Stadium. I marched back and forth across campus as one
office sent me to another. At times I felt like I was getting the run-
around, but I refused to take "no" for an answer and eventually I found
someone who would say "yes".

The woman who finally helped me had a sympathetic heart toward
the American Cancer Society and *Relay for Life*. She happily assisted me
with the paperwork. I filled out the required forms and submitted them.

**"They say surround yourself with great people and great places because
great things will come of it." –R. Bulinski**

The following Wednesday night I walked into a quiet building at
6:45 p.m. My meeting was scheduled to start at 7 p.m. and I prayed
people would show up.

43

When I walked into the room I was the only one there. My own friends and sorority sisters weren't interested in the project, but that didn't stop my enthusiasm nor determination.

I sat down on a desk in the front of the room and waited eagerly as I watched the clock tick. I swung my legs back and forth under the desk like a child waiting for recess.

At 6:55 p.m. three girls walked in and we exchanged casual hellos.

At 6:57 p.m. one guy walked in and I welcomed him.

At 6:59 p.m. nine people walked in and again I said hello.

At 7:02 p.m. five more people walked in.

I glanced at my crowd. Fifteen girls and three guys. *Good enough for me.*

"Hi everyone. My name is Adrienne and I'm going to get started." No one said anything.

"First, thank you for attending this evening. If you are here for the *Relay for Life* Committee Formation Meeting then you are in the right place. Is everyone familiar with *Relay for Life?*"

Everyone nodded their heads. I was relieved that at the very least I had a team of eighteen people who knew about *Relay for Life*, even if I didn't.

Fake it 'til you make It, I reminded myself.

"Awesome. If by the end of this evening you are still interested in helping plan and organize the event then you are on the committee."

Everyone chuckled.

"How about we start by going around the room and introducing ourselves? If you are willing, please share with the group why it is you want to be involved with the committee or what your personal connection to cancer is. Cool?"

Everyone agreed.

"Great. To break the ice, I'll start. As I said, my name is Adrienne and I'm excited to spearhead the first ever *Relay for Life* at KU. I met with the American Cancer Society in Topeka last month to ask for their help in starting a *Relay* this spring. They are excited to have us." Everyone was pleased with this announcement.

"My background with cancer: my grandma and two aunts are breast cancer survivors. They were all diagnosed before the age of fifty. My family is the first reason I want to find a cure. My second reason, but equally as important: one of my childhood friends lost his mom to breast cancer during our senior year. It was tough on our whole class.

She didn't make it to graduation. I guess you could say, for me, not only is 'cancer' a dirty word it's a scary word. I want to take the fear out of cancer by helping to find a cure and the only way I know how is by raising money for cancer research. Since our own university has a research facility in Kansas City, I definitely feel we need a *Relay for Life* here on campus. In fact, I find it crazy we don't have one already." I shrugged my shoulders and looked around the room. "So, here I am."

The crowd consensus found my introduction acceptable. Without much prompting, my peers were anxious to share their own personal connections with cancer.

One by one, each attendee shared his and her heart.

It's an understatement to say I was more than moved by their stories. Cancer had made its way into each of our lives and it had left a lasting impression on all of us. Many had family members who were survivors, while others had lived through the harsh reality of watching loved-ones suffer and die.

Honestly, my heart wasn't prepared for the blunt reality one of the attendees was about to share with the entire group of strangers. Through tears, one of my soon-to-be friends told our group about her mom who was in the midst of her own nasty battle with breast cancer. She hated watching her suffer while she felt like a helpless bystander. Not only was being a witness difficult, but it was frustrating. There was nothing she could do to help her own mother.

When she saw the flyer for *Relay for Life* she knew it would be a good outlet for her to find solace in facing the disease her mother was so bravely fighting. But solace did not mean acceptance because that meant she had surrendered, and in the fight for her mother's life she would never surrender. She was desperate to find a cure to rid her mom, and the world, of such a horrific disease. She confessed her fears as her sorority sisters sat next to her, one holding her hand. The beautiful friendship among the "sisters" was one that could only be understood when built among friends who were battling life's trials together. The sisters were just as dedicated in their mission to destroy cancer as she was.

Their little group was in the midst of a personal fight against cancer. The rest of us choked back tears as we tried to understand the scary journey they were all on. Their personal and relevant story gave all eighteen of us a deeper dedication to see the *Relay* not only to fruition, but to a fruitful success.

A tear of my own escaped my eye and I wiped the moisture from my cheek. I instantly knew I was surrounded by incredible people. People who had a bigger vision for their lives than drinking alcohol and sleeping around, which seemed to be the "norm" for the college students I was somehow associated with.

In one hour I had learned more about my peers than some people do in a lifetime. The people in that room had depth, compassion, and purpose. They wanted to make difference in the community and the world. I was humbled and overwhelmed. I realized, not only were these the type of people I wanted to be surrounded with, but I questioned whether or not I was the right person to lead the group. Hearing their personal stories made me more determined to make the event successful, not for me but for the hope it would bring to others.

I didn't want to let anyone down with my lack of experience in leadership. I stood tall and pretended I had planned major events a hundred times, even though the *Relay* would be my first. The only thing I could think about to encourage myself was the fact I could teach kids to swim. And if I could teach non-swimmers how to swim with gusto, then I could lead a crew of students to plan a successful event.

I pushed the meeting forward and went through the minor details I had in place. "I'm currently waiting on approval for Memorial Stadium. When we get it, it looks like they will give us the date of May 5th. I would like to lock in the date amongst us so we can start planning. Does anyone have an objection to May 5th?"

No one spoke.

With enthusiasm I said, "All in favor of the *first ever Relay for Life* at the University of Kansas to take place on May 5th please say aye."

In unison everyone said aye.

"Perfect!"

I moved on to the next order of business which was designating the sub-committees. I listed the sub-committees we needed and our group efficiently divided into those committees.

Each sub-committee then took twenty minutes to create a game plan (AKA: a business plan) for the upcoming months. As the leader I was overseeing all the committees. I walked around the room answering questions and helping guide the groups with ideas when they needed them.

Once everyone had their plans in place we moved our chairs into a circle. Each sub-committee then shared their tentative plans with the entire group. We critiqued each other's plans to make sure we weren't missing any big items. We all agreed were at a great starting point.

After an hour and half we adjourned our meeting. We each had our personal assignments and would meet back at the same location in one month. We exchanged contact information and said our good-byes. There was an excited buzz among us as we left the building. Not only had we made new friends, but were embarking on a journey that would forever impact the university and the destruction of cancer.

Scene Eleven

University of Kansas, a fraternity house, October 2002
(Four years and ten months *before* the accident)

"The worst we do is wonderful." *–Neil Traylor*

I rang the doorbell and waited patiently. I stared down at my stack of flyers, double checking the spelling. Although, even if I had found a mistake it was too late to do anything about it.

The massive wood door to the giant house opened and a handsome young man, my age, greeted me. He was wearing flip flops, jeans that were slightly frayed at the bottom, a white t-shirt, and a smile. He had gelled brown hair and soft brown eyes.

"May I help you?" he asked very politely.

"Hi. My name is Adrienne and I talked to one of your fraternity brothers about dropping off flyers for *Relay for Life*. He asked me to come by around this time."

"Perfect. Everyone is at dinner. You can come in and make an announcement."

"During dinner?" I clarified with raised eyebrows as I looked down at what I was wearing.

"Yes, if you want to," he said.

I hesitated and then answered more confidently than I felt, "That sounds great."

I hadn't planned on making an announcement to a room full of men - men I could potentially date - and I unexpectedly felt my forehead break into a sweat as I started analyzing my wardrobe selection. I had on a jean skirt that hung over my knees, a t-shirt with a giant KU Jayhawk on the front, flip flops, and a scarf in my hair. *Good enough*, I thought as I stepped across the threshold.

The two of us walked through a grand entryway and around a corner. The sound of our flip flops echoed off the wood floor and floated up into the high ceilings. I could hear a chatter of people, obviously coming from the dining room.

When we reached the dining hall, the gentleman leading me stepped to the side and gestured for me to enter the dining hall first. Before I stepped into the room my eyes bugged out of my head. There were approximately 150 men and one woman – the house mom – eating dinner. For some reason I was picturing eighty at the most.

My heart thumped wildly in my chest and my mouth went dry. Without time to think or allowing myself to chicken-out, I stepped into the room.

Instantaneously the 150 men stood and turned to look at me. Their chivalry sent a chill up my spine and I went weak at the knees.

I started laughing, stunned by the attention I was receiving, and a huge smile washed across my face. I was immediately giddy. "Can I leave and walk in again?" I asked my audience with bright eyes.

They joined in my laughter.

The gentlemen who had shown me into the room stepped up next to me, gestured for his fraternity brothers to take a seat, and introduced me to the crowd, "Everyone. This is Adrienne and she is here to tell us about *Relay for Life*." He turned and looked at me, cueing me it was my turn to talk.

"Thank you for that wonderful greeting," I said to the room, still beaming. "As he said, my name is Adrienne. I am a part of the Greek community, but the reason I'm here is to recruit a team for the first ever *Relay for Life* at KU." I continued with a quick synopsis about the *Relay*.

"The *Relay* will be taking place the first weekend of May and I am challenging your house to field at least one team. A team consists of 15-30 people and by the looks of your numbers I would love to welcome multiple teams. I'm going to leave some flyers. The flyers have my contact information, so please don't hesitate to contact me with any questions (*Including dating inquiries*, I thought.). Does anyone have any questions?"

No one said anything so I closed with, "Thank you."

As if *thank you* was code for "applause" they all began to clap. I smiled ear-to-ear while still looking "professional".

I turned and walked out of the room. The same handsome gentleman who escorted me into the house also showed me out. We chatted as our flip flops smacked the bottoms of our feet in unison and we made our way back across the grand foyer.

I handed my escort the stack of flyers and said thank you once again.

As I walked down the walkway and back out to the sidewalk I tried to conceal my grin, but it was pointless. When I heard the heavy wood door close securely, I did a little bell-kick clicking my heels together in mid-air.

To have a room full of men stand when I walked in made my heart melt. Whether or not they formed a team was the least of my concerns. I was already dreaming up more organizations I could create just to have an excuse to make another visit during dinner. And then I realized I had more than a dozen other fraternities to challenge to a team.

I did a second bell kick.

As the leader of *Relay for Life*, I immediately volunteered to do the fraternity recruiting.

Even at the age of twenty I skipped back to my sorority – maybe not the whole way, but there was at the very least a skip in my step.

That in which you focus your energy is where you will see your results.

My mind was racing with items I needed to accomplish as it pertained to the *Relay*. I was also thinking about my next class: ballet.

Every morning was much the same: I put on my leotard and tights followed by a pair of jeans and my favorite gray hoodie sweatshirt with "Kansas" emblazoned across the front. I would braid my hair in two tight "Dorothy Braids" before I tucked the ends up, securing the braids with hairpins. Next, I would hairspray my hair making sure there wasn't one hair out of place. I didn't want to disrespect my ballet professor with loose hair.

When my appearance met my satisfaction, I slipped my feet into tennis shoes, tossed my backpack over my shoulders, and walked to class. Yes, I carried books and notebooks, but the most important items in my bag were my canvas ballet shoes and the stench they carried with them. The second most important item was my *Relay for Life* notebook.

Over the course of several semesters I had advanced from beginning ballet to intermediate ballet and was finally enrolled in advanced ballet. I had begun training with dancers who were preparing for professional ballet careers. It was intimidating at times, but I used the intimidation to push myself harder. I was preparing for a professional performance career myself.

Three days a week I had to get through at least one "book class" before I reported to the ballet studio for my two-hour ballet class. After ballet I would go back to my "book classes" for the rest of the afternoon. My education had turned into: hurry and go to class so I can go to *class - dance class*. I had elected journalism as my major, but not because I was excited about it.

"Take all the dance and acting classes you want, but we want you to get a degree you can lean on should you injure yourself," my dad said. I heard that statement over and over again from my parents. I knew they were right, but I also hated listening to their wisdom. I was at the young age of invincibility, but I also had no money. They were helping me financially so I had to listen.

I knew dance was an athlete's career, and just like a young boy that aspires to be an NFL player, most athletes suffer an injury at some point. My brothers were living examples. They were both division one football players on full scholarships (one at Kansas State University and the other at the University of Michigan), and both of them had dreams of professional ball. Sadly, both suffered career ending injuries and/or illnesses.

With resistance, I agreed to work toward a Bachelor of Science in Journalism. I actually liked writing essays and interviewing people. Journalism felt natural. I could listen to music while I was doing my homework and it didn't act as a distraction, which was quite the opposite of *trying* to listen to music while doing a math problem. The only way I could tolerate homework was with my ear buds in my head and my mind connected to music.

My parents volunteered to pay for all the dance classes I could fit into my schedule, as long as my journalism grades didn't suffer. If my grades dropped, so did their funding.

In addition to dance, they were always supportive of my leadership role with *Relay for Life*. They never said anything about how much time it took away from my studies - they must have known I was gaining invaluable business experience. Had my grades dropped, however, they would have still cut my funding. That was an unspoken given.

Off to my book classes I went, *every day*. I suffered through the boring lectures, convincing myself I would indeed use the knowledge I was retaining.

Math classes were the worst. For the life of me, I couldn't find a positive spin on how algebra and statistics were going to play into my entertainment career, nor my journalism career, if I ever decided to use it.

I suffered through the classes and did my best to earn As and Bs. The time in those classes drug on and on. Why was it my time in dance class flew by, but five minutes in math was like five hours of torture?

I looked up at the clock to my left willing it to rescue me. The big hand had only moved four minutes since the last time I had looked. Not only was I bored, I was about to explode. The elastic in my tights was squeezing my bladder, and the professor was going on about how a "ranking system" could ultimately produce unexpected mathematical results. I didn't care, I had to go!

I glanced around at everyone furiously scribbling notes. The professor was reviewing the material for an upcoming exam. He was overly excited as he talked. While it was slightly interesting, it wasn't *that* interesting, which was apparent on everyone's faces. I, along with eighty-nine other people, was dying of boredom. Would any one of us actually use the knowledge we were so desperately trying to understand? At the time, I doubted it.

I took a deep breath and tried to focus my mind on the professor as he continued writing on the dry erase board. I tapped my foot up and down furiously. Bladder full. Professor rambling.

Finally, the horn blasted and I bolted.

I had ten minutes to find a restroom, get across campus, strip off my street clothes, and be standing at the *barre*. There was no such thing as being late for ballet.

My favorite ballet professor was a former principal at the Joffrey Ballet in New York City. She was maybe five feet two inches tall, weighing ninety-five pounds soaking wet. While she may have been tiny, she was also a force to be reckoned with. Twenty minutes into class she would have each aspiring ballerina sweating *through* her leotard. If people were going to drop her class because it was *too* hard, they did it after the first class they attended. She knew how to turn wanna-bes into real dancers.

There were thirty-five dancers in the class. Many of the girls were dance majors, but there were a select few of us who danced our way into the advanced classes while declaring a different, non-dance major. The head professor in the dance department didn't like us, but the department graciously accepted our tuition.

I chose ballet and only ballet for my training because it was the foundation for all dance and it kept me in shape. I would have taken more dance classes, but my schedule was already jam packed with other requirements for my journalism major and *Relay for Life*.

Year-after-year I auditioned for "the dance company" but was never selected. It was rare that a non-dance major actually made *the company*. I hated it, but I was forced to accept it. Instead of pouting about it I focused my energy in other areas like *Relay*.

I walked over to a *barre* in the center of the room (my favorite place to dance the warm-up while holding the cold metal "bar" for balance). There were ten metal *barres* spread across the floor with two girls at each. The rest of the dancers lined the walls that held the permanently mounted wooden *barres*. I preferred to be in the middle of the room in front of the fourth mirror from the south wall. It was the skinny mirror.

I turned sideways to admire myself. I mostly looked at the lower portion of my stomach. I sucked my tummy in and tightened the muscles at the same time I placed my hand across my abdomen. I approved of my flat stomach but reminded myself I was also in front of the skinny mirror.

I turned my gaze to the *barre* and reached my hands out to grab hold. With my hands steadied for balance, I lifted my right leg and gently extended it across the cold metal, pointing my foot. I reached my left arm up and over my right leg for a deep ballerina stretch.

"How's *Relay* going?" my friend asked as she stretched on the opposite side of the *barre*.

"Great. We are crazy busy trying to finalizing everything."

My *barre*-mate had joined a team with her own sorority.

"Has your team met their monetary goals?" I asked.

"Almost. We are about $400 shy, but we'll get there."

"That's great," I said as I lowered my right leg to switch to my left.

"Yeah, I think it's going to be a lot of fun."

Before I could respond, our instructor walked in and started demonstrating the first exercise. I lifted my leg off the *barre* and watched her feet intently. She showed us the combination of foot work (AKA: combo) one time before she looked at the accompanist and gave her the tempo. The pianist gave us four counts and without pause class was in session. We didn't stop for the next two hours.

Slowly but surely I had started to advance in my ballet knowledge and I was quickly becoming adept at seeing a ballet combination demonstrated one time before I could dance the same combo with proficiency and eventually perfection. My trained eye and feet were a necessary survival skill to not only audition, but keep up, and eventually excel in the dance and performance world of New York City.

Dreams should make you uncomfortable,
otherwise they belong on your to-do list.

Did I want to compete in a pageant again? My heart said yes, but my ego was hesitant – I didn't want to be crushed.

I signed the application and stared at it.

Deep down I knew I was on the staircase to greatness. One step at a time I would climb my way to my destiny. Yes, I would have to take some steps backward, but if I stuck to my goals and my commitment to myself I would indeed climb to the top. I would find greatness.

Greatness in what? I asked myself.

Anything, I responded.

Everything I was working on was pointing me in the direction of a successful future. I couldn't quite define what success looked like, but I could feel it.

I wasn't distracted by college parties, alcohol, or boys (okay, so I went weak in the knees when the fraternity boys stood for me as I walked in the room, but they weren't really a *distraction*). I had zeroed in on my goals and I was going for it.

I had been dancing hard, studying diligently, and I had a platform of *Cancer Awareness* in which I was proud of. Dancing and the studying was part of my DNA. A pageant made me stretch as a person. It was, after all, the pageant that led me to the American Cancer Society. As a result, ACS had given me new depth and meaning to how I was spending my days. I honestly felt like I was contributing to society, leaving it better than I had found it.

The pageant system helped me grow as a person and a community member. It helped me find my voice, my opinion, and the ability to develop grace under pressure. It was teaching me to take on criticism and apply it in a positive way. All with a smile on my face.

Pageant or no pageant I was getting my first taste of what it felt like to better the lives of people. I was learning what it meant to create hope for those who needed it most. My definition of success was taking on a whole new meaning.

I had decided I wanted to pursue a career in the entertainment industry. My dreams were starting to take shape. The word "Broadway" was becoming something more than a street sign. Pageants, auditions, and performing in general would give me the skills I needed. Winning a pageant wasn't the ultimate goal, but it would be a great stepping stone to propel me forward.

Somewhere in the midst of my goals I was also holding down a part-time job delivering pharmaceuticals to patients. I hated the reality of a real-world job but it started pushing me to work even harder toward my goal as a professional entertainer. Where I focused my energy was where I would reap my rewards.

I knew the only way I would get experience was to go find it. And I was going to find it.

I stuffed the application and paperwork in the envelope and wrote the address on the front.

The packet was headed to the Miss Flint Hills Scholarship Pageant. I would compete in the Miss America system once again, but I would also audition for "Texas" once again. If neither worked out I would go back to my hometown and teach swimming lessons for a second summer.

It was a triple win no matter the outcome.

I stood up from my desk, walked down the stairs of my sorority house, and into our mail room to drop my envelope in the outgoing mailbox.

"You can't ride two horses with one ass."
−*Sweet Home Alabama*, the movie

Four weeks after I dropped my paperwork in the mail I brought home the Miss Flint Hills title and crown. I also had my second ticket to compete in the Miss Kansas Pageant.

A few months after the pageant I went back to the "Texas" audition, and three weeks after the audition I was offered an ensemble role as a "dancer". It was a paid position.

I was beyond ecstatic. For the first time I could see the sparkling lights of a Broadway billboard. I could taste Broadway on the menu of my life.

There was one problem... I couldn't do both as they overlapped in their time commitment. The Miss Kansas Pageant was the same weekend as opening weekend for "Texas".

I was at a crossroads: I had to pick one.

One of my favorite lines from the movie *Sweet Home Alabama*, "You can't ride two horses with one ass." In other words, I had a decision to make.

I weighed my options for two weeks. If I relinquished my crown to the first runner-up, could I ever compete again? I felt it was poor form to win and then say "no thanks". Would that mean my days as a pageant competitor were over? I believed the answer to that question was a simple, but solid "yes".

If I kept the title and competed, but didn't win the Miss Kansas crown I could teach swimming lessons. But if I did win, I would have to cancel my summer of instruction – letting down my students and their parents.

The dancing role was an opportunity to perform fifty-four times in one summer. As a dancer. Gaining experience for Broadway.

I had two winning options: win Miss Kansas or take the dance contract. Winning Miss Kansas was a gamble. I had the "Texas" contract in my hands.

My deciding factor was with my swimming students. I simply couldn't promise those kiddos one thing and not follow through with my promise. My integrity couldn't allow me to do that to them.

I picked up the phone and dialed the number of the executive director of the Miss Flint Hills Scholarship Pageant. When she picked up the phone I explained to her my dilemma.

"Well, what would you like to do?" she asked.

"I would like to pass my crown to the first runner-up. I'm going to take the dance contract."

Scene Twelve

Back in the horse pasture, August 12, 2007
(The accident)

*"Come to me all you who are weary and burdened,
and I will give you rest." –Matthew 11:28*

I originally met Shelly and her mom during my first season with the production "Texas" in 2003. Shelly and I had instantly become friends. There was a connection between us that was a blend of long lost friends and sisters. Shelly was a wrangler for the show as well as a professional cowgirl. She was a "local" in the area and enjoyed spending her summer down in the Palo Duro Canyon State Park, where I was performing that summer of 2003 when I was a dancer. She and her husband made their living working with horses so the production was a natural extension of their day and some extra income.

The show used wranglers to handle the horses. In the early days, the show would use six or seven of the "guys" in the cast and crew to take care of saddling up the horses and to do the actual riding. As the show progressed, it became apparent that people who actually knew something about horses were needed. Wranglers were hired. The wranglers also took over most of the riding scenes for not only safety reasons, but for the authenticity of the look of riders. From the rider appearing during the overture (atop the rim of the canyon wall) to the six riders carrying the six flags of Texas during the finale, the show relied upon those wranglers to add that very unique element of live animals to the production.

But that didn't stop the performers from finding the horses on our days off. Shelly and I became friends over our shared infatuation with the majestic creatures. But my infatuation would end with the severing of my foot.

"Help us Jesus. We need You," Shelly prayed in a slow, calm, and steady voice. "We have faith in You. Please calm Adrienne."

Someone help me, I silently screamed. *God where are you? What just happened? What have I done?*

"Adrienne I'm here with you. Jesus is here with you. Breathe, focus on Jesus." Shelly continued. "Lord we need you," Shelly pleaded.

Why is this happening? I asked silently. *What is going on? It's so hot. I need water. Oh my God the pain.*

Shelly continued to pray. I continued to breathe. I continued to question. I was calm as she prayed and panicked when she stopped.

We were out in the country, which meant we had to wait. Wait for help. Wait for shock. Wait for Jesus.

I had made the ultimate stupid decision of running and jumping on a horse. And I couldn't undo the consequence.

I laid in the hot Texas sun, the heat as unforgiving as my decision. I had to wait for my story to play out. I couldn't speed up time nor slow it down. I had to live through it. One breath at a time. One moment at a time.

My little group was doing their best to keep me conscious. I knew shock, to unconsciousness, wasn't an option. It could kill me. So we did the only thing we could, we prayed.

Slowly, one-by-one neighbors began showing up as they noticed commotion in the neighboring pasture. They approached slowly, cautiously, but when they took one look at the situation they backed off. Did they sense the situation was under control or could they not handle the sight of six inches of my bone protruding and my foot dangling off to one side?

A sheriff arrived. The officer was hesitant, but calm. He approached so slowly I recall being irritated. *Could you be in any less of a hurry?* my thoughts screamed. *I'm only in PAIN! And I can't BREATHE!*

Next I remember someone asking if they should move me into a car to take me to the hospital. Everyone, including myself, shouted in unison "NO!" Our growing group decided to wait for the paramedics.

The waiting continued, and so did the prayers.

At some point I started politely barking orders, "Please call my dad!" I pleaded as I tried to catch my breath. I continued to breathe as though every breath would be my last, "My insurance card is in my purse," I gasped for air. "It's in the bedroom." As if it mattered.

More time passed. More prayers. More neighbors.

I started to panic, "Oh my God, get the horse away from me!" I screamed. "He is going to attack me!" I was panicking and screaming. "Where is he? Get him away!" I pleaded.

"Adrienne, it's okay," Shelly tried to calm me, but I didn't believe her words. "He's on the other side of the pasture. You're going to be okay." I squeezed her hand as sweat ran down my dirty face.

"Get him away from me! He is going to trample me!" I continued in panic.

"Adrienne, it's okay he is not going to hurt you. He isn't close to you. We are here with you. We won't let him hurt you," Shelly assured me.

I started hyperventilating again. Shelly started praying again. Paula cried while Richard, her husband, was the solid rock that held me up. At some point he had joined us. He was on his hands and knees, bracing himself behind me so I could lean against him, lessening my movement. I don't remember him saying a word.

I half lay, half sat in the hot sun staring at the blue sky wondering what had just happened. One second I was flying through the air and the next I felt my foot snap off. At first it didn't hurt, but my mind knew exactly what had happened.

My ankle had disintegrated. There was a sickening sensation in my stomach something had happened I couldn't undo. I imagine it is that same feeling when you hear a parent has died, or your spouse is leaving you, or a child has cancer. That sickening feeling I felt that day will forever connect me to the survivors in life. We survived when we didn't want to. We survived what we didn't think was possible. There is an unspoken bond. It is what conjures up the tears when you witness someone else going through the hurt you know so well. You would do anything to take the burden for them, even a complete stranger. You don't wish that kind of pain on your worst enemy.

Never through the experience in the pasture do I remember crying. I was focused on surviving.

The ambulance arrived. I could hear them racing down the highway, sirens blaring. *Faster.* It was the sound of help. *Faster.* The sound of pain relieving drugs en route. *Drive faster!*

When they finally got to me it was a blur of questions yet a sense of calm from the paramedics. They didn't appear afraid of me, or the situation. They were trained. They were there to help.

They moved me to a body board and braced my neck. I stared at the sky as they lifted me out of that pasture and into the back of the ambulance. I knew my foot was with me, on the board, because I could still feel the screaming pain.

"Please give me something," I pleaded with them, referring to painkillers.

"We can't," one medic responded.

"Why?!" I asked as I grimaced in pain.

"The doctor has to assess you first."

Even in my state of frenzy his response seemed to be the stupidest thing I had ever heard. But looking back at the severity of the situation I'm sure they were making sure my nerve hadn't been severed. If it had, I wouldn't have hurt, and if I hadn't hurt they would have no option but to amputate my foot. Pain was actually a good thing.

My paramedics loaded me into the ambulance and as we drove away one paramedic was immediately on the phone with the hospital describing my injury. As I heard him describe my physical state, it was more than I could handle and again I started to panic.

"Shelly!" I screamed. "Where are you?"

"I'm right here Adrienne. I'm in the front seat."

I looked at the other paramedic, who was on my other side - not on the phone. He was my new friend so I started to talk. I started to talk because that is what I do when I'm in a situation that makes me nervous or uncomfortable. I talk. I talk. I talk. And then I talk some more.

"What is your name?" I asked my new friend.

"I'm Tommy." He told me.

"Tell me about yourself," I tried to ask as though it was typical Sunday evening. "Where did you go to school?" I winced.

"Here in Texas."

"Did you like college?" I interrupted and tried to extend a smile through gritted teeth and my piercing pain.

"Yes."

"What was your favorite bar in college?"

He told me, but all I remember is it had the name "chicken" in it. I was trying to listen but I was struggling to hear. I could feel every bump and every turn on that very long forty-five minute ambulance ride.

To pass the time and keep my mind occupied I decided to sing campfire songs to my new friend Tommy. "Do you know the song *Fireman Bill?*" I asked.

"No I don't think so."

That was all I needed as my cue to start singing, *"Fireman Bill was a fireman boy,"* I gasped, *"cause he puts out fires."* I felt the ambulance go into a turn and I gripped the edge of the backboard with all my strength, stabilizing myself. *"He went to a fire one night I'm told,"* I took two big breaths, *"cause he puts out fires."*

I took a long pause and tried to swallow the pain. "It's a boy scout song. My dad was a boy scout. Were you a boy scout?"

Before I even let him answer I started rambling on about a new subject: the story of Doris Day.

I had studied Doris Day that particular summer and I remember being amazed and inspired by her. She wanted nothing more in life than to be a dancer yet fate had something else in store. At the age of sixteen, a car Doris was a passenger in was struck by a train. Her right leg was crushed, as were her dreams of becoming a professional dancer. During her recovery she started singing, which was how she became the amazing Doris Day we know today. She took a negative in her life and turned it into a positive. I thought she was pretty cool and I was doing my best to relay Doris's success story to my new best friend, Tommy.

I'm 90% sure everyone heard me rambling on and on about Miss Day because I told anyone who was in earshot. And if I thought they didn't hear me the first time, I told them again. If I would have been more quick-witted I would have also told everyone the story about my favorite male ballet dancer whose career came to an end because of his horrible knees... that's why we knew Patrick Swayze the actor who could dance, versus the dancer who could act.

Scene Thirteen

The University of Kansas Student Union, the *Relay For Life* Planning
Committee, May 2003
(Four years and three months *before* the accident)

*"Things rarely go exactly how they are planned. It's not personal, it's what
happens in business." –George Rosel*

A few months prior to KU's first-ever *Relay for Life* I had a major
crisis. I received a call from our t-shirt printing company announcing
our order had gone awry. They weren't sure I would receive my
complete order in time for the event. I was immediately furious which
sent my mouth running wild and my tears quickly followed.

Why was a t-shirt order such a big deal? Because the t-shirts were
for all the participants, volunteers, and cancer survivors.

I called my dad to tell him about my dilemma and I fully expected
him to jump on board and tell me I needed to ream the owner of the t-
shirt company. Instead, my dad - a veteran business owner - told me to
pull it together. "Things rarely go exactly how they are planned. It's not
personal, it's what happens in business," he told me. "Really? Major? If
you can't learn to go with the flow and pull yourself together you need
to give up your leadership role."

I was stunned and upset with my dad's comments. I cried harder as
he got louder and he told me to calm down. I was upset because my
dad was right. I was freaking out about *t-shirts*. Was a t-shirt really
worth losing sleep over?

It was because of that t-shirt fiasco I learned my first big business
lesson: it's not personal, it's business. I also learned our hobbies and
our businesses should never define us. In life, things go wrong... it's
just the way it is, so go with it and be flexible on your journey.

But now I know the drama really stemmed from the fact I had little leadership experience and I didn't know how to deal with even the smallest of things going askew. In the grand scheme of things it's pretty hilarious I had such a meltdown about t-shirts.

"If you take care of your people your people will take care of your customers and your business will take care of itself." –JW Marriott

------

My mom and dad had made the six-hour drive from my hometown of Liberal to my college town of Lawrence. They wanted to show their full support and they wanted to see the event I was pulling off. I had been talking non-stop about *Relay for Life* for the past ten months. In fact, I talked more about the *Relay* than I did about my seventeen credit hours of classes in which I was enrolled.

They arrived in town the night before the big event and met me and my *Relay* crew on campus. We were finalizing as many details as possible. We had posters, luminaria bags, permanent markers, t-shirts (yes, the t-shirts arrived) and paperwork scattered across the room.

The girls were making posters while the guys were organizing the shirts – all of which had arrived with no defects. Everyone was excited for our big event which was set to start in less than twenty-four hours.

When my parents walked in I gave them bear-hugs and introduced them to my friends. I put mom and dad to work and everyone welcomed their help.

Mom was assigned to posters with the girls while Dad *watched* the guys organize t-shirts. Within ten minutes of their arrival my dad pulled his phone out of his pocket and left. A few minutes later he walked back in. He resumed watching the organization of shirts and the overall business of the room. He had a broad smile spread across his face. I could see his chest puff out at the "business" training his baby daughter had ambitiously sought out and was seeing to fruition.

Forty-five minutes later pizza arrived.

Dad taught me another valuable lesson that evening without even speaking: *take care of your people, even if it is as simple as ordering pizza.* People determine the success of any organization or event.

Sometimes the unexpected journey creates lasting memories.

Finals were in two weeks and the *Relay* was our focus, school our hobby. We were all busting our tails for the two biggest events of the year... a *Relay* and finals. We were all running on pure adrenaline.

The next day I blew off my classes (a very unusual event) in order to arrive at Memorial Stadium by noon to start setting up. My team was joining me between noon and 2 p.m., depending upon their class schedules.

Participating teams, including a team from the fraternity house that stood for me when I interrupted their dinner, were scheduled to arrive at 5 p.m. The *Relay* was scheduled to start *promptly* at 6 p.m.

I had several dignitaries arriving at 5:30 p.m. – including the chancellor of the university, the top research scientist from the University of Kansas Cancer Research Center, state representatives, and many more. I loved it when people asked me how I got so many dignitaries to our event. My response was simple, but truthful: I asked. It's amazing what you get if you simply ask!

My favorite dignitary was our very own committee member's mom who was still fighting her personal battle with breast cancer. Yes, she came to the *Relay*!

I had submitted a request with the United States Air Force for a fighter-jet flyover at 6:15 p.m. They had an airbase located thirty miles away. The Air Force sent me a letter wishing me well on my event. Had I thought of the flyover earlier in the year, instead of two weeks before the event, I knew I could have made it happen.

Our food committee had organized donated food to be delivered every two hours from 6 p.m. to 6 a.m. Our entertainment committee had dj's, bands, dance teams, and singers scheduled throughout the event. Our logistics committee was in charge of bathrooms, trash, and the overall well-being of the stadium for the entire event. Our luminaria committee had hundreds of bags to organize up the hill – the hill being the visual signature of the university while the luminarias were the visual signature of the event.

Our recruitment committee had thirty-five teams registered with $65,000 in raised funds. I don't remember having a goal other than to raise money. I would have been proud of $30,000 from broke college students. You could say we exceeded even *my* expectations.

The unexpected cherry on top: one of our committee members surprised our team of organizers by recruiting his buddies to deliver the sofa from their house. And the sofa was reserved for the planning committee *only*. The best part: the buddies ran off anyone who tried to sit on it. It was entertaining to watch the amateur security guards guarding a sofa.

The event started at 6:05 p.m. and in true Adrienne fashion I was freaking out we hadn't start on time. Why? Because I was a control freak still learning my balance.

We started by taking roll-call of all the teams. Given that we were over-enthusiastic-college-students, it was a fun welcome.

When the enthusiasm calmed, I welcomed our dignitaries one by one and several of them gave "quick" speeches. And of course I had to take the microphone away from our legislators. The *Relay*, after all, wasn't a political podium to solicit votes.

Our opening ceremony concluded by inviting all the "survivors" to the track. The cancer survivors led the way in a victory lap as we, the participants, enthusiastically cheered them on.

Next, as a large group everyone took a lap – signifying the event was officially underway.

We had eleven hours and twenty minutes to go.

**When you do reach a milestone in your journey,
don't forget to stop and look around.**

Around 8 p.m. my dad grabbed me and said, "Adrienne, I want you to stop and look around."

I stood still.

My dad stood next to me in silence as we observed the event. I looked at the hundreds of people on the track and the band playing in the end-zone. People were laughing, dancing, playing Frisbee, and walking around the track. Mom was at the edge of the track chatting with Melinda from the American Cancer Society – they were both laughing. Dad put his arm around me and quietly said, "You made this happen."

I beamed as we stood silently, pressing the memory into our minds.

"Fake it 'til you *become* it." –Amy Cuddy

At 10 p.m. I made my way back to the microphone and invited everyone to join me at the starting line. It was time for the luminaria ceremony.

What is the luminaria ceremony?

(from the ACS web site) Relay For Life participants and donors remember loved ones lost to cancer and honor those battling the disease by dedicating luminaria bags (AKA: paper bags). Luminaria bags are transformed and illuminated after dark (with a candle) at every local Relay For Life event. Each luminaria is personalized with a name, photo, message, or drawing in memory or honor of a friend or loved one who has been affected by cancer. Each luminaria represents a person. They are our mothers, fathers, sisters, brothers, aunts, uncles, nieces, nephews, friends, coworkers, and so many others.

Our luminaria ceremony was one of the finest in the country. You see, the University of Kansas is built on a hill. At the top of the hill is a giant clock tower that is the center of campus. At the bottom of the hill is Memorial Stadium. That evening we covered the entire KU hill in luminaria bags. The hundreds of candles inside the bags lit up the night sky, illuminating the names of cancer patients that had personal relationships with our participants. There were so many names of people who had fought or were fighting cancer. It was humbling to say the least.

Our crowd of *Relay* participants grew silent as we honored those who were the reason for our grand event. It was the awe-inspiring moment of the evening. There was a sense of sadness, like that of a funeral, as you walked the hill and read the life spans of some of the people being honored. There were too many who had lost the fight.

As I walked the hill reading the names for a second time I wondered how many of us would fight our own battles with cancer. The statistics in 2003 said one out of three of us would fight the battle in our lifetimes. Yet, at such a young age we were all invincible. We thought of cancer in a young person's body as an incomprehensible and foreign idea.

When I reached my own luminarias I stopped to honor those that were *my* reason to form *Relay For Life* at the university. Three out of four of *my* people were survivors.

We allowed the candles to burn until the wicks were exhausted.

Melinda approached me shortly after I finished walking the long pathway of luminarias. "I'm going to take off," she said. We stood shoulder-to-shoulder and observed the *Relay*. "Adrienne, you did an outstanding job pulling this together."

"Thank you." I said as we watched the energy circling the track.

"Can I count on you for next year?" she asked.

"Hmmm," I paused, "I guess so," I giggled with sarcasm.

"You know," I paused again, "now that the event is in full swing and is a success, there is something you should know." I paused and she looked at me. "This is the first *Relay* I have ever attended. And the first event I have ever organized."

I turned to look at her. She had a stunned expression.

"Are you kidding?" She asked with raised eyebrows.

"No. I was afraid if I told you earlier you wouldn't help me put this together."

"I may not have," she laughed. "By the looks of things I would have never guessed that. I always assumed you had participated in several. I had no idea."

"I'm a great actress," I said with flair and she laughed.

We hugged and said our good-byes. She asked that I call her during the summer to talk details for the 2nd Annual *Relay for Life* at the University of Kansas. I told her to expect a call in July.

I walked out to the track and joined one of the groups walking laps.

I push myself to know my own capabilities.

At 3 a.m. I walked over to the food table and grabbed a sandwich and a cup of coffee. I had only slept six hours in the past forty-eight. I had three hours to go. I was sleepwalking.

At 5:55 a.m. I gathered the exhausted participants for the closing ceremony, which consisted of "Thank you and good night."

My planning committee voted on a team breakfast. My parents drove me to the restaurant. Before the food arrived I fell asleep sitting in the booth. I think several other committee members did too.

My parents got me back to my bunk-bed in my sorority house and told me to call them when I woke up. They were headed to their own bed to make up for a missed night of sleep.

Scene Fourteen

At the emergency room, August 12, 2007
(The accident)

"H.O.P.E. – Hold On, Pain Ends" –unknown

I was pulled out of the ambulance feet first, blood splattering. I was met by someone I barely knew, a man named Bill Anderson. Bill was the producer for "Texas". He was a familiar face, but not much more as I had more interaction with my director than producer.

Bill came to the hospital because he received a call from someone, "Adrienne has broken her ankle. Will you go check on her?" He showed up thinking it was no big deal. He would check on me and be back home within an hour, two hours at the most. However, when he was greeted with my right foot dangling, and blood flying, he instantly knew he had underestimated the situation. He later told me my blood stained his shoes, his pants, and the concrete in the ambulance bay where he first met me.

Our friendship started as Bill raced into the ER next to my gurney. Our friendship was sealed as he held my hand and offered me his warm presence. Due to the situation, Bill and I had a connection that would bond us for the rest of our lives. We were experiencing a tragedy together. I the patient. He the witness. That evening Bill became one of my best friends.

Into the ER we raced. As we passed the nurses' station I remember their jaws on the floor as they saw my severed foot race by on the bloodstained gurney (the tennis shoe still on my foot). Their reaction wasn't up-lifting. I tried to say "hi" and make a joke, but I quickly realized it was neither the time nor the place for being a smart-ass. My situation was about to challenge everyone's medical education and training. I didn't realize the extent of my own situation.

The next hour was a blur of emotions. I remember crying, laughing, being angry, being grateful, and every other emotion the human spirit could conjure up. My dear circle of friends never left my side. They took turns holding my hand and being the solid rock I needed. My friends consisted of Bill, Shelly and the director of the show. The director arrived sometime amongst the chaos. He took his place as my teammate and never wavered in his strength. They listened as I cried and screamed. I watched them fight back their own tears as they let me vice-grip their hands.

"I don't regret my decision," I gritted defiantly between my teeth. "I was living my life to the fullest! When I'm dead I want to come sliding into home plate," I gasped for air, "with one hell of a story."

The nurses came into my room and shooed my team of friends out. They began cutting off my clothes and prepping me for surgery. But my friends were my life line. I didn't want them to leave. Yet I was in no place to argue and they did as they were told.

"We'll be right outside the door," Shelly assured me.

Almost immediately they started cutting off my pants. As they got to my underwear I realized I had failed miserably at the age-old wisdom: *always wear cute underwear in case you are in an accident.*

By the time I had processed my underwear situation they had already cut through my sports bra and shirt. I was lying naked on the table. Once they had the hospital gown in place they let my friends back in the room and they resumed their position of taking turns holding my hand.

That's when a new face entered my world. "I'm your doctor and I'm going to take care of you," the good doctor said.

He was wearing a typical white doctor's coat, his name embroidered over the chest. He stood at about 5'5" and had a thick head of brown hair with chocolate brown eyes to match. He was holding one of those new black iPhones in his left hand. I noticed how small his hands were. Perfect for an intricate surgery.

I said "hello" as politely as I could, but the next thing I knew the doctor was walking around me taking pictures of my ankle.

"This isn't a photo shoot," I said hastily at him. He ignored me and snapped on.

"What is your pain level on a scale of one to ten?"

"13!" I gasped.

"On a scale of one to ten," he repeated.

"13!" I gasped again.

He didn't repeat his question. I think he knew my response.

"Where are my parents?" I asked as I started to cry.

Bill stepped up to me and grabbed my hand. "They are on their way," he assured me. "I talked to your dad right before he was taking off."

When my parents got the call they dropped everything, literally leaving raw hamburger patties on the kitchen counter to head to the local airport. My dad pulled his Cessna out of the hanger and they flew to me.

Someone announced it was time for surgery. My team didn't leave my side as they pulled the guard rails of my bed in position and pushed me back out into the hallway. Our group had now doubled in size as my team and nurses pushed me down the hall. I watched the ceiling lights go by overhead. I felt like I was in a horror movie and the editor had cut away to the ceiling lights for dramatic effect. I wanted to turn the movie off, but the switch was stuck.

I desperately wanted my parents. I was twenty-four-years-old and all I wanted was my mommy and daddy.

My team said their good-byes and I took a deep breath. I had to be brave. I had no choice. I was focused on survival. My team was focused on prayer.

Everyone, but me, knew I may not wake up with both of my feet.

Scene Fifteen

West Texas A&M University, the choir room, rehearsal, May 2003
(Four years and three months *before* the accident)

"Move out of your comfort zone. You can only grow if you are willing to feel awkward and uncomfortable when you try something new." –Brian Tracey

"Adrienne, I need you to not only sing, but sing out," Lee Kendle, the music director of "Texas" said in his commanding voice. Giving me little room to argue he continued with, "It is a huge stage and we need everyone's confident voice."

"But I thought I was hired as a dancer," I tried to argue lamely.

"And *our* dancers sing," Lee said not buying my excuse.

I took a deep breath and exhaled with my lips pursed together making the sound of a horse. I was terrified to sing.

In middle school I had embarrassed myself while singing a solo on stage and vowed to never sing again. During high school cheerleading I even tried to yell wrong (because we had been taught the difference) in an effort to damage my vocal chords. Now I was being paid to dance in a show, but I had a music director commanding me to sing, and telling me I *had* to sing.

"Again. From the top," Lee said to the accompanist, but loud enough for the entire musical cast to hear. Everyone was silent as we flipped our sheet music back to the first page. I looked down at my book. All I could translate were the words, not the notes on the page.

The music started and Lee didn't budge from where he stood in front of me. He directed everyone in our musical entrance and then refocused his energy *and ear* on me.

He pressed his ear within two feet of my mouth and listened as I squeaked out the lyrics. My attempt was shaky and pathetic. I tried to

71

raise my folder of sheet music, which I couldn't read, in front of my mouth. It muted my sound and he looked directly at me and then lowered the music book back to the appropriate level.

Sweat was forming on my temples. I desperately wanted him to go away, but I also wished for him to share the secret ingredient for confidence.

He waved his arms frantically overhead, signaling the pianist to stop. "Adrienne," he said, staring at me. And I could feel the entire cast focusing their energy on me, just as Lee was. "You have a voice. You're simply afraid of it."

I looked at him with raised eyebrows trying not to cry, but I could feel my chin quivering.

"Do you realize that dancers who can sing get more work? And more work means less waiting tables. Do you want to be a professional dancer?"

"Yes," I said timidly.

"What?" He asked.

"Yes," I said more boldly and managed a meek grin.

"That's better. And do you want to be a starving dancer or a dancer who always has work?"

"Always has work," I responded with an embarrassed, apprehensive smile.

"Well then, this summer we are going to teach you how to sing." He smiled at me warmly. "*And* sing with confidence! Lesson number one, I want you to stand in that corner," he pointed to a corner off to his right "and sing as loud as your voice will let you – without straining of course. Only you will hear yourself. I won't even stand next to you."

My chin stopped quivering.

"You aren't familiar with the sound of your own voice and we need to change that."

As I separated myself from the cast, Lee turned to address the other performers, many of which were also dancers. "Everyone can sing. Singing is nothing more than training and using a muscle. That muscle is called your larynx. And just like you train your muscles to dance, *Adrienne*, you can also train your larynx to sing!"

He paused to let us digest his lesson before he continued, "The problem is, some of you are scared of your own voice. This is the first obstacle we must overcome! One of the best ways to hear yourselves is to sing into a wall," Lee continued his explanation. "The sound will bounce off the wall and back to your ears. As a matter of fact, as an exercise let's spread out around the room. I want everyone to face the wall and sing."

Without questioning his expertise everyone quickly scattered around the room and I was grateful to have the company of my cast members.

"How can you expect an audience to listen *and enjoy* your voice if you don't?" Lee paused while everyone got situated.

"From the top!" he said excitedly to all of us. "And remember, sing out!"

As I sang so did everyone else, but my own voice bounced off the hard wall and back into my ears, just as Lee said it would. I was the loudest vocalist in the room, from where I was standing anyway. The sound frightened me. It was foreign and unfamiliar.

I could feel Lee pacing behind us as he allowed us to sing through the whole song. It was the most volume our group had produced. When the song came to a close Lee immediately shouted, "Again. From the top!"

The accompanist started and we all entered on cue. I heard myself. Again, I wasn't sure about the sound. I wanted to cringe, but I was also thinking about what Lee had just told us. I pushed myself to sing louder.

·The volume in the entire room increased yet again. The vocalists and the dancers sang as one unified ensemble. We even produced a professional sound. I felt chill bumps run up my legs and arms. When the song came to an end, Lee was silent. One-by-one we all turned to look at Lee, and we were greeted by a face that was smiling.

"Now that is a professional group of entertainers."

We all let out a sigh of relief as we glanced at each other and laughed.

"Okay... from where you are, let's go from the top again. This time as you sing I want you to look at each other and perform for one another. Remember, I need volume. You just proved to me you are capable of it."

We sang. My volume decreased slightly but I pushed myself through my insecurity. Lee walked around the room stopping in front of each of us and pressed his ear close to our mouths so he could hear our individual voices. When he stopped in front of me he smiled and then sang along with me. I smiled back.

If my path has no obstacles, I have no sense of accomplishment.

As we progressed through the three weeks of rehearsals I was becoming more and more confident as a singer. I was definitely not ready for a solo, but I was making progress in the group setting. Even if I felt like I was faking my confidence.

The first time we sang in the large outdoor amphitheatre I understood why Lee was pushing all of us to sing in the capacity of a *professional* opera singer. There were no walls and there was no ceiling, which meant the sound drifted up into the air and spread through the sky, dampening the sound the instant it left our mouths.

I had thought I could hear myself when I sang into the wall. Singing in the great outdoors, even with fifty other people, didn't matter as you didn't have the blanket of other people's voices. You could hear your own voice loud and clear, or soft and meek. I realized I had to step up to the plate and sing as though I had sung my entire life.

I had fifty-four performances to learn the sound of my own voice. I was determined to find my vocal confidence.

My favorite moment from those performances came during performance number forty. I was standing next to Lee's wife, Kathy, who was also an incredible vocalist, and I sang as though "no one was listening". During that performance I finally broke down my own barriers, and she heard the transition. She knew I had been fighting my insecurities that entire summer and she too felt the release in my voice and the exhaustion of self-judgment. She reached out and grabbed my hand and squeezed. She glanced my direction as we continued to perform for our audience. She smiled as she sang, our eyes met, and I squeezed her hand in return.

I was, for the first time, singing with passion and conviction in a way that made an audience *want* to listen.

I was a dancer who was officially singing. *Now if I could just learn to read my darn sheet music.*

"You must do the things you think you cannot do." –Eleanor Roosevelt

------

When I returned to school that fall I reassessed my goals. Yes, I picked up where I had left off in terms of *Relay for Life*, but I also

74

decided I wanted to become a dancer who could sing *and* act. Since I was dedicated in my book studies as well as the dance department, I added theatre as my minor in order to focus on my acting and vocal skills.

I buckled down and found teachers and classes that taught me to read sheet music and act out monologues. I even auditioned for a vocal musical theatre class. Whether the teacher selected me by accident, out of pity, or as his "pet project", I didn't care. For a semester I was surrounded by some of my university's best performers and greatest singers. I knew their talented presence alone would make me a better singer. I was by far the weakest link in the class, but my twenty classmates cheered me on every time I stood in front of them to sing and workshop my vocal selections. That semester my confidence grew and I strengthened my vocal chords.

And by that spring we held the second annual *Relay for Life*, again at Memorial Stadium. It was a full blown success, except we were missing one of my favorite dignitaries: our committee member's mom who had lost her own battle with breast cancer.

Scene Sixteen

Outside the Amphitheatre, July 2007
(One month *before* the accident)

"Life is really simple, but we insist on making it complicated." –Confucius

After the show the cast would graciously meet the thousands of people who ventured out to the canyons in order to take in the theatrical version of the settling of Texas.

As our audience exited we greeted them with laughter and music and appreciation. We would visit with people from around the country and sometimes from around the world. Our characters became memories in family photos and photo albums that captured summer vacations. For some families it was their first theatrical experience.

I found myself wondering how many of those young faces, who sat under the stars that summer, had set their destiny into motion because of our performance. It was, after all, the magic of theatre on a young and impressionable mind. For I was that young and impressionable mind only a decade prior.

I remember a young lady around the age of nine, approached me in the meet/greet line. Her eyes were the same color as her brown hair. Her parents stood behind her with their camera ready. I could tell she was nervous as she handed me her program book and a pen.

I crouched down to be eye-level with the reflection of myself.

"What is your name?" I asked her gently as she handed me her program book.

"Madison."

"Madison. It is very nice to meet you. My name is Adrienne."

She said nothing, but continued to stare star struck. What she didn't realize, I was just an ordinary person and only a few years older than she. I tried to pull that pedestal out from under my feet as I flipped to my page in the program book.

"Madison, where are you from?"

"Tulsa."

"Very cool. Are you on vacation with your family?"

"Yes."

"Are you having fun?"

"Yes."

"And what do you want to be when you grow up?"

"A dancer."

I looked up from signing my name next to my picture, "And I have no doubt you will be."

She smiled a broad smile and stepped forward to give me a hug. I hugged the little girl and thanked God for the opportunity to not only perform but reach people beyond the stage.

Scene: Amarillo, Texas. A trauma hospital, private patient room, August 13, 2007
(The day *after* the accident)

I woke up almost a day later with my dad at my side. He was crying.

"There is no crying," I slurred boldly. Dad just kissed me and held my hand.

I looked up at the clock and it said 5:05. Was it a.m. or p.m.? I was confused. "How long have I been asleep?" I asked my parents.

"Almost twenty-four hours," my mom responded.

I looked down and my foot was in a cast and propped on a pillow. It still hurt, not as bad as it did in the field, but it was indeed painful. Because of the drugs, and the trauma, I drifted in and out of consciousness. I didn't have dreams.

Thankfully, my mom or dad were always holding my hand when I awoke.

My nurses would come and go from my room changing my IV bags, giving me medication, taking my blood pressure, bringing me food I wouldn't eat, and checking my catheter. When I was awake and alert, I finally asked one of them, "What are you doing?"

That time they were checking for a pulse on my foot, but every time they came in the room it seemed to take longer and longer.

77

On the third day my doctor came to my room and tried to find my pulse in the top of my foot, just as the nurses had previously done. I watched him as he felt for my pulse with his fingers. He moved his hand around the top of my foot. I cringed. He furrowed his brow and grabbed for his stethoscope. He listened. He moved the stethoscope again. He listened.

His eyes filled with panic.

He called for a nurse and before I could register what was happening, the doctor himself began frantically cutting through the fiberglass cast with a power tool. I could hear the scream of the saw as I watched sweat drip down his face. The dust was quickly filling the air. My parents were huddled together at the side of my bed. I was lying there, dumbfounded, confused, and waiting. My mind was empty. I was empty. Why was he in such a panic?

When the cast was sliced open, he ripped and pulled with all his strength, trying to separate the cast into two halves. The worry and fear on his face was as evident as a Texas thunderstorm. He dug through the cotton dressing as he hastily stuck the stethoscope further up my foot. Everyone fell silent.

He listened. We stared. He moved the stethoscope. He listened. We stared. He moved the stethoscope. He listened. We stared.

This time he let out a sigh, "I found it."

Had he not found my pulse I would have been in deep doo-doo and probably without a foot.

Scene Seventeen

University of Kansas, graduation day, May 2005
(Two years and three months *before* the accident)

"I find the harder I work the more luck I seem to have."
–Thomas Jefferson

When I returned for my senior year of college I wanted to lead *Relay for Life* for my third and final time, but I couldn't. I had forty credit hours left to complete my degree "on time". While I loved being in charge of the event, I reminded myself the *Relay* wasn't the reason I went to college. College was to arm myself with an education, and if I was going to graduate debt-free I had to buckle down and focus.

The *Relay* had given me the experience in leadership I needed and it was time to turn that opportunity over to the next person in line. I am very proud of my team who raised $110,000 in a mere two years.

My scholarship funding was running out and I needed to get done on time. So I said good-bye to my "baby".

My funding was determined by my parent's, which they explained before I left my hometown for the first time in 2001. "The George F. Rosel scholarship foundation," my dad, George F. Rosel, explained, "is good for the financial equivalent of four years of in-state tuition, which means you can go anywhere in the country you like, but we (mom and dad) will only fund equivalent to Kansas' tuition rate. Your four years must be consecutive. If you drop out, but decide to go back you are on your own. If you go longer than four years you are on your own. If your grades fail you are on your own. If you get pregnant, tattoos, or piercings you're on your own. The final requirement: you can study anything you like, but when you leave college we want you to have a degree you can rely on. Meaning if you choose dance, great, but you must choose a second degree in the event you get hurt."

The above seemed harsh, but I couldn't argue. My parents were offering me a four-year full-ride scholarship and I didn't think their stipulations were all that crazy when compared to the dollar amount. After all, they never said I *had to* take their offer. It was my choice.

My senior year I did indeed buckle down and focus. I lived on campus from 6 a.m. until 10 p.m. five days a week. I started my mornings at the gym, advanced to journalism classes, "passed go" to ballet, and eventually ended my days in the theatre department as the *mistress of costumes* for shows, which also allowed me the appropriate credit hours to complete my theatre minor.

I signed up for a total of twenty credit hours the first semester and twenty credit hours the second semester. Twenty credit hours seemed like a lot, but I told myself I didn't have a choice and so I simply did it. And with my determination I received the best grades of my entire college career. I also had the most fun with friends I had ever had, and I finally dated someone for the first and only time during college. I was focused and happy, and when graduation day rolled around I couldn't wipe the smile off my face.

That same hill at the university I had lined in luminarias for the *Relay*, was the hill graduates have the honor of walking down on graduation day. It was symbolic for overcoming obstacles and taking a step in the direction of your dreams.

On graduation day I couldn't quit smiling. As I laughed with friends my dad took pictures of me with my journalism flag. That journalism flag lead the newest J-School graduates down the hill, into the stadium, and into the ceremony that congratulated us on our achievements.

My dad was with me on graduation day because he also walked that hill over thirty years before I had... but he walked behind the engineering flag. Dad beamed right along with me. Not only was he proud, but he knew I had worked through my frustration, even when all I wanted to do was drop-out, move to New York, and pursue my dance dream full time.

The gift of a college education is one of the greatest gifts I could have ever received. I am so grateful to my parents for such an amazing gift. Because of them I was able to graduate college 100% debt free. And while my dad was with me at the University of Kansas, my mom was at home handing my younger brother his high school diploma on the same day, during the same hour, but six hours away.

While I didn't particularly want to do anything other than dance my way through college I still found myself grateful for my journalism and marketing degree, which I have put to use every single day of my life. I even used my education to market myself when I lived in New York chasing my dream. But my daily gratitude for the gift of education is being demonstrated at this very moment as you read this book. A book written by a dancer with a journalism degree.

I think this is a good time to mention, even though I was walking behind the journalism flag, I had decorated my graduation cap to say "New York or Bust". I was headed to New York City, right after I competed in the Miss Kansas Pageant one last time.

How did I get back to the Miss Kansas Pageant? Funny you should ask...

"Be a weed. Reach for the sky and don't be afraid to grow where no one wants you." –R. Bulinski

------

During Christmas break my senior year of college I read the book *Rich Dad, Poor Dad.* The book opened my eyes to my lack of financial knowledge which caused me to panic about my financial future.

When I finished the book I had one semester left in my college education and the only financial education I had received in my *sixteen* years of formal study (all within the public school system) was that which my parents taught me at home. Nowhere in all my years of study had *anyone* taught me *anything* about finances. Except of course the elective class I took in seventh grade when I was taught how to balance a check book.

I started observing the world around me and the financial disarray so many of my friends were in – from student loans to no savings in their bank accounts to co-signing on friend's credit cards. The co-signing had resulted in massive amounts of damage to everyone's credit scores.

My frustration sparked something within me which forever altered the course of my own life's journey. I began questioning where the educational system was breaking down. The journalism department at the University of Kansas was the number two school in the nation for their journalism program. I knew everything I needed for a journalism/marketing career, yet I had no clue about personal finance. I was baffled. More importantly I was irritated.

On top of my final twenty credit hours I began lobbying my state legislators asking about financial education in the school system. "Where is it?" I asked anyone and everyone who would listen. No one, and I mean no one, had a good answer let alone an answer. As far as I was concerned my education meant nothing if I didn't know how to take care of myself financially. Isn't that one of the reasons we go to school in the first place? To become assets to society versus a burden on welfare?

Haven't these people ever seen *Cabaret*? *Cabaret* is one of the world's most famous musicals and even those theatre geeks figured it out. As a matter of fact they sing it: *"money makes the world go around the world go around the world go around."*

How could the public education system teach us 1+1=2 but not teach us how to apply that equation to real life? Aren't we required to pay our bills and manage our bank accounts? Doesn't the government want us to pay taxes? This was a huge disservice to Americans and I was determined to find out why Congress wasn't making a stink about this oversight. I was beginning to connect the dots why our country was so far in debt. Our own congressmen and congresswomen were not educated (through the public school system) on financial literacy.

My financial enthusiasm somehow caught the attention of Miss Kansas 2004 Megan Bushell Bennett. I had never met Megan and honestly I didn't know she was Miss Kansas until she started calling. Our first conversation was in February and went something like this... "Have you considered competing for Miss Kansas?" Megan asked. "You have the talent and it sounds like you have a platform. I've heard about your work at the state capitol."

"Yes, I've been lobbying our legislators. But no, I don't have any interest in competing," I responded.

"Adrienne, do you realize with the title Miss Kansas behind you the kind of attention you can attract for your cause? You have the ability to make a difference and the crown gives you a taller platform. *And a megaphone!*" Megan encouraged.

I hadn't thought about the Miss Kansas crown being a master-key to opening doors. But I also reminded myself about the Miss Flint Hills crown I had walked away from. I had spent two and a half years reminding myself it was poor form to go back and compete again. Poor form according to... well... me.

I threw out an excuse, "I appreciate your phone call. Really, I'm flattered. But I plan on moving to New York City when I graduate in May," I explained. "I competed at Miss Kansas several years ago. It's not for me." The truth was *it was for me*, but my pride was too nervous to express my interest loud enough for anyone to hear.

Thankfully Megan didn't accept my response and so our conversation continued. We talked back and forth for forty-five more minutes. She kept encouraging me to compete and I kept declining.

"There is one more preliminary in the state. Will you please consider competing?" Megan again pushed.

I was starting to realize, just like the Miss Liberal Competition, the only way I was going to end the conversation was to either hang up or say yes. Being the polite mid-west young lady my parents raised me to be I responded, "Sure. When is it?"

"Three weeks. In Wichita."

I think Megan was more excited than I was, but I knew the little girl in me covered in fish guts and ketchup shared Megan's enthusiasm.

We finished our conversation and hung up.

My next call was to my mom. "I don't know what I just got myself into, but I'm competing for Miss Wichita in three weeks. Will you help me get ready?"

"What formal gown are you going to wear?" Mom asked.

"I don't have any here at school that would work, but I have an idea. Is the bridesmaid dress from Eric (my brother) and Kaely's wedding still hanging in my closet?"

"Yes, I think so."

"What if you re-made the bottom of it so it hangs in tiered layers? Under the layers you could attach a circle of tutu fabric."

"It's called tulle," my mom corrected.

"Yes. That's it. The tool would brush the ground when I walk. Think Audrey Hepburn style."

"That sounds interesting, but you won't have a chance to try it on before the competition."

"That's okay. Play with it and I'll meet you in Wichita the night before. Whatever you end up with is what I'll wear," I said with a chuckle.

"Send me your current measurements," Mom said.

"I will. And mom... thanks."

"If you follow your heart, if you listen to your gut, and if you extend your hand to help another, not for any agenda, but for the sake of humanity, you are going to find the truth." -Erin Brockovich

------

Three weeks later I wore my navy blue strapless bridesmaid dress that fit like a glove and rivaled Miss Hepburn's wardrobe from *Breakfast at Tiffany's*. My mom hand delivered my dress to Wichita. No alterations were needed.

That evening I joined the ranks of Erin Pattee, or as the world knows her, Erin Brockovich. Yes, Erin and I both claim the title Miss Wichita. But that's not completely true. I claim the actual title Miss Wichita while Erin technically claims the title Miss Pacific Coast (a pageant held in California). When the movie *Erin Brockovich* was being produced the director thought it would be fun to change her pageant title to a title from Kansas since she was born in the *Land of Oz*. I spent years thinking I shared something in common with the famous Miss Brockovich. While I may not share the sisterhood of a crown I do share her stubborn spirit.

More importantly, I was once again back in the running for the Miss Kansas title. I needed a dynamic philanthropic platform if I was going to be a strong contender for the Miss Kansas crown. You would have thought the American Cancer Society would have been my platform, but ironically it wasn't the ACS. I knew I had already found my success with ACS. What I saw the world so desperately needed was a financial education.

I considered my own situation and how money played a role in my life. It wasn't until I established a dream that I realized the vital role money management played in my ability to become successful. And I'm not just talking about success monetarily, but success in seeing a dream come to fruition (and success in being able to help others).

I realized I had to have money to compete for Miss Kansas. I had to have money to get an education. I had to have money to move to New York. I had to have money *to be able* to take off from work to attend an audition. I had to have money to obtain healthcare.

Whether we want to admit it or not, money plays a vital role in every part of our lives. I wasn't obsessed with money; I was merely realizing the knowledge of *how* money works would give me a broader ability to unlock my world of opportunities. Knowledge is power and somewhere the education about money was being overlooked.

"For the _love of_ money is a root of all kinds of evil." -1 Timothy 6:10

It took me establishing a dream before I really cared about the financial investment it would take to get me there. With the Miss Kansas crown in mind I had declared a two-part platform which I titled *Small Towns Big Dreams*. The first part of my platform was to help students learn to dream and determine a plan of action in order to obtain that dream. The second part was to plant seeds for a strong financial foundation. I would also use the crown to continue lobbying our state legislators.

The "financial" aspect of my platform was an idea I doubt the Miss America Organization had ever seen (financial literacy) and I was sure it was bound to cause some controversy. I was okay with that. I preferred to be an original rather than a duplicate. Besides, controversy over money versus the height of my heel when in a swimsuit seemed deserving of our country's attention and energy.

But my greatest quality I was taking to the Miss Kansas Competition: a care-free attitude. I was either going to spend a year making a financial difference as Miss Kansas or I was a step closer to my Broadway dream and my move to New York. It was a win-win situation I had worked my butt off for no matter the outcome.

Scene Eighteen

A hospital room, August 15, 2007
(Two days *after* the accident)

"In life, just as in music, harmony makes life beautiful." –Olivia Kent

"You have visitors," my mom whispered as she leaned over my hospital bed.

I opened my eyes and looked up at her. "Who is it?" I asked.

"You want these visitors," she responded with a smile as my dad ushered in three of my musician friends, guitars in tow.

I smiled and weakly said, "Hey guys. What's up?"

The leader of the pack was a friend of mine. He was a tall, big man with long straight black hair. He towered over me and anyone else who was in the room, but Ben was nothing short of a gentle giant.

Ben and I had met at the beginning of the summer at our first rehearsal: he was a musician and I was an actress. At first I was intimidated by his grand stature, but I quickly learned he had a gentle soul. It was so easy to be in Ben's presence: he was kind, patient, and accepting. He had all the qualities that seemed to be hard to find in my line of work and in life in general.

Ben and I got to know each other as we hung out at parties and with the same people. While I dated his roommate for a few months Ben's was the friendship that lasted.

"We wanted to cheer you up," Ben said on behalf of the other two musicians as they got situated.

I grabbed my bed controller and pushed the button to sit up. Despite the pain they were a welcomed distraction.

Ben counted the guys in and they began making a glorious noise.

As they played my mind calmed. My pain level remained at a woozy "nine", but the music was peaceful and melodic and wonderful. It was a noise those hospital walls had never heard. I was, after all, in the trauma ward.

My parents had grins on their faces as they stood off to the side and watched my personal serenade unfold.

Wow. This is what friendship is, I remember thinking. *When someone in your life is hurting, and you don't know what to do, you do what you know how.* Ben had gathered some friends and they were serenading me with their hearts, which translated into music. And music could not have been more powerful, or more meaningful, to me in that moment of my life.

I watched my three friends as they played and sung. They were there in my hour of need. They couldn't fix my body but they were helping mend my mind. They were helping me in a way they knew how. It was the absolute perfect medicine. At the perfect moment. In the perfect place.

I watched their fingers dance across the guitar necks as they transitioned from the first song and straight into the second song. I clapped for their amazing performance, the best performance I had ever seen. We may have only been an audience of three, but we were the most grateful audience any performer had experienced.

Ben started singing to me. I wanted to smile and I did. I closed my eyes to listen and to free my mind. I was trying to forget my pain but it wouldn't subside, it wouldn't even ease. The music was beautiful and the pain was horrifying. The blend of beauty and horror was like the flip side of magnets rejecting each other - if I could have flipped the magnet that held my pain, I would have gotten up and participated. The music was healing to my ears and my soul, yet my body was fighting for survival and quickly developing a massive infection.

I opened my eyes and saw a gaggle of nurses looking into my room. A few of them had tears in their eyes. They too could see the love in my friends' actions.

I was doing my best to take in the music, but my eyes started getting heavy. I was trying desperately to stay awake, but I couldn't. I was drifting. My medication was kicking in.

"Adrienne smile," my dad said. I opened my eyes and my friends leaned in for a picture.

"Thank you," I said with deep gratitude to everyone in the room.

"It's okay, you can go to sleep," Ben said quietly.

"Thank you so much," I said once again as I reached out to squeeze his hand.

I closed my eyes and drifted into a deep drug induced sleep.

Scene Nineteen

The Miss Kansas Pageant, final night of competition, June 2005
(Two years and one month *before* the accident)

"If you can dream it, you can do it." –Walt Disney

The Miss Kansas Competition lasted exactly one week.

When the final night of competition arrived I remember being backstage securing my blue opening number outfit, fixing my hair into a half-up half-down stylish hair-do, and dreaming about what the night had in store. There was a nervous chatter among the contestants. Our hopes were floating on top of the plume of hairspray particles that had overtaken the dressing room. Deep inside I had a calmness and peacefulness about how the evening would unfold. Yes, I was excited and nervous, but my heart knew God had already selected the winner. I knew the superficial nerves I did have would calm once I got on stage, they always did.

After the opening number we took our assigned places and awaited the announcement of the top seven. I stood under the hot stage lights, my feet were numb from my four inch heels, and my smile was quivering. I looked at the women standing around me. All of them beautiful. All of them talented. All of them smart. Yet only one of us would walk away with the crown. Would it be me? I had no idea, but no matter the outcome I had done my best. I couldn't have asked for any more than that.

The negative voices in my head wanted to remind me I had no edge on the competition. I had only spent three months preparing for the job of Miss Kansas. But the positive voices reminded me I had been preparing for the crown of Miss Kansas since I was eleven-years-old.

In the midst of my thoughts the announcements began.

"Welcome to Miss Kansas 2005," the emcee announced as the crowd cheered.

"Let's begin the process of naming that special young lady. First, let's narrow the field of contestants," he paused as he walked across the stage, clearing the way for the top seven finalists to step forward.

"Our top seven will be competing in all phases of competition until we reach the on-stage interview. At that point we will narrow the competition to five contestants and then we will announce our new Miss Kansas."

The crowd cheered.

"First, we need to see which are in the top seven. This is in random order."

The crowd hushed.

"Our first finalist," he paused and the auditorium went eerily silent "is Sarah Jump, Miss Emerald City."

The crowd came to life with a cheer.

Without hesitation the announcer continued, "Erin Kruse, Miss Southern."

Again the crowd cheered and the emcee pushed forward.

"Hillary Gaston, Miss Capital City."

He was reading through the names so quickly I hardly had time to think.

"Michelle Walthers, Miss Cheney Lake."

Miss Wichita, Miss Wichita, Miss Wichita I was chanting in my head.

"Casey Belmar, Miss Arkansas Valley."

Only two left.

"Adrienne Rosel, Miss Wichita"

I took my place on the front of the stage, my smile beaming from ear-to-ear.

"Our seventh finalist is... Alaina Fenton, Miss Topeka."

The crowd cheered even louder.

"Congratulations ladies," I heard the announcer say as we rushed off the stage. I could finally breathe. I was in!

The seven of us dashed to the dressing room and striped our clothes: into our bikinis and four inch heels we went. One by one we lined up and the dressing room attendants applied our butt glue as we adjusted our jell-boob-pads in the mirror. Once everything was in place, we crossed our fingers a pad wouldn't fall out halfway across the stage. It never ceased to amaze me that even as bare as we were, we could stuff breast enhancements into the small triangle of fabric that covered our chests.-

The seven of us dashed back to the stage wings. As I waited my turn to strut across the stage, I watched some of the other contestants as they did squats and pushups behind the curtains. I was dumbfounded as I watched them try to get their muscles to "pop". *Seriously, if they didn't look good ten seconds ago they aren't going to look better in the next ten seconds either,* I thought to myself.

I peeked around the curtain and looked out at the judges and the crowd. Everyone was transfixed on the contestant on stage. She was walking with confidence and working the crowd. The music that was booming through the speakers was upbeat and fun. The energy from the crowd gave the song an extra amp.

"Adrienne," the stage manager cued me. "Go!" he whispered.

I took a deep breath and stepped out from behind the curtain. It was my turn.

I strutted my half-naked body across the stage – my chin high and a confident smile spread across my face. *This is a typical Saturday evening. I always walk around in a bikini, four inch heels, stage make-up, and false eye lashes. Don't you?*

It was a weird sensation to feel the heat of the stage lights with the coolness of the air conditioning on my bare skin. Chill bumps stood on my arms and legs as I walked in front of the judges. I looked at each of them in the eyes as I passed. I breezed across the stage in less than fifteen seconds.

I hustled back to the dressing room and striped down to my birthday suit. I pulled on my tights intensely focused on not puncturing a hole in my nylons with my acrylic claws. I was proud of my next costume I stepped into. It was a costume my mom and I designed and my mom built.

Next up: talent.

I had selected a talent that showcased my ability but also pushed me as a performer. Since I was still working through my insecurity of singing in public, I saw the pageant as the perfect place to push my personal boundaries. I knew I wasn't comfortable with simply singing, but I knew if I paired singing *with* dancing I would be okay. So that is exactly what I did. I performed a song and dance to *America* from the musical *West Side Story*.

Something about singing *and* dancing made me feel more talented even if I was faking it. And the more talented I *felt* the more confidence I portrayed.

I stepped out on the stage in the dark as the emcee introduced my talent selection. I walked to my starting place and got into my pose. I grabbed the edge of my full circle skirt and dramatically tossed it around, pulling one side high enough to expose my thigh. I pointed my right foot in front of me proudly displaying the small hole worn into the toe of my shoe.

The emcee exited the stage as the lights shifted to me. I was blinded by four spotlights and immediately felt like a solar-powered-energy-bunny soaking up the rays of the artificial beams. I smiled at my crowd as the music started. I took two dramatic steps forward and I began to sing. Not an ounce of nervousness could be detected in my vocal chords. My voice was crystal clear. I was solid and on key.

I may not have been on Broadway *yet*, but it was only a thought away as I sang the lyrics *"I like the island Manhattan."* I pranced back and forth across the stage singing to my audience and acting out the lyrics. I could feel my eyes sparkling under the powerful lights. But most important: I was having genuine fun.

The vocal portion came to an end and I started a series of turns across the stage as the music grew with intensity. I kicked my leg to my nose, not once but twice. With the second kick I kept my leg extended, foot pointed to the sky, as I bent backwards into deep backbend. I continued with a series of turning power leaps across the stage, doing the splits in mid-air several times.

I danced my way back to the center of the stage where I went into a series of *fouette* turns, turning on one leg while my other leg pumped me around in circles. The turns took me to the end of my ninety second talent showcase. I hit my final pose with enough gusto and flare to rival even the best flamenco dancers of Spain.

The crowd cheered. I was breathing heavy. I could hear my dad yelling in his deep, masculine voice "Yeah! Yeah!"

My smile stretched ear to ear. I was satisfied with my efforts. I had faced my insecurity and I had officially rocked it. I took a huge bow and when I stood straight my time in the spotlights was over. I dashed back to the dressing room to change into my next set of competition clothes.

The rest of the evening was easy-peasy. I had already competed in the ten minute private interview a few days prior, I had pranced across the stage in a bikini, and now I had faced my biggest insecurity of singing in public. All I had left was the casual wear competition and evening gown competition. If I made the cut I would advance to the on-stage question and then the crowning.

I changed into my business suit and was hustled back out on stage. The top seven finalists lined up across the stage. It was time to eliminate two women.

"It is time to narrow our field of finalists to five. Only one competition remains, the on-stage interview," the announcer said and without any delay he started naming off the finalists.

"Sarah Jump, Miss Emerald City."

The crowd cheered as Sarah left our group of seven to stand on the opposite side of the stage.

"Erin Kruse, Miss Southern."

The crowd cheered again.

"Hillary Gaston, Miss Capital City. "

Adrienne Rosel, Miss Wichita. Adrienne Rosel, Miss Wichita.

"Michelle Walthers, Miss Cheney Lake."

I broke into a cold sweat. Only one spot left.

"Miss Wichita, Adrienne Rosel."

I took a dramatic sigh of relief as I walked to the other side of the stage where I joined the other four finalists. The two eliminated were escorted off the stage.

One-by-one the remaining five of us answered our final questions before we were escorted back off stage to change into our evening gowns. It was a mad dash to get out of our business suits and looking red-carpet-ready. We had approximately four minutes to get our butts back on stage.

I had three dressing room attendants helping me get into my gown and lace up the corset. The corset ran from my tailbone up to my shoulder blades and considering it was a strapless gown it had to be secured properly. It needed at least two sets of hands to cinch the corset and pull the laces tight. Picture Scarlet O'Hara, in *Gone With the Wind*, as Mammy squeezes her into her corset. Now do that in four minutes, hence I had three women helping get me into my gown. Needless to say, I was the last one in the dressing room as *my* three attendants frantically worked. When I heard the finale music start, the stage manager was instantly at the door yelling for me to hurry.

One of my attendants looked at me and said, "Are you ready for your new title?" I could tell she was genuine with her question, but I didn't know how to respond and I didn't have time. Instead I smiled, squeezed her tight to my heart, and dashed out of the dressing room.

The stage manager was in full panic mode as I ran past him and onto the wings of the stage. I barely made my entrance, but walked on stage as though I had all the time in the world.

The contestants paraded around the stage in true pageant fashion. There were smiles glued on our faces and five of us wondering *"Did I win?"* Was my attendant in the dressing room just being nice or was she serious? Did she really think I was going to be named Miss Kansas?

We took our designated places on stage and the awards started. First they went through all the "add-on" awards, such as "Best Stage Presence" and "Outstanding Vocalist" and several more. I was actually named the top scorer in the private interview competition at that point.

"Now I would like to ask our five finalists to step forward," the announcer said. He continued to talk as five of us made our way to the front of the stage.

This was it. How would history write itself? Whose life was about to change? Who was about to win a ticket to Miss America?

I was excited, but I was more or less focused on enjoying the moment.

Without delay the eliminations continued.

"Our fourth runner up and winner of a $750 scholarship is… Hilary Gaston, Miss Capital City."

The crowd cheered. *One down three to go.*

"Third runner up and winner of a $1000 scholarship is… Michelle Walthers, Miss Cheney Lake."

The crowd cheered. *Two down two to go.*

"Our second runner up and winner of $1250 scholarship is… Sarah Jump, Miss Emerald City.

The crowd cheered. *Three down one to go.*

Erin and I looked at each other. We had both finished at the top of an outstanding group of women. We turned to face each other and grabbed hands.

"Oh my goodness," I said to Erin.

"For one of us our life is about to change," Erin said.

"This is a dream come true," we agreed.

I studied Erin's eyes as we continued to whisper about our mutual dreams of the Miss America crown and our move to New York City. One of us would be moving to the Big Apple that same summer while the other would be delayed a year. We squeezed hands and looked deep into each other's eyes.

"One of these two remaining women," the emcee interrupted, "will be our Miss Kansas 2005. She will win a $5000 scholarship, free use of a car, and an amazing year."

My stomach did a loop and I quit breathing. My skin went cold as I felt sweat drip down my back, slithering its way between my shoulder blades.

"First runner up and winner of a $1500 scholarship is…"

I looked down at our hands clenched together. My palms were sweaty and I could feel the cool air swirling around us.

"Erin Kruse, Miss Southern."

The crowd roared.

I won!

"Our new Miss Kansas 2005 is Miss Wichita Adrienne Rosel."

I really won!

Erin hugged me before she was escorted away from center stage. I sucked in a breath of air as I tried to absorb the announcement. I was speechless and without much thought. I turned to face my audience who was in the process of standing as they applauded. A feeling of incredible pride mixed with love mixed with overwhelming gratitude mixed with humility swept through my heart.

Confetti was released from the ceiling as music roared through the sound system. I bent at my knees to allow Megan to pin my new crown to my head. Flowers were thrust in my arms and I was handed a set of car keys. I was suddenly too excited to cry. Instead I twirled my car keys above my head and pumped my arm like a basketball player.

I pranced down the runway waving, celebrating, and pumping my arm several times like any athlete but *not a beauty queen.* I was so excited I couldn't contain myself. It was an atypical celebration for pageant winners around the globe. The press loved my reaction.

Miss America here I come, I thought with humble cockiness.

After my crowning moment was complete I was whisked off the stage to be prepped for my first press conference. I was taken into a private room where I was given a chance to gather myself. I reapplied lipstick while someone took my favorite accessory, that matched my gown, out of my hair. I had specifically picked a large red orchid to tie together "my look" for my red strapless gown. I had pinned the flower to my hair for the finishing touch, like a cherry on top of a perfect sundae. But apparently the two women helping me in the dressing room felt the "Miss Kansas" look was something slightly different.

"What are you doing?" I asked as one of the women removed my flower.

"It takes away from the crown," the woman responded as she tossed the flower off to the side. "Congratulations on the win. I need to remind you, you are Miss Kansas now. No more pumping your arm." She was referring to my arm pump moments ago on stage.

It seemed like a weird comment, but I smiled and said, "Okay."

I was escorted down a long hallway where I entered a room and was greeted by the press: my first press conference where I was the center of attention.

Later that evening I attended parties and celebrations, first with my judges and then with my family and friends.

The next morning I woke up as Miss Kansas and it was time to get to work. I was confident the Miss America Organization had no idea the personality that was about to take Kansas by storm, and eventually America.

My eleven-year-old self *is* proud of the crown I now claim as my own.

Be brave to be you.

My care-free attitude is what won me the Miss Kansas crown. I was confident in who I was, what I stood for, and where I was going in life. If someone didn't like me I really didn't care. I didn't need an organization to tell me I would be successful, I knew it in my soul. I had figured out how to dream and work hard. I had figured out how to accept disappointments and celebrate successes, all with a positive attitude. I was confident and determined. I was also willing to face my insecurities head on and turn those insecurities into strengths. Little did I know that same determination would later serve me in ways I could have never dreamt.

I believe that panel of judges saw my determination and confidence. After all, isn't that the type of person you want representing your state?

By the time I reached the Miss America Competition it was a whole different story.

Scene Twenty

*"I know God won't give me anything I can't handle.
I just wish he didn't trust me so much." –Mother Teresa*

I escaped the hospital on the Friday after my accident, but I was instructed to stay in the area. My medical team wanted to monitor me and my lack of progress.

But where was I released to go? I couldn't walk. I couldn't feed myself. I couldn't even shower on my own. Where was home? Was I to go back to Kansas with my parents? Could I ever go back to New York where I had performance contracts waiting for me?

The doctors and nurses pumped me full of every medication they legally could and sent me on my way. I was armed with prescriptions for anything that might take my pain levels from a ten to a nine. But nothing worked.

Since no one thought I could get any worse my parents agreed to my request of going to the amphitheatre for closing night that Saturday. I knew staying for the show was unrealistic. I simply wanted to say good-bye to my cast of friends so my parents took me. But the only thing I remember is from the pictures showing proof I was there…

For weeks I was in a constant state of pain. When I was awake I was in agony and when I closed my eyes I dreamt of things lost. More often than not, I would wake myself crying. I quickly became grateful there were only twenty-four hours in a day.

Scene: a girl, her mom, a coffee table heaped full of pain meds, September 2007
(Twenty days *after* the accident)

97

My pain was constant. Relentless. If I was awake I was in excruciating pain and when I slept I dreamt of the agony. There was never a break. Never an escape. Not a moment to breathe a sigh of relief.

One of my doctors finally prescribed a drug by the name of Methadone. Methadone is the same drug doctors prescribe for heroin addicts as they are weaning them from their heroin addictions. My doctors were hesitant about the prescription, but nothing else was working.

After I took my first dose of the potent drug, I had my first taste of pain relief, not 100% relief, but enough relief that I wanted more. Within forty-eight hours I began vomiting uncontrollably. I already wasn't eating so most of what I vomited was bile and water. My doctors retracted the prescription, which meant I had to live with the pain (note: I would have rather continued to vomit – it was more pleasant than the pain).

Through it all my mom and dad didn't leave my side. They accompanied me to all my doctors' appointments. They administered my IVs. They prayed for me. They fed me. My mom even showered me. All because I was helpless.

"Adrienne, please try to eat," my mom begged as she set a plate of five pain meds and two saltine crackers next to me. "This medication is going to burn a hole in your stomach."

My mom stood anxiously next to me watching. I took my pills one-by-one followed by one bite of one-hundredth of a cracker. The sight of the crackers alone made me dry heave, but I tried my best. Not for me but for my mom.

"Mom, I can't do more than that."

"Hey, you took a bite," Mom said with a weak smile.

"I'm sorry. I really can't do more than that."

My mom graciously accepted my pathetic apology and started the process of hooking me to my IV for the second time that day.

During the first week of my new life, I had a PICC line inserted into my chest. The line ran internally from my left shoulder and stopped above my heart. The majority of my medication was administered by my parents through that PICC line. It dumped the medication above my heart so it would spread through my body more quickly.

Every week mom and dad were instructed to administer two IV bags of meds (three times a day) along with my piles of oral medications. My parents diligently and lovingly administered all of my medications according to my doctors' instructions.

It was my infectious disease and control doctor that was monitoring my IV medication. I went to see him at least once a week for many months. He later explained he was giving me such strong medication to kill off the growing infection that it was comparable to the chemotherapy doctors give cancer patients. He didn't tell me about the possible side effects because it didn't matter. I had to take the medications. I would learn the effects on my own.

"If you leave the crackers I will try to eat more," I told my mom without looking at the plate.

She smiled as she started my IV drip.

I watched the medication begin to trickle into my IV in a slow rhythmic beat. The first bag would take approximately fifteen minutes to flood my veins. The second would take forty-five minutes. Mom set her timer and began prepping my second bag of medication.

I felt my eyelids gaining weight.

"I love you mom," I said quietly.

"I love you too," mom smiled. "Have a nice nap."

As I started to doze off I asked God to send me a pleasant dream. I asked for a dream of dance. God knew what dance was in my life. He was the only witness that knew the freedom it gave my mind, my body, and my spirit. God had given me the gift of dance as a place where I could work out my frustrations and find my place of solace.

I want to be dancing, I whispered to Him in my thoughts. I knew He was with me and so I focused my mind on my college ballet studio, allowing Him to do the rest.

The room was an impressive 1200 square feet with tall ceilings and a series of mirrors along the front wall. There was a beautiful black grand piano nestled into the right corner of the room. As I walked into the room I could feel the spring in the floor under my feet. I set my bag off to the side and walked to the center. I turned toward the mirror and stared at myself as I began to fasten my hair back into a high bun. I looked at my body. I was proud of my curves, of my athletic build, of my muscle. I didn't have a ballerina's stereotypical body, but I had the perfect body for me.

I had on my favorite black halter-top leotard that zipped up the front and hugged my breasts nicely. I finished my look with black tights that hooked over my pinkish-peach canvas ballet shoes. My legs were long and lean, toned and perfect. I didn't have the best arches in my feet, but they were my arches and I did the best I could with them.

I pointed my right foot and glanced at the holes I had worn into the edges of the shoe. I was proud of those holes. I had earned those holes. I was a graceful dancer, but those holes also screamed that I was fierce.

I finished fastening my bun and I walked over to the single barre that was placed in the room. I positioned my left hand on the cold metal and my right hand out to my side, like any ballerina preparing for class. I prepared my feet in *first position.* The pianist began and four counts later so did I.

I began with a series of *rond de jams* into *pliés* into *relevés.*

I studied myself in the mirror and watched the muscles in my arms as I stood with a tall neck and pleasant expression. I stretched my arms as long as I could. I glanced out over my right finger tips and allowed my gaze to gracefully focus off in the distance. I had the package to be any kind of dancer I wanted to be. I was healthy. I was strong. I was determined. I was talented.

I started a series of *battements* – I kicked to the front, to the side, to the back, to the side, to the front. I was pleased with my form, with my endurance, with my flexibility. With my two perfect ankles.

When the song concluded I walked to the right corner of the room. I stood on my right leg with my left foot pointing beautifully behind me. My arms were gracefully waiting in first position. My neck was long and my nose pointed up into the air. I glanced at the pianist and gave her a nod. I was ready and so she began.

This time I gave her two measures before I began my series of big leaps across the floor.

tombé - pas de bourrée - glissade - grande jete - glissade - grande jete - grand jete

As I glided across the floor I felt weightless. I was soaring. I was at peace. I was in my element. My legs were dancing while my upper body was telling the story. The story of grace and charm. A story of beauty and endurance. I was dancing beautifully.

As I came out of my final leap and my feet connected with the ground my hair fell from its bun.

The pianist continued as I tried to re-secure my hair, but I couldn't get it situated. As I began combing my fingers in the upward motion toward a pony-tail, I turned to look at myself in the mirror. That's when I noticed the long strands of brown hair piling at my feet. I pulled my hands away from my head and to my horror clumps of hair were in my hands. I reached up again and ran my right hand through my hair and again a clump of hair came out.

I stood, motionless and expressionless, staring at my hands with the mounds of hair. Tears began to silently fall down my cheeks.

The piano started producing a harsh sound; it was changing from a beautiful aria to an alarming wake-up call.

As I gasped for air, pain rushed in and I shocked myself awake. I opened my eyes and my mom was hooking up my second bag of medication.

The tears kept coming, but this time without any sound. My mom continued her task as there was nothing more she could do for me.

When she was done hooking my second IV to my chest, she reached her hand down to my forehead and moved her fingers through my long hair. She leaned down and gave me a kiss on the forehead before she wiped my tears away with her bare hands.

Scene Twenty-One

Twelve hours after the crowning of Miss Kansas, June 2005
(Two years and two months *before* the accident)

"God made you as you are in order to use you as He planned."
—J.C. Macauley

My first meeting after I won Miss Kansas was interesting. We – me, my parents, and the executive directors of the Miss Kansas Organization – met around a large conference table to discuss the national competition and my upcoming year of service.

First, we started by discussing the Miss America Competition and all things I needed to change, or perfect, before I arrived on the national stage. We discussed things like my physical appearance, wardrobe, platform title, talent, hair, etc. Since I wanted to be a fierce competitor and the executive directors had helped so many girls prepare for the competition-of-a-lifetime, I took what they said to heart. I knew their constructive criticism was their way of helping me create the best version of myself I could. I listened and heeded their advice. I knew they were using their years of experience to help prepare me to win.

We discussed how I could further slim my thighs for the swimsuit competition. We also dissected my "options" for the talent competition. My directors asked if I would be willing to consider a *ballet en pointe*, but I hadn't been in my pointe shoes for five years. I took their suggestion off the table. I wasn't interested in the pressure of getting my feet "performance ready" for a *ballet en pointe*. I had years of experience with blisters, calluses, and toe nails falling off thanks to the wooden shank that held my toes in the ballet slippers. It was a painful process getting your feet conditioned for pointe shoes. I couldn't justify the months of blisters and ugly feet for ninety seconds in the talent portion of the competition. I knew I was a great dancer without pointe shoes. I gracefully said "no thank you" to their suggestion of a ballet number. I further explained my reasoning, "I don't know who will be in the audience and Miss America is the ultimate audition venue for Broadway." Because I wouldn't budge, it was settled I would keep my talent selection of *America* from *West Side Story*. The only change would be my costume, which my mom and I designed and constructed.

But I wasn't emotionally prepared for them to pick apart my platform, which I had won the crown with less than twenty-four hours earlier. My platform I had titled *Small Towns, Big Dreams*. My platform was the cornerstone of the legacy I wanted to leave as Miss Kansas and I was told it may not be strong enough to win the national crown.

Small Towns, Big Dreams was born out of the idea that just because the odds might be stacked against you (like being from a small town) didn't mean you were less capable of big dreams (like making a global impact on our world). My platform was focused on the students across Kansas, and Miss Kansas (me) giving those students the self-confidence to utilize his/her potential to do anything with his/her life he/she could dream.

I had selected a sub-platform of *financial literacy* to add to my over-all platform of *Small Towns, Big Dreams*. Students first, money second. I understood money creates opportunity and since our public education system had failed to teach *me* the basic principles of being financially savvy, I felt the educational system had limited my opportunities. I had a vision of changing that small thinking on a state and eventually national scale.

So while I was encouraging kids to pursue greatness, I had the crown to get my foot in the door at the state capitol to influence the addition of financial education in our public school system. My platform was born out of frustration and instead of doing nothing I was doing something to make a difference. Like many great things in our world, when people get frustrated enough that frustration fuels the desire to implement change.

As we discussed my philanthropic vision my directors raised a valid point, "As Miss America the platform title doesn't work. Not everyone is from a small town. Does your platform title relate to the inner-city schools? Does your platform reach corporate audiences?"

After much discussion I realized their point was valid. While I didn't want to forego my *Small Towns, Big Dreams* vision I leaned on my advisors' wisdom and agreed to make a change. I understood there was an "image" of who Miss America was. My advisers where helping me fit into those shoes in order to win. So with their help I shifted my focus to the financial aspect of my platform and renamed my platform *Fin Lit 101* (Financial Literacy 101). The pressure was on for this dancing journalism major to become an overnight financial guru. But I liked the pressure, so I dug my heels in deep and went with it.

I was going to take my financial knowledge, or lack thereof, to a national competition and convince a panel of judges I was a financial expert or at least deserved to be. I was an actress so I knew I could do it. Since the Miss Kansas directors had been in charge of the organization for more than a decade I leaned on their guidance and allowed them to start shaping me into what *they* thought Miss America *should be* versus who God created me to be. Slowly I was trying to conform to what I thought would win the title. While everyone's end goals were the same and our hearts were in the right place, I was also heading toward a tough lesson.

After the talk of Miss America and everything I needed to change, we moved on to my job as Miss Kansas. First, I was instructed I could no longer be seen in public without make-up whether it was grocery shopping or going to the gym. "You never know where someone might recognize you," one of my co-executive directors had told me. Everywhere I went I was expected to look and act like the stereotypical Miss Kansas. When I didn't look the part complete strangers did indeed feel it was their responsibility to tell me. I gave up the acrylic nails and went natural, but my audiences didn't approve. Complete strangers would say things like, "your nails don't look very nice" or "I don't like your outfit". My directors were right: people liked to pass judgment on a Miss *Anything*.

I recall conversations about how I *shouldn't* wear my hair, which was half up, half down because it attracted attention to my nose. Apparently my nose wasn't my best feature. Prior to winning Miss Kansas I never thought about my nose. But again, I took the criticism constructively and filed it away for future reference.

In that meeting I was also given my first set of scheduled appearances. My directors explained how very little money I would make that year. I had heard this fact from previous Miss Kansas', but until I wore the shoes of the queen the reality wasn't real. Everywhere I went the Miss Kansas Organization charged a modest fee, but I would only get a small percentage of that payment while the organization would keep the rest. I'm not sure how they (the organization) spent their portion of the money, but I was too busy to ask or even care.

I was less concerned with the payment structure, which was skimmed over, and I got stuck on the next order of business: details about my sponsored car and where I would be living for the year, which was nowhere.

I had ninety days of free hotel rooms in Wichita, but I was not allowed to stay for a consecutive ninety days. I remember sarcastically asking my directors "Aren't there more than ninety days in a year?" It was up to me to find a place to stay for the other 275 days in that year.

Some of those days would be spent at host homes. A plethora of Miss Kansas' before me and after me had host homes in the community where they hold the pageant. A wonderful community known as Pratt, America. For some reason I was not lucky enough to have a host home or host family. I was on my own for a year with no permanent address and not enough hotel rooms to add up to 365. I didn't have enough income to afford rent for a place of my own. My parents lived in southwest Kansas and it wasn't exactly easy access to *anything*. I felt as though I was left high-and-dry by the very organization I was selected to represent, but I stayed focused on the bigger picture which was winning Miss America and affecting the lives of people I had the chance to meet. Yes, I may have been a "homeless" Miss Kansas who couldn't be seen in public without make-up, but I would make the best of it. It was a year of opportunity to open doors and make an impact.

I assigned my first project to myself: finding a roof to put over my head. I started soliciting more corporate sponsorships with the hopes I would find a place to live. I did end up securing sixty days at another hotel in Wichita and an apartment complex in Lawrence (where I went to college) agreed to give me a free room until I went to Miss America. I wasn't worried about post-Miss America because I was preparing to win. The downfall of my shared apartment: I was living with someone I didn't know. But I was happy to have a place to lay my head. After a few months of coming and going my new roommate became a friend that didn't mind seeing me in sweatpants with no make-up on my face. And my late night spoonfuls of peanut butter were a secret safe with her.

Since I didn't have a permanent address for 365 days I turned my car into a closet on wheels. When I told friends about my mobile closet they didn't believe it until I showed them. I literally had a stack of drawers in the back of my SUV: underwear drawer, sock drawer, workout clothes drawer, and jewelry drawer. Next to my drawers I had stacks of boxes of shoes. Across the top I had a utility rod to hang my clothes. At all times I had a business suit, cocktail dress, and formal gown. It wasn't abnormal for me to change in the car from one appearance to the next.

But not having a home is a challenging situation, especially when you are supposed to *look* put together at all times. When I was dog-tired from appearances and wasn't in the city where I would sleep that night I would find a nice neighborhood, lock my doors, and crawl in the backseat of my car to take a nap.

Eventually I worked a deal with the restaurant food chain for a $500 gift certificate in exchange for eight two-hour appearances across the state. I was, at the very least, relieved I had a plan to feed myself. Thankfully the restaurants had a great selection of salads with a grilled protein to top it off.

My business office quickly became the restaurant *Panera Bread* because they had free reliable Internet access and coffee. But of all the challenges the worst was the loneliness.

I was on my own for a year. I didn't see friends or family on a regular basis. It was hard because I had just left college where I had four roommates and sorority house of 180 "sisters". I was in and out of schools, in and out of host homes, trying to promote my platform, and spending countless hours behind the windshield of my car. Yes, I was grateful for my array of opportunities, but I did get lonely.

I have no idea how many miles I traveled that year. I literally lost track. I do know my car sponsor traded out my vehicle three times because they didn't want me to put too many miles on just one vehicle. It would kill the resale value.

On top of a busy travel schedule I was sleeping very little. I was driving myself to appearances and when I had downtime I was in the gym. No one wants to see a fat Miss Kansas. If you gain a pound someone was sure to point it out to you. How do I know this? Because it happened.

I was honestly worried how I was going to maintain my weight leading up to Miss America. During college I worked out six days a week and took dance classes three days a week. As Miss Kansas I was in a car and eating at banquets and restaurants. It was a recipe for easy weight gain.

During those first 2-3 months of my reign I pushed my body so hard and ate so lean I actually lost my period. In fact, I went without my period for over two months. It was one less thing to worry about so I really wasn't concerned. When I was running high school track the same thing happened. I was an athlete. It happens. The only reason I finally called my doctor was because of the acne taking over my skin.

"Adrienne, your skin looks horrible," an acquaintance had told me during my Miss America gown fitting. Sadly, I agreed with her as well as her next comment, "You need to get that fixed."

That same conversation was followed by the suggestion I needed full body Spanx to make my body look better in my gown. I had never owned a pair of Spanx. When I tried to put on my first pair it was as though the elastic was trying to squeeze everything out of me, like ketchup from a bottle. But I didn't have anything to squeeze. I was solid as a rock, which meant I looked better without the Spanx rather than with (and I tell you this because it is probably the last time in my life I get to make such a statement)!

One evening when I was attending a private Miss America training session, I was told the reason my hair always looked like a mess was because I fidgeted with it way too much. I was grateful for this critique and applied the criticism to my advantage. I started to notice I did indeed mess with my hair when I was nervous, a quality I proudly share with my sister. But with a little effort I learned to control my nervous tick and leave my hair alone. To this day, if I know I am entering into a tense situation, such as a business negotiation or interview, I pull my hair back so I leave it alone and focus on the business to be discussed. But don't kid yourself, when I pull my hair back I never fix it half up, half down for fear someone may notice my pointy nose, a poor quality in a former beauty queen.

Not only was my skin, hair, and wardrobe being picked on by others, but so was every other area of my life. I was quickly learning the spotlight was very unforgiving.

This all may sound superficially silly, but after so many little "picks" (at *who* I was and what I looked like) it started to add up. I gradually started questioning my appearance, my talent, my business sense, and everything else a person could question. Slowly it started breaking me down as I was trying to turn myself into what everyone else expected me to be, or rather what I *thought* they expected me to be.

That was the beginning. Beginning of questioning if I was good enough - a dangerous question to ask. As I look back I realize it wasn't anyone in particular, or the opportunity of being Miss Kansas that caused me to question myself and impose self-doubt. My self-doubt was a flaw within my character and that flaw was finally surfacing. We all have flaws. The flaws may be different, but that is what makes us perfectly imperfect.

Sadly, it was during my year as Miss Kansas I discovered my first signs of depression. Although, I didn't know it was depression preying on my happiness. I thought it was loneliness.

Scene Twenty-Two

A modest hotel room, September 2005
(One year and eleven months *before* the accident)

"Without the rain there will be no rainbow." –G.K. Chesterton

I paced around my room. I had no plans and no events scheduled for a few days. It should have been a welcomed break, but I was alone in a community in which I had no pre-Miss Kansas friends.

I walked over to the window and opened the curtains. I was on the second floor with a view overlooking the parking lot and a busy street. I stared at my car and the other three vehicles scattered throughout the lot. It was a Wednesday at 9 a.m. and everyone who was in town on business had already left for their important destinations of the day. I had no appointments, no appearances, and no obligations.

The sun was shining and the trees stood still. It looked as though Wichita was experiencing a break from the wind and the heat. The news broadcasters had said it was going to be a high of seventy degrees and an unseasonably beautiful Wednesday. It was one of those extraordinary picture-perfect serene days that came very rarely.

I watched a woman as she jogged down the sidewalk against the flow of traffic. She looked sweaty and peaceful. I envied her. I considered going for a run, but I reminded myself of the countless conversations revolving around the size of my thighs and the infamous swimsuit competition. I didn't need bulk anywhere on my body and running naturally made my muscles pop. The Miss America crown was on my mind (as were the Spanx) and I had another four months before the competition.

I considered going to the gym *again* to work every cardio machine in the building. But I had already done that every day for the past ten days and ten consecutive days before that and ten before that. I knew my muscles needed a break, but it also meant I would have to cut my calorie intake for the day.

Somehow I was maintaining my weight even with my busy travel schedule. I knew my weight was on target because I drug my scale in and out of every hotel room. I treated my scale like a delicate and breakable gold-plated leaf. A prized possession. An award I had won. In reality it was a ball and chain that produced numbers that haunted my mind until the next time I stood on it. Then the new number would haunt my mind. And then the new number. And then the new number.

I thought about how to spend the beautiful day, but I felt isolated and alone. I was trapped in my thoughts. If I left my hotel room I had been instructed I must "look" like a Miss Kansas. I was expected to wear make-up even to the grocery store and the gym. I was always supposed to be *put together*. The pressure of perfection felt crushing.

I had nowhere to go. I was in a hotel room *alone*. My friends had graduated when I did (three months prior) and all of them had started their careers. I couldn't call anyone on a weekday and expect them to have time to talk.

I felt my breath shorten and my chin began to quiver. I felt lonely isolation.

I considered again going to the gym again, but I didn't want to.

I knew I needed to get out of the room for my mental well-being.

I debated going for a walk, but I didn't want to.

I could feel my emotions turning black.

I considered calling one of my sponsors and inviting them to lunch, but I didn't feel like Miss Kansas, *and I didn't want to.*

I considered driving four hours to my parents, but I didn't want to.

A tear slipped down my cheek.

I didn't want to cry, but I could feel it boiling under my consciousness. As I began to recognize the lonely isolated feelings surfacing I surrendered to my emotions; or rather my emotions took over my mind. I quickly slipped into a dark, negative emotional place. A single tear turned into a steady stream that flowed down both of my cheeks.

I didn't understand why I was crying. I didn't understand why I was upset. I was Miss Kansas for crying out loud, *literally*. I had achieved a dream-come-true for so many women. I was on the ride of my life. I was preparing for Miss America. I was a college graduate.

And yet *I felt miserable.*

I began counting my blessings, but the darkness had encompassed my entire mind. My silent tears turned into an audible hysteria.

I slinked down to the floor and put my head between my knees. I cried fiercely until I started choking. I couldn't breathe and I began gasping for air.

Why was I crying? Why was I upset?

I rolled over onto all fours and pushed myself up to my feet. I closed the curtain and it was instantly black in the room except for the light coming from the right side of the curtain. I grabbed a chair and leaned it against the curtain, blocking the sliver of light.

I climbed back in my unmade bed and pulled the blankets up to my chin. What I would later learn is the fastest way to spiral into depression is to be lonely. The other ingredient is to be self-absorbed. "I" can be the root cause of many problems. When we are too focused on ourselves we lose sight of the bigger picture. *I* had not learned my lesson *yet.*

So on that lonely day I cried until I passed out from exhaustion.

"Be kind, for everyone you meet is fighting a hard battle." –Plato

------

Depression is an ugly monster that can flare its fangs with the same intensity as a supercell thunderstorm. At first you see the storm in the distance, but *it's in the distance.* You watch as the rain drenches the community miles away. It is a problem *they* should obviously deal with before it destroys their city.

As you pour your energy into your opinions about how your neighbor should deal with their issues, you don't see the storm as it creeps up on you. You don't see the sky break overhead. Before you know it, you're drenched but you ignore it. You don't see the rushing waters forming around you.

When you least expect it, the storm sucks you up into a cyclone of negativity and lack of self-worth. As you spiral upward into the eye of the tornado it's as though you lose the ability to think straight. *You know you know* the difference between right and wrong, happy and sad, life and death. Yet you can't bring yourself to differentiate the contrasts. If there is such a place as a spiritually negative space it is where you go. How do I know? Because I have been a visitor to that horrible place one too many times. And my first-class ticket to the destination is usually issued out of loneliness.

111

When you look back you can see the storm so clearly. You curse yourself for not seeing it coming, for not listening to the warning signs. *It was so obvious.* But hindsight is 20/20.

I first started experiencing signs of depression when I was a sophomore in college. I chalked it up to a bad case of PMS and my pride dismissed it. I didn't have a problem and I didn't need to talk to anyone about it. Besides, if you don't have a problem what is there to talk about?

The fangs started small, like the fangs of a spider. Yes it hurt, but it was temporary. It itched after the bite, but if I didn't scratch it went away.

I learned to cope with the emotional struggles through vigorous exercise. I would go for a run or go to the gym. I would push my body until I hit exhaustion. I would focus on competitions and dance and school. I would block the struggles from my mind. I would do anything so I didn't have to face the real issue. I was filing the fangs' sharpness down to a tolerable bluntness through hard work and perspiration.

But the fangs were always there. While I ground them down, they kept growing in width and depth. It was a slow growth so I didn't recognize it. In many ways, my pain tolerance was growing too. Those spider fangs slowly turned to the fangs of a monster.

It would be years before I realized I had a problem.

**Every day the sun comes up and the sun goes down.
What will you do in the sunshine?**

I found my joy in the Miss Kansas journey every time I had the opportunity to share my heart and my message with an audience. Be it in a school, a business, a gala, a convention, or a community meeting, I *lived* for my presentations. I still do. It is the place I feel my love for the stage and passion for people come together in perfect harmony. My presentations are less about me and more about my audience. I genuinely feel the urge to help people. With a microphone I can scatter seeds of greatness. I scatter hope, inspiration, self-respect, leadership, dreams, and motivation. If I'm honest, it was the crown that led me to my God given gift as a speaker. That crown opened doors so I could put my gift into action. We all have gifts. Have you found yours? The opportunities to develop your gifts can be found in the strangest places or by overcoming the darkest moments.

112

As Miss Kansas I spent a lot of time in the schools across my state. It was the best part of my job. My heart would sing when I could feel, and see, a student's "light bulb" turn on. A light when they began to realize their own unique greatness. I could see the welcomed fear in their eyes, fear because they were realizing they had the power to turn their lives into anything they could imagine. That kind of power when felt for the first time is overwhelming indeed. Instead of questioning whether or not they could achieve *it* they began to question *how* they could achieve *it*. It is a humbling opportunity to witness a student's heart feel harmonious potential for the first time.

You cannot fake your heart in front of any audience, but especially teenagers. They have superpower abilities to see straight through an imposter. Students accepted me for who I was. They embraced my flaws and even celebrated them. It made me more relatable. I couldn't be anything, or anyone, but Adrienne when I was in front of them. I suppose that is why we connected on such an intimate level: intimate whether or not it was a gathering of two or two thousand.

With my students I got to live the dream of what a Miss Kansas was to *me*: a promoter of dreams, a promoter of positive attitudes, and a promoter of making the most out of life despite life's challenges. The platform (*Small Towns, Big Dreams*) I won the Miss Kansas title with, and the message I was sharing across the state, was what the students wanted *and* needed to hear. Yet my directors had suggested my platform would never work on a national level. I let them *try* to change me. I let them change me for the Miss America Competition, but not for my students. I suppose it was one of God's ways of keeping me right where He needed me most.

As I look back on my journey as Miss Kansas I have much to be thankful for, but a part of me will always wonder what would have happened if I was encouraged to be myself. Would I have claimed the crown of Miss America?

I knew my own confidence was developed from a community of people who told me I "could" versus I "couldn't". I wanted to be that person who made my young audiences believe in their own beautiful possibilities. Yes, I believed in the power of a strong financial education, but first you had to have a dream in order for the financial aspect to make sense.

So every time I walked into a school I focused on the positive impact I could leave on the community. I knew that impression would eventually affect the town, then the state, then our country, and eventually our world.

I knew the power of one person with a dream. I still do.

Scene Twenty-Three

Kansas, an unnamed lonely highway, a girl on a mission, November 2005

(One year and nine months *before* the accident)

"Success doesn't come to you, you go get it." –Marva Collins

I was driving down a lonely Kansas highway looking for my destination – an elementary school located in mid-western Kansas. According to my map I should have been there, but there was nothing around. I was scheduled to give a school presentation in thirty minutes and I had no idea where the town was. On my map it was a tiny dot, but according to my odometer and compass I was in exactly the right area. This was what it was like to navigate the quiet highways of Kansas before the days of a smart phone, GPS, or satellite radio! And I'm not eighty-years-old as I write this, I'm thirty-three!

As the highway curved it dipped down into a wide open valley. I could see for fifty miles in every direction. There was nothing that resembled a town. There was a line of silos for grain and feed, but not much more.

As I blew past a highway turn-off there was also a sign with an arrow that pointed to my destination.

No way, I thought. *That row of silos can't be where I'm headed.*

I slowed my car to make a u-turn in the middle of the abandoned highway. It had to be my destination as it was the only cluster of structures I could see for miles. I turned down the road following the arrow's direction.

As I rolled into "town" I laughed at the four stop signs that were placed at the only "major" intersection in the community. I was on the only paved road in the whole settlement. If I turned left or right I would be on a dirt road.

115

I giggled. "Now this is Kansas," I said aloud.

I spotted the school from the stop sign and turned right onto the dirt road. When I pulled up to the school I parked next to a short row of pick-up trucks and mini-vans.

I slipped on my purple lizard stilettos and stepped out of the car. I had on pageant make-up, perfectly styled hair, a purple ruffled blouse (that matched my shoes precisely), and black crop pants that were flawlessly pressed. I opened the door to the back seat and grabbed my crown box, plate of gum, autograph pad, and purse. Yes, you read that right... my plate of gum.

I carefully walked up to the school being mindful not to kick up the dirt. I didn't want my lizard-skin-shoes dusty. I opened the front glass door and stepped inside. It was obviously an elementary school by the low hanging children's art. Above the art was a large sign that read "Welcome Miss Kansas". I smiled as I walked past my sign and into the office.

"Hi," I said to the woman sitting behind the counter. "My name is Adrienne. I'm Miss Kansas."

She smiled warmly and said, "Welcome. It's nice to meet you. I'm Susan."

"Thank you. It's nice to meet you too. I'm happy to be here."

"The kids are so excited to meet you. I'll show you to the gym."

As she got up from her chair she explained there were thirty-two kids in the entire school (kindergarten through fifth grade). She also explained my audience would be closer to sixty attendees as many of the parents were driving "in" to meet Miss Kansas. The students were farm kids and that was why their little town was... well, little.

I smiled. I loved being in rural Kansas. I was just "Adrienne" but since I had a tiara in tow I was being treated like a celebrity. I was flattered, but I also found that treatment frustrating. Had I just been "Adrienne" arriving in the small community would I have received such a gracious welcoming? That bothered me the entire year I was Miss Kansas. I loved being Miss Kansas, but there was more to me than a crown.

It took me years to accept the fact it was the "crown" that opened doors "Adrienne" struggled to open on her own. But it was "Adrienne" that would leave a lasting impact on every room she walked into. I recognized the pedestal I had and respected it. I learned to use it to my advantage even, but at the end of the day I always reminded myself I was an equal. I was an equal that happened to win a pageant and an opportunity. It would have been wasteful to not capitalize on that opportunity. Whether I was "Adrienne" or "Miss Kansas" I had a message to share. For the time being it was "Miss Kansas" that got everyone's attention.

As we approached the gym I excused myself to the girl's room. I stepped into the bathroom to pin my crown to my head and reapply my lipstick. I literally had to duck to see the top of my head in the low hanging mirror. As I secured my crown I giggled at the used paper towels scattered about. Apparently the waste bin was too tall for the tiny elementary school students.

I could hear the buzz increasing in volume from my crowd on the other side of the wall. It was show time.

No matter the size of my audience or the location, I was only as good as my last performance. One hundred percent of my focus was on my tiny audience on the other side of that bathroom wall. I knew I may be the impact on just one person that would give him/her the courage to become something great in their life. I knew I could give him/her the boost to make a lasting impact on their community and our world.

No two days as Miss Kansas were ever the same. The day before my small town appearance I had been standing in front of eight hundred high school students sharing my message. The day before that I had emceed an event on the other side of the state. The day before that I had shared my heart with a Rotary club.

On this particular day I was preparing for one of my smallest school appearances. I would have never predicted I would remember the details of that small school versus the excitement of a school with two thousand students.

When I walked into the gymnasium my little crowd applauded. I giggled and waved. The "Miss Kansas treatment" was something I never got used to. Even in my frustration, I was always honored.

My crowd was twenty-five students and thirty-five parents. I felt my nervousness kick in as the principal greeted me and then introduced me to my audience. I had an hour to entertain my crowd. While I was hired to speak to the elementary age students, more than half of my crowd was older than I was. It was going to be an hour of thinking on my feet and blending multiple presentations. An audience is an audience and a professional knows how to captivate *everyone* in the room even when their ages were so diverse. My job as Miss Kansas was to share a message with the students. My job as Adrienne was to share a message with the entire room, no matter the age gap.

I pulled a CD out of my purse and handed it to the principal. As I had requested they had the sound system prepared. A staff member handed me a microphone while the principal popped my CD into the player.

The music started and I walked to the middle of the gym and stopped. I began to sing with a confident powerful voice. I sang the first lyrics of the famous song *At Last* before I walked up to my first kiddo. I knelt on one knee and grabbed a young man's hand and gestured for him to stand. He did. I held his hand and sang a couple of lines directly to him. His precious smile melted my heart. The kids around us giggled as the parents snapped photos. I gestured for him to sit and I walked to the other side of the room, still singing.

I found another young man and again knelt on a knee and sang directly to him. More giggling and more pictures. I had my audience's attention, young and old, and everyone in the gym was smiling and laughing. I had knocked down that invisible fourth wall, along with the Miss Kansas pedestal, within the first five minutes I was in the room. It was a good start.

My presentations for middle school and high school students started the same way but with a bit more flare. Before I even spoke I would walk through the crowd and pick eight random young men to take a seat on the stage in one of the eight chairs I had spaced across the stage, or the front of the room, or the center of the gym. The audience would go silent waiting to see what I was going to do with the eight gentlemen.

Once my men were seated and their faces blushing red, I would stand in front of them and say to the audience and audio engineer, "Music please." Without delay my music would start and a classic love song would roar to life. The crowd immediately knew I was about to serenade the eight young men with a mushy love song.

My crowd would go nuts as I would sing. Ninety percent of the time I sang my song from memory because the crowd was so loud I could hardly hear the music. I walked up and down the row singing to the young men. Some I danced with while others I played with their hair or sat on their laps. It was the perfect ice breaker.

Why did I decide to sing? Remember my fear of singing in public? I knew if I turned the attention on my audience I wouldn't be judged on my singing ability, or judged quite so harshly. It gave me an avenue to grow as a performer, and a person, and it ended up being a ton of fun. From that point I could deliver my message of dreaming big and seeing those dreams become a reality. The fact I started my presentation with a song would later play into my message when I talked about stepping outside your comfort zone. I had demonstrated before their very eyes I was putting my money where my mouth was. I was taking the steps from good to great to awesome. I was following my dream, and while Miss Kansas was a great stepping stone, it wasn't my ultimate dream. I was a living, breathing example of hard work and determination. I was also actively overcoming my insecurities in order to push myself to greatness.

Immediately after my song I transitioned into my message, which started with a question. *What do you want to be when you grow up?*

No one could prepare me for the first grader, in that tiny town, that looked at me with big eyes and said with a tone as serious as a cancer diagnosis, "I want to be a garbage man." I had to fight back a chuckle as I never thought in my wildest dreams I would hear such a dream.

Indeed I was used to hearing dreams of race car drivers, ninjas, teachers, moms, doctors, lawyers, and truck drivers. But never a garbage man. That young man trumped my far-out-there dream of becoming a professional dancer on Broadway.

My response to such an unexpected dream: I looked at that young, bright-eyed first grader and said "you can be anything in this life you set your mind to and I have no doubt you will indeed be a great garbage man." His smile was priceless and hearing his dream made a lasting impact on me.

I never wanted, nor do I want to be, the person who says "you can't do that" or "find a new dream" or "your dream is stupid". I have been told it all and it is crushing to the soul. I believe the people who crush dreams are the people who didn't have the courage to chase their own.

So I continued to ask and continued to encourage people of all ages with the simple, yet loaded question: *What are you going to be when you grow up?* When really I was asking *what is your dream?* Or *what interests you?*

Asking my older audiences the same question became much more complicated in their responses. Why? Because in my experience most kids know exactly what they want to be when they grow up yet most adults "have no idea". The confusion starts somewhere in the teenage years of insecurity. Somewhere in our teens we start judging ourselves and become too insecure to speak our vision out loud. Any successful dreamer knows the first step to achieving your goals is by saying your plans out loud.

Which is more powerful, your insecurity or your voice? Your voice will fuel your will-power to continue through tough times. Insecurity is an excuse. Everyone has both: will-power and insecurities. Which will you focus on in order to create the life you envision? The choice is yours.

I once heard a comedian say "wouldn't it be great if we became the first thing we said we wanted to be? We would have a bunch of superheroes and princesses running around."

That comedian made me laugh, but I laughed because in many ways I did become that princess he was poking fun of as being non-existent. I was, after all, the queen of Kansas. I had the crown to prove it.

But being the modern day version of a princess was for a limited time. After 365 days I had to pass the crown to my successor, but during my Miss Kansas year I discovered new dreams to live. Life is a journey and the landscape is constantly changing. Enjoy the view while you have it, but don't get stuck.

As people we are constantly growing and changing. We are not the same people we were yesterday and we are not the same people we will be ten years from now. Life experiences give us different perspectives. Different perspectives show us new paths to discover, and different journeys we would have otherwise missed.

Why do so many people feel they have failed if they don't achieve their original dream? Why are we not being encouraged to have many dreams? I believe in dreams, plural, not a dream, singular.

I wish I knew where that little first grader is today. Did he fulfill his first grade dream? Is he indeed a garbage man? Did he find more dreams that he is now seeking? Today I don't know the answer to that question, but in this small world I know someday our paths will cross yet again. For those of you who think his dream of a garbage man was strange, I will remind you that our dreams grow and change as we grow and change in the world, as they should. No dream is silly. No dream is small. What is silly is if you don't dream at all.

Let's pretend you are twenty-years-old and I promise you will live to be one hundred. Do you really think in the first twenty years of your life you will discover what it is you want to do with the next eighty years of your life? Did you figure out in twenty years what is going to keep you motivated for the next eighty? If you don't achieve your goal will you punish yourself with thoughts of failure?   Well… I'm here to call your bluff on that hand of cards.

I will ask again: *what do you want to be when you grow up?*

Now I will encourage you: be many things. As people, we are always growing and changing, which means you will ask yourself this question your entire life. Get used to it. Don't be scared of it; rather welcome it.

Life is like a river. Both are constantly moving and changing. Sometimes the water will be smooth and peaceful, other times it will be swollen from a storm and yet other times there will be unavoidable raging rapids. There is no such thing as treading water in a river. You are constantly moving.   The scenery is always changing and the experiences are always new. Some may be similar, *but they are only similar.* When the river dries up so does the life around it, bringing your journey to an end. So make the most of the journey before it is over.

What do you want to be when you grow up? It's a tough question, and a question you better get used to asking *and answering.* You're not grown up until your dead, and if you're not dead you better be dreaming. Being one thing for eighty years is boring. As long as we are going to be many things, why not be awesome at each one of those things? Life is for a limited time. You get one chance *at many things.* Don't suck at your one chance. And guess what? The only person that gets to decide the level of awesomeness you reach is *you.*

Let me clarify, I didn't encourage my students to be scatter-brained with many dreams; quite the contrary actually. It is important to focus on one thing at a time. While you can be many things over the course of your lifetime, don't try and be everything all at once. Instead, know there is a season in life for everything. Just like the weather has four seasons, it is impossible for it to snow and be ninety degrees at the same time. Nature focuses on one thing at a time. At the end of the day, the weather is still the weather but has many different stories to tell.

If you don't have many dreams in life, and if those dreams don't scare the socks off you, then you aren't dreaming big enough.

Scene Twenty-Four
A girl conveying a life lesson to an audience of any age
(Two years *before* the accident)

"Do something today your future self will thank you for." -unknown

Once you determine a dream, how do you make it happen? *It's simple. And it only takes five minutes.*

Imagine if you spent five minutes a day working toward your dream. Can you imagine? Five minutes is nothing. Every day you are given 1,440 minutes: *one-thousand-four-hundred-forty-minutes. Seriously*, what do you do with all that time? Once you use it (or not) it's gone forever.

I'm suggesting five minutes. Translation: you can do what you have to with the other one-thousand-four-hundred-**thirty-five** minutes in your day. For example, if you work eight hours a day and sleep eight hours a night (which most people DON'T) you still have 480 minutes in your day. Four-hundred-eighty minutes to do *something*. *Anything!* I'm only suggesting you dedicate five minutes. That's peanuts, right? This is your dream, after all.

Are you reading this as a skeptic? Are you asking: if that dedication is *so* little, how can it get me to the bigger picture?

Let me shift gears for a second and ask you a different question: If you dedicate 110% of your focus and energy for 1,825 minutes would you accomplish something? Anything? Of course you would!

Now, imagine if you dedicated just five minutes of your day for one year toward your goal. In one year you would have *simply* (easy as peanuts remember?) dedicated 365 tasks toward your dream, and you would have put 1,825 minutes toward your dream. This is more than most people do in ten years to accomplish what they *think* about achieving.

Five minutes a day is all it takes. No you can't bank your time. It's every day. Five minutes a day. A simple task which you agreed with a few paragraphs ago.

To better demonstrate my message I came up with a visual example that has traveled with me for the past ten years. For every day I spent five minutes working toward my dream, I chewed a piece of gum. Once I exhausted the flavor I put the gum on a plate. Every day for 365 days I chewed a piece of gum and stuck it to a plate. Yes, I have a pile of gum that is four inches tall and five inches wide. It's disgusting *and beautiful*. A piece of art if you ask me. It represents the stepping stones of my dream. A little bit *every day* goes a long way over the long haul.

Imagine if you dedicate five minutes a day for ten years: that is 3,650 sessions of five minutes *or* a total of 18,250 minutes dedicated toward your dream. I'm not even including leap years! Don't you think you can accomplish something in EIGHTEEN-THOUSAND-TWO-HUNDRED-FIFTY minutes? That's 304 hours dedicated to your dream (remember: no bathroom breaks, sleep, or food breaks. That's 110% dedication for 304 hours). Yes, I know basic math. Do you? Have you broken down your goal to be as easy as chewing a piece of gum once a day?

In five minutes a day you can accomplish your dream.

Shall we discuss what ten minutes a day would do? Or an hour? I recently read it takes 10,000 hours to become an expert at something. What are you waiting for? It's time to get started.

Need a non-visual example? If I asked a non-runner to run a marathon, right here right now, they would physically be unable. If I trained that same person for a year they would cross the finish line with ease *and* pride.

When you discover your dream, you want to have accomplished it yesterday, but how do you get there? It's easy, and it only takes FIVE MINUTES.

You cannot know success without tasting failure.

Some people talk themselves out of their dream before they even start working toward it. Why? Fear of failure? Fear of success? You will never know your possibilities unless you push yourself. And if you fail… you fail and start again.

Why are we so afraid of failure? Failure isn't bad. No, it doesn't *feel* great, but it isn't a bad thing either. If you gave your best effort then you found an answer. It may not have been the answer you were looking for, but it was an answer nonetheless. Learn from it, accept it, and move on. With the right attitude you will learn failure provides the greatest opportunities to learn life's lessons. Those lessons set you up for greater success in the future.

What if you didn't give your best effort and you failed? Well, I'm here to tell you GET OFF YOUR TUSH AND TRY HARDER. Failure because it wasn't meant to be is one thing; failure out of laziness is something in which I have zero tolerance. And remember, you may only get one shot at your opportunity. Don't cheat yourself by half-assing your efforts.

Life is a series of goals and dreams. Knowing how to identify a dream and set goals to achieve those dreams are the first steps in finding a successful future and a fulfilling journey. I like the way Steve Harvey puts it, "Goals are dreams with their feet on the ground."

"A great attitude becomes a great day which becomes a great month which becomes a great year which becomes a great life." –Mandy Hale

------

"When the going gets tough, the tough get going." I grew up hearing this famous quote which is sometimes attributed to Joseph P. Kennedy (JFK's father) or a Norwegian-born American football player and coach, Knute Rockne. No matter who owns this quote, the quote resonates with me and my message. The tough truly are strong in mind and spirit – **the tough know it's all about attitude.**

Your attitude takes you from simply dreaming to actively achieving. Your attitude will give you the power to continue when things get tough, or your attitude will give you the excuse to quit. A positive attitude is like a muscle. You must exercise it *every day*. You must feed it with the right nutrients *every day*. And you must keep it in a healthy environment *every day*.

A positive attitude is an everyday *decision*. It is one thing in your life you can control. No matter your circumstances you *can* choose a positive attitude. It is a choice. Yes, sometimes it is an easy choice and sometimes it is difficult, but if you have conditioned your mind correctly, you can always find the positive attitude it takes to persevere through any situation.

How do you condition your attitude? It's easy, and you can do it at the same time you brush your teeth.

"Look in the mirror, that's your biggest competition." –unknown

------

Growing up with two brothers, one sister, and one bathroom made mornings at our house a competition for privacy. A competition we failed at miserably. It was a race to claim the toilet and the shower. Thankfully, there were two sinks in a separate room so we learned to share.

I am the third child out of four. Yes, I am loud, boisterous, and head strong, but in the mornings I want to be left alone (I still do). I had to wake up on my own accord or the whole day was bound to be a cranky one. But my dad knew no such thing as a cranky teenager.

To this day I still have my alarm on the other side of the bedroom. If I'm out of bed then surely I can stumble my way to the bathroom. The first stop: the toilet. The second: the sink to brush my teeth.

Still half asleep I would scrub the morning fungus from my teeth and tongue. Without saying a word, Dad would strut his way down the hall and into the bathroom. He would proceed to butt his way in between me and my siblings. In an effort to get our attention, he would make faces at himself in the mirror. In return, my brother and I would give him the death glare of *get out of the bathroom*, but he ignored us and continued his performance.

As the three of us stood in silence my dad (the only stooge) would proceed to pull his shorts up as high as he could and lean backwards. His intention was to imitate Steve Urkel from the hit TV show *Family Matters*. We did our best to pretend we didn't notice his efforts, which of course was next to impossible. After several silent minutes of making faces and exchanging death glares, dad would finally break the silence and look at us in the mirror. He would say in an Urkel voice "Are you going to have a good day or are you going to have a bad day?"

We, the teenagers, continued our morning routine in silence, not giving into his desired response. Again his question would come, "Are you going to have a good day or are you going to have a bad day?" Each time he asked the question it became more dramatic and more escalated, "Are you going to have a good day or are you going to have a *baaaaaaad* day?"

The stares and glares continued along with the question.

I was usually the one who broke first. "Yes, Dad," I would say in my best annoyed teenage voice and roll of my eyes. "I'm going to have a good day. Now get out of the bathroom!"

As he Urkel-ed out of the bathroom, satisfied with my response, my brother and I would snicker, although we would have never admitted it to anyone!

This was the routine *every* morning: Dad as Urkel, and my brother and me as two annoyed teens. Eventually we started the morning by saying, "Hey dad, it's gonna be a great day." Or "Yo Dad, it's gonna be an awesome day."

Dad, a little confused his Urkel routine had been hijacked, had a huge smile on his face. He was happy his annoyed teenagers were grasping his lesson. I suppose that is one of the reasons I loved high school. I started every day saying "I'm going to have a great day." As I advanced to college I continued to arm myself with a positive attitude. It didn't matter what the day tossed my direction, I handled it. Sure I had bad days (remember the *Relay* t-shirts?). I had meltdowns, but deep down I knew everything was going to be okay. I had the right attitude. My positive attitude transitioned from something I said to a habit to a way of life. When life would later become more than I could handle on my own, I would know how to reach out for help.

My attitude began driving my passions and my passions began steering me toward a successful future. So yes, first you must have a dream, but you must add a positive attitude to the recipe.

Do those two items alone guarantee a successful future? Not necessarily, but they do set you on a promising path to achieve many great things in your life.

I had six months to perfect my motivational message while I prepared for the Miss America Competition. My message began to develop and grow in depth. I was beginning to use my own personal challenges to reach out to audiences to show them I was relatable. It broke down any stereotypes I carried with my crown. And through the process of helping others I helped myself. We helped each other.

There were some high schools that invited me for full school assemblies with "agendas" and I happily shifted my message to meet their students' needs. For example, I walked into one middle school prepared to give a full sixty minute message, but just before I walked in the gym the principal informed me the assembly was for their "DARE" program (a program to keep kids off drugs and away from alcohol). I had twenty minutes, not sixty, to leave a lasting impact.

I took a few minutes to gather my thoughts and take a deep breath before I walked in the gym to deliver a message on the fly to four hundred students. I still started with a song, but I immediately transitioned into a story I had never told before. I told them the story of when I was three-years-old and my cousin (who was in high school at the time) decided he was invincible enough to drink and drive. I described standing on the stairs of the church as the pallbearers carried his casket to the hearse. I remember my sister crying and I didn't understand what was going on. I explained to the students about all the people "your one decision" can affect… and continue to affect for years to follow, including "a three-year-old girl who becomes Miss Kansas and shares your decision with a group of four hundred students."

You could have heard a pin drop in the gym. That was the presentation I realized "story telling" and sharing my message would always be a part of me. My dream had expanded that day in that gymnasium in front of four hundred students trying to grasp the ways of the world.

I know my audience heard my message. After that presentation the girls' basketball team invited me to stay for practice, and I did. I had all my workout clothes in my car, remember?

Another school asked me to address teen pregnancy. I did. I told the story about my freshman year of high school when one of my best friends, who was just *messing around*, ended up pregnant. At fifteen-years-old, pregnancy changed her entire game-plan for life. It also changed me.

But I didn't just tell stories; I weaved in the value of attitude and the importance of dreams. For it is your attitude and your dreams that keep you on the right path when faced with life's obstacles. I talk about obstacles people rarely want to talk about, but we are all faced with (such as: sex, drugs, alcohol and suicide). When the inevitable, or accident, does happen it is your dreams and your attitude that help get you through your healing.

And my message was resonating with audiences. How did I know? Because people of all ages waited around to tell me and share their own stories. There was one girl in particular that left the biggest impact.

After a presentation, as I was chatting with a group of students, I noticed a young lady standing off to the side. I noticed her because of her insecure actions and her wardrobe. She was entirely too skinny and dressed in an extra large t-shirt and baggy pants. She wouldn't make eye contact with anyone.

As I was trying to listen to the group of students in front of me, I noticed she was going to leave. I stopped my students, asking them to hold on a moment, and I looked directly at the skinny young lady, and said "hi" directly at her. She looked at me and I continued, "I really want to meet you too. Will you hold on a second?" She nodded her head, giving me a few more moments with the group standing in front of me.

When the little group dispersed I walked over to the young lady. It was just the two of us left standing in the auditorium. With a little prompting she opened up. She explained she didn't feel she could talk to anyone in her school, or her small town, but because I was an outsider she felt she could confide in me. She proceeded to tell me about her thoughts of suicide and her step-dad who was molesting her.

We talked for a long time. Before I left that little community I found her help.

I had learned being a "speaker" is more than just "speaking". You have to be willing to listen to other people's stories, many of which are hard to hear. You have to be willing to help people. You have to be willing to problem solve.

At some point during those six months leading up to Miss America, I realized yet another dream: I was tossing around the idea of being a full time motivational speaker. My performance background paired with my love for people had led me down a path to not only realize a new God-given gift, but to understand speaking was a way I could leave a bigger impact on our world.

I began to see the Miss America crown as more than a crown. The national title was a bigger key to unlocking more doors and share my message with more people.

I was beginning to want that tiara... *bad.*

Scene Twenty-Five

Back in Texas, September 2007
(Thirty days *after* the accident)

"As the heavens are higher than the earth, so are my ways higher than your ways and my thoughts than your thoughts." –Isaiah 55:9

It was a beautiful fall morning in Texas. There were streaks of wispy white clouds scattered across the vast light blue sky. The birds were chirping and all seemed to be right in the world. The wind was at a welcomed rest and the temperature was cool. The ground was finally experiencing relief from the long summer weeks of the scorching sun.

I had never been in Texas that late into the year and I was really grasping the beauty in the landscape. I understood why people lived there. My mind was loopy from the medications, but I was still grasping it. It was a magical place. Peaceful and serene. I couldn't quite comprehend how such a beautiful place could also be the setting of my worst nightmare.

The three of us – Mom, Dad, me - were staying in the country with Paula. I had been welcomed into Paula's home for the duration of the summer show. When my accident occurred Paula had extended my welcome and even invited my parents to move into her second spare bedroom. My parents were welcomed as family.

I crutched out the front door and onto the circle drive where my car was waiting. My dad held the car door open while my mom was behind me carrying her purse. Her purse held my insurance card and more pain meds.

It was time for my daily doctors' appointments with two of my three doctors. I was headed to my infectious disease and control doctor before they sent me over to my wound care doctor, which had become a daily visit since my wound was growing at an exponential rate. My wound was up to five inches across at its widest point. It looked like raw hamburger meat and every day it seemed to be growing in size.

My parents helped me get situated in the car; my back was against the door, a pillow between me and the door, and my feet were stretched across the seat. My crutches lay on the floor at my side. My dad crawled behind the wheel and my mom slipped into the passenger seat. The three amigos were off.

"Dad, please lock the door," I requested. I hated riding in the car while I was leaning on the door, but it was the best way to get me from point A to point B.

My dad slowly accelerated and we were off on our thirty mile daily trek. I leaned my head back and closed my eyes. I focused my energy on my breathing as I listened to my parents chatting about how beautiful it was outside. I couldn't look around. The motion of the car mixed with my meds on an empty stomach left me in a constant state of nausea.

As Dad turned onto the highway, I could feel my heart begin to race. I was terrified of the high speeds. I did my best to keep my mind away from the visions of a car accident at 70 mph, crunching metal, and another ambulance ride. I tried to tell my mind to let go of the visions and the feeling of another broken bone. But the more I tried to distract my mind the more I thought about it.

I didn't say anything to my parents because there wasn't anything they could do. I just continued to take deep breaths with my eyes closed. When that didn't seem to work, I released some of my anxiety with silent tears that escaped down my cheeks. I had to go to my doctor's appointments. My parents knew it. I knew it.

If a car accident happens, it happens, I kept reminding myself.

I had a team of physicians and nurses doing everything they could to save my foot. At one of my follow-up appointments, my orthopedic doctor explained to me I was a textbook case for an amputation.

"Why didn't you amputate?" I asked him.

I don't remember his response. I'm not sure there was one. I do remember grabbing his hand and crying as I told him "Thank you". The tears we shared were more powerful than any words we could have exchanged. We both knew God was the reason he was able to save my foot. I also knew he was nervous, for many months, I might still end up with an amputation. He would tell me more often than not "You're not out of the woods yet."

I asked my great doctor why he decided to become a doctor in the first place. He told me his story. When he was in his twenties he was in the Colorado Rockies training for the Olympics. He was skiing moguls when something went wrong. He severely trashed his knee and the surgeon who operated didn't do a good job. Several surgeries later, and still a bum knee, he decided he was going to become the best orthopedic surgeon there was. He didn't want another young athlete to lose a career from a hack-of-a-surgeon. I suppose that is why he put me back together instead of taking the easy way out: an amputation. He saw I had the fight in me. The will power. The ability to overcome. He wanted me and my body to determine my fate, not him.

"I need to stop for fuel," my dad announced, which stunned me back into the present and away from my thoughts.

"I'm going to get a cup of coffee," my mom said. "Adrienne, do you want to try one today?"

"Sure," I said. "Maybe today I will like it." I knew that was highly unlikely. I'm not sure coffee was the greatest thing for my body. I'm sure my mom didn't think it was either, but she knew how much I loved coffee and it was something other than medication in my stomach.

As we turned off the highway and into the gas station I saw an ambulance at the far bay refueling. There was only one EMT by the ambulance and I didn't recognize him, which meant it wasn't Tommy. I looked over toward the convenience store and I could see two EMTs inside. I wondered if one of them was *my* EMT. I couldn't fully remember what he looked like, but that was okay. I would find him. He would understand. I was, after all, under a massive amount of stress when we first met. I had an overwhelming sensation that I wanted to tell Tommy "thank you".

"Mom, I want to go inside with you," I announced.

"Serious?" she asked. I nodded.

Mom helped me scoot out of the car and she handed me my crutches. She paced her stride to match my crutching ability.

The automatic doors to the convenience store opened and I crutched inside and over to the counter where the two EMT guys were paying for their purchase.

"Excuse me," I interrupted them.

"Are one of you Tommy?" I asked.

They both looked at each other before the one on the right said, "No, we don't know a Tommy."

"Really?" I asked with disappointment.

"Do you mean Johnny?" the other one asked.

"Maybe. A Tommy, or perhaps a Johnny, was my EMT a month ago. I was thrown off a horse and had a horrible break," I explained. "It wasn't just broken though. I'm told it was pretty ugly to walk up on."

"It was Johnny," the one on the left said with a smile. "He told us about you."

"Is he here?" I asked.

"No, I'm sorry. He's out on a maintenance run with another truck."

"Bummer. Will you tell him that we met?" I paused, "But more importantly, will you please tell him thank you? I'm so grateful to him."

"We'll tell him," the one on the right said with a smile.

"Thanks," I said. "And thank you for what you do."

My little outing was exhausting so I turned to head back to the car. My dad was just finishing fueling and he opened the door for me.

"His name is Johnny not Tommy," I said to my dad as he looked at me a little confused. "Johnny was my EMT that helped me stay awake, and alive, from the field to the hospital." My dad nodded, still not saying anything.

My dad silently helped me get situated in the car as my mom climbed back in the front seat, coffees in hand.

"Okay," she said as she handed me a cup. "Here is your coffee. Half cappuccino from the machine, half coffee."

"Thanks mom."

I cupped my hands around the Styrofoam. The warmth felt nice. The aroma drifted upward and my nose welcomed the familiar, comforting smell. I enjoyed the fragrance. My dad started the car and pulled back out onto the highway.

We went another five miles before I decided to try a sip. I lifted the cup to my mouth, but before I connected the cup to my lips I took another deep whiff of the pungent aroma. I closed my eyes. I tried to imagine myself in a different place, in a different time, and in a different state, but my mind wouldn't let me escape. I didn't have the energy to fight it so I opened my eyes and took a sip. It was hot and bitter, just as my situation. But I could taste the sugar through the bitterness; the sugar represented my parents among the bitter drama.

The coffee wasn't awesome, but it wasn't horrible. Perhaps my situation was much the same… it could have been worse. I took another sip.

My mom glanced over her shoulder, while my dad looked at me through the rearview mirror. They both smiled, yet neither one of them said anything. Somewhere deep down in their own emotions, they knew their baby daughter had the strength to overcome this horrible time. They knew my determination. They knew my ability to persevere. I may have been questioning my own abilities, but they knew me better than I knew myself. Their mission had gradually turned from helping me survive to helping me overcome. They knew, better than I did, I was still at the beginning of a very long, hard journey. I suppose that is why one of them was with me at all times. They were my arms, my legs, my emotions, and my drivers. They listened when I cried. They cheered when I had bowel movements. Mom helped me shower and Dad would put me in a wheelchair to take me for walks around the block when it was time for some fresh air.

I couldn't have done it without my parents. The phrase "thank you" became my most frequent expression that came from my mouth. It was everything I could offer. It was all I could offer.

My taste buds for coffee eventually came back and I once again resumed my favorite morning ritual. But most notably, I no longer take a morning cup of coffee for granted. I'm more thankful today than I was before my accident for that small gift God gave us – the coffee bean. It may seem so routine to you, but for me, enjoying a cup of java is anything but routine. Praise God for the small, ordinary things we so often take for granted. It is the ordinary things that bring joy to our journey as we pursue our dreams and live from day to day.

In a few months I would discover another ordinary joy: the joy of stepping off a curb. Yes, a curb. As in, step from the sidewalk to the street. I went months without that simple ability so when I was able to do it again, I was grateful through giggles. It was so fun in fact, I would step back up the curb just to step off again.

Scene Twenty-Six

Medical/physical therapy clinic, three hyperbaric chambers, a team of
medical professionals, a patient and her parents, October 2007
(Sixty days *after* the accident)

"Troubles are often the tools by which God fashions us for better things."
–Henry Ward Beecher

By my eighth week, post injury, I had received forty wound care
treatments by my wound care doctor (Dr. N) and his team. That is a
wound care treatment everyday Monday through Friday for two solid
months.

I would crutch into the clinic, past the receptionist, and straight to
the bathroom where I would change into scrubs. I would exit the
bathroom and head to my designated wound treatment table. It took
me an average of thirty crutches from the car to the table, which meant I
had to muster up the energy for at least sixty crutches, round trip, five
days a week. That didn't include my weekly visits to my infectious
disease and control doctor nor my orthopedic doctor, both of which I
visited at least once a week. Most days I refused a wheelchair, which I
was proud to refuse.

There was one day I only made it twenty crutches before I vomited
all over the checkered tile floor. I asked if I could skip that day's
treatment, but my medical team handed me a puke pan and told me
"no". They conducted our normal routine: wound care treatment
followed by an hour (or two) in the hyperbaric chamber.

Whether or not I was throwing up, the forty treatments went much
the same. I would situate myself on the exam table and prop my foot on
a stack of hospital blankets in front of me as I waited for Dr. N's next
clever treatment option. Most of the time I would lay over on my legs,
in a full hamstring stretch, and prop my chin on my hands so I could

casually watch him clean and manicure my wound. As he worked we chatted about nothing in particular.

The treatments Dr. N administered were interesting. In fact, some of the treatments consisted of mango extract and pig intestine. Eventually we moved on to the major leagues and he introduced me to an alternative skin graft which was made of a baby boy's foreskin. Yes, I have baby penis on my ankle. I'm sure there is a more sophisticated, medical term for the skin he used, but the reality was, it was baby penis. The graft is a technology where scientists take the skin (after a circumcision) and grow it in a Petri dish. That foreskin can then be used as a skin graft. Very cool, right? I thought so too. It didn't work for me, nevertheless I still brag about baby penis on my ankle.

Every day with Dr. N was an adventure. I enjoyed our growing friendship and I appreciated the education he was giving me. But every time he unwrapped my ankle I seemed to be getting worse rather than better. My body was eating away at itself and my wound was growing instead of shrinking. Nothing seemed to be working, but Dr. N never lost his positive attitude or optimism. At least three days a week he would sit next to me and stare at my ankle. He would always assure me, "There is more than one way to skin a cat." His statement always made me laugh because he was the gentlest soul I had ever met from the medical industry. I'm sure he had never, and would never, skin a cat. As a matter of fact, I would have placed a bet that he had a cat or two at home.

On my forty-first treatment my situation went from bad to worse. It started out normal as I made my thirty crutch journey from the car to the bathroom to the table. I laid over on my legs for another educational session of wound care treatment, but when Dr. N removed my wound vacuum and began cleaning my wound, something caught our attention and I asked, "What is that?"

I pointed at a white chord (that looked like a 1/8" wide rubber band) that was lying in the middle of my gaping wound. I had never seen that chord during any other treatment sessions. I waited for him to pick at it with his scissors, or forceps, as he told me about skinning cats. Instead he asked, "Will you pump your foot back and forth?" Gently I did as he requested.

The white chord moved.

"It is your tendon," he confirmed with a sigh.

"Is that bad?" I asked.

The tendon we were looking at was the specific tendon that picked up my foot when I walked. (Note: You can actually see this tendon in your own foot. If you pump your foot back and forth, and around in circles, you will see a tendon move on the front of your ankle. That is the tendon Dr. N and I were looking at, but outside of my skin.) My situation: my tendon was exposed. If left the way it was, it would dry out. The result: I would lose the tendon as well as the ability to move my foot. In other words, I would be left with a "drop foot" when, and if, I ever got the chance to walk again.

"It's time to get you to Dallas," he responded solemnly.

Dr. N repositioned my wound vacuum over my wound. He flipped the switch on the vacuum and the pad sucked down on my ankle. He gave my parents instructions while I started my final thirty crutches out of the clinic and back to the car.

Life is full of challenges,
but it is the challenge that makes the victory so sweet.

The next morning I was in Dallas meeting with more wound care doctors, infectious disease doctors, orthopedic doctors, and a now a plastic surgeon. In less than 24 hours I would be back in surgery. They were prepping me to receive a free flap, a procedure where they would take muscle from one area of my body and transplant it to another. The free flap would do two things: 1) cover my tendon and 2) reconnect the blood supply from my leg to my foot (blood/circulation = healing).

My plastic surgeon, who would perform the free flap surgery, wanted to take the muscle from my left scalp "because that muscle is less bulky." Some of the side effects could be muscle loss in my facial expressions on the left side of my face. In short, I may appear as though I had a stroke. The backup plan was to take my inner thigh muscle instead of the muscle from my scalp. They wouldn't determine which muscle until they got me into the operating room.

Another warning from my surgeon: this was a risky procedure as the muscle doesn't always "take" to its new location on the body. I still preferred to gamble with the free flap procedure versus jumping straight to a "drop foot" or an amputation. My surgeon explained to me I would be on bed rest for two weeks, with my foot above my heart, and in the hospital for seven nights. If everything went according to plan I would graduate at the two week mark and be allowed to have my foot below my heart for five minutes, three times a day (enough to go to the bathroom), and nothing more. For each week I graduated I would gain five minutes. If all went according to plan, by week four I could have my foot below my heart for ten minutes three times a day. By week eight I could have my foot below my heart for thirty minutes three times a day. My doctor was so emphatic about my foot being above or below my heart he informed me I needed to use a timer, *literally*.

"What if it doesn't take?" I remember asking.

"We start over and use a different muscle," my plastic surgeon answered.

After our meeting with the doctors, Mom and Dad voted we do something to distract ourselves. They loaded me into a wheelchair, with my wound vacuum and bone stimulator securely at my side, and wheeled me into the mall.

I insisted we go to a shoe store. Why? To be a pain in the ass.

In we rolled, well, I rolled and Mom and Dad walked. The three of us laughed as we made jokes about the fact I only needed one shoe.

I immediately spotted a gorgeous pair of flat leopard-print dress shoes. A woman who worked there saw me admiring the shoes so she came over to help.

"May I help you?" she asked.

"Yes," I said. "I need a size nine… but I was wondering, since I obviously only need one shoe will you sell me one shoe for half the price?" I asked.

I sat silently, stone cold serious, staring at the poor girl as she processed my question.

"Umm," she said confused.

"Well you can plainly see I only need one," I responded as I gestured to my splinted foot that had tubing coming out of it.

"I don't think I can do that," she said nervously.

I waited and there was a long awkward silence as I stared at her in anticipation for her response. She was getting uncomfortable.

As I realized she was about to cry, I burst out laughing and told her I was joking. She wasn't sure if she should laugh or cry but I told her the situation and she let out a sigh. I felt bad for making a joke at her expense, but the three of us had a good laugh, a much needed laugh. The girl remained confused. I didn't buy the shoes, but it was a welcomed distraction and I appreciated her being a good sport.

That evening Mom and Dad turned their head when I took my Percocet with a beer. I was scared.

137

Scene Twenty-Seven

A girl prepping for Miss America, October 2005
(Two years *before* the accident)

"Wanting to be something else is a waste of the person you are."
–Marilyn Monroe

I thought I had to heed the advice of those around me as it pertained to *winning* Miss America. So I circled back around to my appearance and what I needed to do to be my best. It seemed my biggest issue was my skin as I was having massive breakouts.

Two months before my departure to the Miss America Competition, I called my doctor and he assured me he could help with my acne. My doctor's primary concern wasn't my breakouts, it was the fact I had lost my period. My doctor prescribed a hormone medication to get my body working, or re-start my period. I remember reading the warning label and it said it may take up to fifteen days before the first signs of a period. The side effects: weight gain and bloating.

Great, I thought.

Sure enough it took the whole fifteen days as I anxiously watched the scale advance in weight. I reduced my food intake as much as I could without compromising my energy levels or being severely unhealthy, but it didn't make a difference. After the fifteen days my doctor started me on birth control pills in order to maintain my monthly periods, which meant more weight gain and more bloating.

I was losing control. I felt powerless, hungry, and irritable as I prepared for the biggest competition of my life. I was fighting ugly internal battles and as the numbers on the scale continued to creep higher, I continued to eat less while exercising more. It was becoming more than I could handle and more than I could sustain.

138

I began to question: *is my life going to be determined by a tiny number on a scale I can hardly read without my contacts? Adrienne, wake-up, your health comes first. The Miss America Competition will come and go. This body is your temple and the only one you get. Enjoy this once-in-a-lifetime opportunity, but don't let a tiny number, based off a ball and chain, determine your self-value.*

With much heartache, I decided my health (both internal and emotional) came first. I abandoned my scale. It was hard, but I left it behind at my aunt and uncle's house. When I drove away I had no weighing mechanism, and I didn't have enough money to buy a new one.

By the time I boarded the plane to Miss America in January, my clothes were bulging at the seams. I was trying not to freak out, but my hormones were out of whack and the meltdowns came with the territory. I was at the competition of a lifetime at least fifteen pounds heavier, but I'm not really sure because I had quit weighing myself.

I was the furthest thing from being at my best, physically or emotionally. To add to the nightmare, I had a team of people down my throat about my appearance. I will never forget a particular moment at Miss America when I ran into a woman I knew and she asked, "What did you do to yourself?" She was referring to my weight gain. Her question was more than warranted but I remember thinking *maybe you should ask "is everything okay?" versus criticizing me for details she had no idea about.*

"Periods. Why can't it be like fairy dust or something?"
– Miscellaneous teenager

My hormones hit an all-time-raging-high the day of the televised final competition. It started the moment I awoke. Actually it's what woke me up. I was uncomfortable and *wet*. To my horror I had an unexpected visitor: Aunt Flo.

Apparently *Auntie Not-Invited* didn't want to miss the big occasion and she packed extra for her time at Miss America. She was upset she hadn't been invited to this once-in-a-lifetime event, so she planned on being smack-dab in the middle of the action, whether I liked it or not.

I tip-toed to the bathroom to get some towels.

Is this really happening? Am I having a nightmare? I asked myself.

I tip-toed back into the room to scrub my bed, trying not to wake the sleeping beauty in the bed adjacent to mine. I silently but furiously cursed my visitor as I cleaned her mess.

When my efforts were satisfactory I grabbed my phone and went back in the bathroom. I immediately called my mom. "Mom, I'm sorry to wake you, but I need your help." I whispered.

"What is it Adrienne?" she asked.

"My period came early and I don't have any supplies," I said. "Will you go to the store and get me some heavy duty help?"

"Yes, I'll have it to you in an hour," she said and hung up immediately.

I finished getting ready, doing my best to calm my nerves.

Dear God, of all the times for this to happen... please, please, please make it go away.

By the time I arrived in the dressing room one of the security guards was looking for me. "Miss Kansas I have a package for you," he said in his deep booming voice.

I walked over to one of our big burly male security guards. If I had a tail it would have been tucked between my legs. "Thanks" I said as I retrieved my package.

"Sorry we had to inspect it before we could bring it back to you," he said and then walked away.

I opened the bag and pulled out the box of tampons that had "Miss Kansas" plastered across the front. I was humiliated and relieved; although I wasn't sure one box of supplies would last for the next 24 hours let alone the telecast. It would have to do as security wasn't about to let me run over to the nearest drug store on a tampon shopping spree.

I disappeared to the ladies room and fought back tears as I took care of business. I also stuffed my pockets with tissues for tears, and tampons in case I wasn't back in the dressing room for a while. I took a deep breath and opened the door to face the world.

I would get through today and I would do with a big freakin' smile on my face. My attitude would be positive, damn it.

We were being summoned to the stage for our final rehearsal. I quickly slammed back some ibuprofen and filed past the food table to grab a handful of chocolate. My butt was already twice the size it was the day I won the state competition. A handful of chocolate wasn't going to make a difference.

Desperate times call for desperate measures and I was desperate.

My cramps hit at an all-time raging high. Of all the times to have cramps and a mad Aunt Flo. I popped a piece of chocolate in my mouth and gracefully stomped my way out to the stage.

I survived the first few run-throughs of rehearsal. To my surprise the tampons and chocolate were behaving themselves and staying in my pockets. Finally, something was working for me, not against me. To add to my successes, the ibuprofen was kicking in and the more relief I felt the taller I stood and the more genuine my smile became.

This was it. This is my journey and I better like it for better or worse.

"Kansas," Miss Hawaii whispered to get my attention. "Rough morning?"

I rolled my eyes as a response.

"Are you okay?" she asked with concern.

Without saying a word, I pulled both my hands out of my sweatshirt pockets for a show and tell. One fist was full of tampons, the other was full of chocolate and tissues. She gave me the most sympathetic look followed by a hug.

"I'll be fine," I laughed as I heard the director holler "From the top."

I was fine. I survived rehearsal and the rest of the morning; even while Aunt Flo continued to rear her ugly face.

"Be careful how you are talking to yourself because you are listening."
–Lisa M. Hayes

Two hours before the telecast, the contestants spread across our designated private area of the hotel grounds. Each contestant was going through her pre-show warm-up rituals. To an outsider, I suppose it was quite the dramatic scene.

Many of us had our hair in curlers, make-up caked on our faces, and fake eyelashes twice as long as normal lashes. Some girls were running around in bathrobes and house slippers. We were a beautiful bunch, but had we been sixty years older we would have looked like a washed-up retirement community of women in the midst of a makeover.

Several of us walked across a small staff parking lot to an adjacent, vacant building. We spread out through the rooms, each of us taking our own private room. Within moments, the quiet building lit up with beautiful sounds bouncing off the walls and up through the ventilation system. Girls were warming up their voices, including myself. We sounded like an opera house before opening night. I smiled as I went through my vocal warm-ups and cemented the memory into my mind.

This was it. Fifty-two of us little girls were living out the final moments of our Miss America dream. One girl would get an extension of that dream, but ultimately we were all at the end. Most of us played "princess" growing up and there we were at the end of our journey. We had sparkly gowns, boob pads that made up for any lack of personal endowment, scholarship money, free cars, and there was another crown up for grabs.

I planned on making it into the top ten (extra pounds and all) and if it was God's will I would be the last one standing. I wasn't being conceited, quite the contrary actually. I was honored to be among those talented and beautiful women, but I had worked my butt off in preparation and I was there to win, as were all the gorgeous contestants.

I thought about the little girls all over Kansas glued to their TV sets just as I was eleven years prior. I had 125 people who had traveled from Kansas to Las Vegas in support of their local Kansas girl. My family and friends were in the audience. So was my sixth grade science teacher, Miss Sharon, and my high school track coach, Coach Cornelsen.

For my track coach, a pageant was a stretch. I had the utmost respect for that man. He was one of the people who instilled the winning spirit within me and reassured me that pain meant I wasn't dead yet. Every year he would run us so hard we would throw-up at least once a week, but year-after-year the athletes returned. Why? Because we won. Not only were we fierce athletes, we had a winner's attitude instilled in us. Let's just say, my senior year of high school our girls track team won our twelfth consecutive state championship. He trained us to win and he was in the audience to watch one of his athletes win Miss America. That same year he would also follow the Pittsburgh Steelers, and Jerame Tuman, to the Super Bowl to watch another of his high school athletes compete for another national title.

Yes, I was there to win.

The preliminary awards had been handed out and the *Quality of Life* winner had been announced. I had not won any preliminaries nor the *Quality of Life* Award; however, I was a *Quality of Life* finalist… and there were only seven of us. Since the creation of that portion of the competition, no girl had won the Miss America title without first having been a *Quality of Life* finalist (at least to my knowledge). I was positive, but with no actual guarantee, one of the seven of us would have the Miss America crown on our head by the end of the evening.

If I can survive the swimsuit competition, which was first, *I can sweep the competition.*

As I continued to warm-up, I remember thinking *this* warm-up was *the* ultimate warm-up. The warm-up that all other warm-ups had led to. I also thought about who might be in the audience that would recognize my talent, which could lead to something greater than even Miss America.

As I continued to sing I looked down at the bandage on my little toe. The blood had finally quit soaking through.

Earlier in the week each dancer was given the opportunity to skip lunch and rehearse her talent on the stage. We didn't have music, it was merely a rehearsal time in order to get used to the stage layout and the texture beneath our feet.

The stage had a beautiful design made out of some sort of Plexiglas material. It was beautiful, but slick as snot. As I went through my routine, my shoes were sliding all over the place. I decided to take my shoes off and dance barefoot. It was the right decision as I had the perfect amount of traction but it was still slick enough that I could turn with ease.

After about twenty minutes of rehearsing something caught my attention. There were little swirls of red all over the white portions of the stage floor, but when I looked closer it was all over the black too.

I looked down at my feet.

My baby toe was nearly sliced in half and gushing blood, but I hadn't felt it because dancers usually can't feel their feet anyway. I looked at the stage again. There was blood *everywhere*.

I sliced my toe somewhere on the stage where it had been pieced together. I wasn't that concerned about the blood, but the Miss America staff quickly called the ambulance and pulled my parents out of a "If Your Daughter Wins Miss America" meeting.

When my parents arrived in the dressing room to join me and my medics, my dad looked at me and laughed, "Only Adrienne ends up with the EMT at Miss America."

From ketchup as an eleven-year-old to blood as a contestant… I still loved the Miss America Pageant.

My vocal warm-up was coming to an end and I giggled at the memory from earlier in the week.

After my voice was warm I went back to the dressing room to grab a pair of socks. Socks were my preference for dancing on carpet (and the Miss America staff told me I couldn't go barefoot). There was a red carpet that linked the dressing room/trailer to the stage. It was the perfect place for the dancers to warm up.

I joined the next set of girls for a dance warm-up. First I sat on the carpet and stretched. As my legs became more limber I moved into my right splits and then my left. While in the splits I laid the top half of my body over my leg and took a deep breath before I stretched my body tall and into a backbend, all while remaining in the splits. I finished by rolling back and forth through my middle splits.

I thought of all my students I had shared my dream with, and encouraged big dreams of their own. They would be watching that night. I felt more pressure to finish well for my kids than for anyone else, even myself. I wanted to show them anything was possible, even for a young girl from a small town in Kansas. I thought about that first grader who wanted to be a garbage man.

Most of the girls had completed their warm-ups, but since I was warming up both my body and my voice I was still on the red carpet. I was eventually alone except for our security guards, or as I referred to them, our body guards.

I took my tampons and chocolate out of my pockets and set them on the concrete next to the carpet. I stood and did a series of turns followed by a few leaps. I finished with two sets of ten *fouette* turns, turns on one leg while the other leg works through the air to keep a dancer spinning. I was spot on. My body felt energized and alive.

I retrieved the curlers that had flown out of my hair, as well as my goodies on the concrete, before I returned to the dressing room to get ready for the telecast.

Our dressing room was in a portable trailer just outside the stage doors. It was a large trailer, but it reminded me of the trailers surrounding a school. The kind of temporary buildings they install when the student population grows beyond the planned space. But the trailers surrounding a school usually have bathrooms in them. The Miss America contestants had a luxurious port-a-potty.

"Everyone's a star and deserves the right to twinkle." –Marilyn Monroe

------

I sat down at my dressing room mirror. Miss Oklahoma was on my right, and little did we know she would become Miss America in approximately two hours (and yes, she was a *Quality of Life* finalist).

"Happiness is the best make-up." –Drew Barrymore

There was an exciting buzz in the air. Twenty minutes before the competition began, the fifty-two contestants were escorted from the "dressing room" to the backstage wings. We would be entering the stage through two tunnels. Both tunnels opened to grand staircases. The staircases were large enough for twenty-six of us to be spread across one set of stairs and twenty-six on the other.

As we waited backstage some of the girls were quiet and solemn, while others were all smiles and wishing their new friends good luck.

"Sixty seconds ladies," one of the stage managers hollered to our group of girls on stage right. I squeezed hands with some of my friends standing next to me and we all took a deep breath. The evening was in God's hands.

They started a count down on stage and you could hear the crowd settling into their seats.

"Thirty seconds," the stage manager updated. We got into our lines, ready to walk through the tunnels.

There was a two minute lead-in video going through the history of Miss America and the excitement of winning the crown. The video started playing on the big screen and I forgot about the aching in my feet and the drama of the morning.

"Go! Go! Go!" The stage manager yelled at us in a panic.

We all advanced through the silver tunnels and emptied out at the top of the staircases. The lights on stage were dimmed, as the video was in its final thirty seconds. When we appeared the crowd went nuts. I could feel their energy. I saw my group of supporters on their feet cheering. I spotted them in a matter of seconds because of their signs. Each person had a letter. One series of signs read "K-A-N-S-A-S" and another said "Y-O—A-D-R-I-E-N-N-E". Even my track coach was holding one of the letters, but upside down. There was a third sign, or rather a giant flag, made out of red sequins and the word "Kansas" stitched across the front.

My heart soared. It was by far the coolest moment of the entire competition. There were no bright stage lights. No one knew who would make the top ten. We were all hopeful equals. You could feel the love and support in the auditorium. Our family and friends were determined their contestant would win. Everyone was optimistic. Everyone was nervous both on and off the stage. It was a love and excitement, in a theatre setting, I have never found again. For a stage production, not a national competition, the actors may be nervous on opening night, but not the crowd. The crowd is looking for a fun night out. At Miss America, people traveled from all corners of the country to be a part of the once-in-a-lifetime event. There was a lot at stake for the fifty-two contestants and their families. At Miss America, everyone shared the nerves, the dream, and the hopefulness.

We were on stage dancing to the opening number and going through our introductions. There was a cameraman with a giant camera attached to him floating around the stage. A second man was running behind him. He was in charge of the cables so the cameraman didn't trip. It was a fun choreographed dance between the two.

The opening number went by in a blur and we transitioned to our designated places for the announcement of the top ten. By the time they called out the fourth girl, I knew I wasn't in. The judges weren't going for my personality type.

After the ten girls were named they shooed the rest of us off the stage. I picked my jaw up off the floor and painted a fake smile on my face. My heart was broken. My energy was gone. I was in shock. The only thing still inflated was my fanny.

As we walked behind the curtain and back to the dressing room I was fighting back tears – while many others let them stream silently down their faces. Secretly I was relieved I didn't have to model a swimsuit on national TV.

A photographer jumped out from behind a curtain and snapped a picture of the "losers". The flash blinded us and it took everything in me not to yell obscenities at him. It was a cruel moment. He had taken the knife and twisted it. I feared where I would later see those pictures circulate.

We rushed past the heartless photographer and my chin began to quiver.

As I stepped out into the fresh air behind the theatre I took a deep breath and told myself to pull it together. I choked back my tears as I thought about all the people in the audience I had let down. And the little girls in Kansas… But there was nothing I could do about it. I was out.

I told myself God had bigger plans in store than what the Miss America title could deliver. I told myself to keep my faith in Him and I would find the right purpose in life that was specially designed for me.

When we walked back into the dressing room to change into our swimsuits for the swimsuit production number, my heart sank further, as did the hearts of many of the other girls. The attendants had moved the top ten to the front of the room and it felt like they had barricaded them from the rest of us.

We licked our wounds as we changed, silently, into our swimsuits. We had to go back out on stage as the background "decorations".

After the swimsuit production number we were held captive in the dressing room until the crowning moment (when we could serve as the decorations once again).

The losers huddled around the TV and watched the telecast. Our disappointments eventually turned to laughter over M&Ms and bagels with cream cheese.

Ironically, to this day I have never actually *seen* the Miss America production *live*; I have only experienced it on TV.

"You only live once but if you do it right once is enough." –Mae West

------

It finally came time to put on our evening gowns and go back out on stage for the crowning moment. I put on my long dangly earrings, five inch heels, and walked over to where my gown was hanging.

My sponsored gown was a $3600 Stephen Yearick. It was a tightly fitted silky Champaign-colored gown with glass and crystal embedded all the way down the front, from my chest to my toes. It also had a silk overlay that opened when I walked. With my extra weight my chest was naturally enhanced, but add to it the three sets of boob pads that were stitched inside and I was very well endowed. I was the modern day version of a Greek goddess.

I unzipped the gown and dropped my black silk robe to the floor. I was completely naked as I stepped into my gown. I started to pull my gown up, but I had a problem. I couldn't get it over my hinny. My gown was stuck.

There I was, butt-naked, nothing on but earrings and heels and I started jumping around the dressing room trying to wiggle into my dress.

I was a sight to be seen, to say the least. Not to mention, as I was hopping around the dressing room the floor was shaking under my weight, which meant the mirrors were shaking as were all the beverages on the food table.

Everyone turned to see who was making all the commotion. It was Miss Kansas in her birthday suit. Maybe I needed the Spanx after all!

"I can't get my dress on," I said in a panic. "Help!"

"Kansas needs help," one of the girls said as she looked my direction, eyebrows raised.

A few dressing room attendants raced over to help me. We were on a TV commercial break and I had moments to get my fanny, literally, in the dress and on stage. I kept hopping around the room, willing my butt to shrink.

My will must have been strong because I finally wiggled the gown over my rump. And then, to my horror, the dress wouldn't zip.

"We have to sew her into it," one attendant said to the other.

"Oh my goodness, this is humiliating," I responded.

"Don't worry, we'll get you into it," they assured me.

One gal went to work on my zipper while another was tucking my skin inside so it wouldn't get caught between the zipper's teeth. A third attendant was racing around the room looking for a needle and thread.

"Should I put on a different gown?" I asked in a panic. But I knew my gown sponsor would be watching to see her dress on TV.

Suddenly the zipper moved and I went flying out of the dressing room and onto the stage. I held my breath for the entire crowning moment. How the zipper didn't break was beyond me.

I stood in the back of the stage, squeezed in my gown and trying to breathe, as Jennifer Berry, Miss Oklahoma, was named Miss America 2006. It was indeed a magical moment from where I stood, even if I saw it from the back. I was happy I didn't have a wardrobe malfunction.

Since my tenure as Miss Kansas many people have asked me what it is really like backstage at Miss America. Are the girls cutthroat? Are they catty?

My answer: yes and no. You have to understand what is at stake. It's not *just* a pageant.

First and most important, the women on that stage were, and are, each amazing women in their own right. They are talented, smart, and beautiful. Many of the ladies from my year had ambitions of starting businesses, becoming state senators, going to medical or law school, or pursuing a career in the entertainment business. The Miss America contestants are determined women and most women who are determined also have a stubborn streak. You do not get to a national competition without having a competitor's spirit. So is it cutthroat? Yes. But do you also create lasting friendships that are genuine? Yes.

No one prepares for Miss America with the attitude *I hope I do well.* You prepare to win. You prepare to present the best version of yourself you can. Sort of like life.

I grew up hearing the phrase "show me a good loser and I will show you a loser". Yes, it is harsh, but it is true. Second place is still the loser's seat.

The Miss America Organization says (on their web site) they are "the nation's leading advocate for women's education and the largest provider of scholarship assistance to young women in the United States, awarding millions of dollars annually in cash awards and in-kind tuition waivers."

Miss America is the ultimate job interview. The winner typically walks away with $30,000 -50,000 in scholarships. *And that is just for the title Miss America.* That does not include any preliminary competition awards nor does it include the scholarship money from the state and local levels. There have been Miss Americas who have ended up with over $100,000 in scholarships by the time they add up all of their winnings over the years. With that kind of money a girl can buy a pretty impressive education! So let me ask you: if you were going to Miss America would you be a cutthroat competitor or would you show up hoping to finish well? Remember, $50,000+ is on the line.

Miss America has the opportunity on a national level what I had on a state level. It opened doors. It continues to open doors. It is the ultimate job for a young woman between the ages of 17-24. That organization has been a launching pad for my career and I will be forever grateful.

I do believe there were forty-six out of fifty-two girls who stood on the Miss America stage with me in 2006, that were ready to take on the Miss America title and would have been amazing Miss Americas in their own right. It is a similar feeling I have had when I snagged roles in well-respected musicals. Yes, there is a leading lady, but what the audience doesn't always know is that 90% of the ensemble has the same level of talent the leading lady has, yet the leading lady gets the standing ovation and the larger paycheck. Every contestant (and performer) knows: *give me a different set of judges (or director) and I'll give you a different outcome.*

I realize during my one shot at the Miss America crown I had a lot of health issues. I look back at my time at Miss America and it makes me sad I didn't present my best self. It was a missed opportunity. I believe it was God's way of keeping me on the path he had laid out for me.

I have learned a lot from that missed opportunity. You get one shot at many opportunities in life. Be prepared. Always put your best foot forward. Most important, learn from your mistakes and celebrate your accomplishments.

And remember… **"Luck is when preparation meets opportunity." –Seneca, a Roman philosopher (and one of my dad's favorite quotes)**

"It's all about the journey, not the outcome." –Carl Lewis

Yes, I dreamed of becoming Miss Kansas and eventually Miss America. I accomplished one, but not the other. I was so self-conscious, too focused on myself, and concerned with pleasing other people that the Miss America title slipped through my fingertips. My attitude was focused on other people's expectations and not my own. And when you lose sight of who you are, you lose.

Sometimes you learn more from a loss than a win. A loss makes you stretch. A loss challenges your character. A loss makes you work harder.

My year as Miss Kansas was a year of growth and challenges, but if I was to make a list of some of the greatest lessons I learned they would be:

1. Be exactly who you are.
2. Listen to those who have walked before you. Use their wisdom as *guidelines,* but don't allow their experiences to determine the joy in your own journey.
3. If I can walk across a stage in a swimsuit then I can walk into any room with confidence in who I am and what I bring with me.
4. Bring on the interviews! I can interview anywhere, anytime, with anyone. Period.

5. Meet everyone: from the people waiting the tables to the trash man to the governor. Everyone is working hard in life and you can learn some of life's greatest lessons from those in places you least expect.

Final note (about pageants):

I'm happy to report by the end of my tenure as Miss Kansas I got my hormones under control and I was eating more than just salads. *And my Miss America gown fit perfectly.* In fact, the night I passed on my title I was in the dressing room to take off my gown and I unzipped it, by myself, and laughed as it fell to the floor. There was no wiggling the dress over my bum.

Normal is boring. Perfect is boring. Bumps, bruises, blood, sweat, tears, and tiaras are what make the story so special. I bet there isn't another girl who went to Miss America and her hinny was too big to fit into that size six gown that fit four nights prior. I bet those dressing room attendants remember me and I bet they laugh about their memory. It sure makes for a laughable story today.

Laugh at life. Laugh at challenges. Laugh at failure. Laugh in general. Life is a journey. Enjoy it!

To keep laughing I only wear my Miss America sweatshirt, which is unique to the state title holders that competed for Miss America in Las Vegas in 2006, when I have on no make-up and I don't feel like getting dressed. *Oh the irony.*

But the best part: I'm still pursuing my work (eleven years later) which I began during my year as Miss Kansas. My platform I had titled *Small Towns, Big Dreams.* Without the crown, the hardships, and the experience as a whole I may have never found my life's calling. I cherish my experience I gained through the Miss Kansas and Miss America Organizations. I will always be grateful to the thousands of volunteers who help young women become their best.

Scene Twenty-Eight

A hospital room in Dallas, a patient and her dad, October 2005

(Sixty-seven days *after* the accident)

*"Come to me, all you who are weary and burdened,
and I will give you rest." –Matthew 11:28*

My dad and I were sitting in my hospital room chatting about nothing in particular while the movie *Happy Feet* was playing in the background. Mom was taking a well-deserved break to get a bite to eat and take a shower. Earlier that afternoon my mom helped the nurses wash my hair while I lay in bed with instructions not to move. My mom and dad had become my arms and legs, and sometimes the only laughter that filled my ears.

It had been four days since my six-hour surgery and thankfully the swelling in my toes had finally decreased for the first time since my injury: a good sign the surgery had worked. My dad was the most ecstatic about the decreased swelling as he was concerned my "sausages" were going to explode from the fluid that was trapped inside. I could tell he was breathing easier. The decrease in swelling was the first positive side effect of my free flap. It was the first positive advancement I had experienced. Still, I hadn't seen my ankle and no one knew what to expect.

My surgeon ended up shaving half of my head before determining he couldn't get the proper amount of muscle for my transplant (from my left scalp). The hair on my head would grow back. He went with his second option which was my inner thigh muscle (AKA: my gracilis).

I had yet to see the scar on my inner thigh from where my doctor had harvested my muscle. It was still wrapped in bandages. I had, however, seen the area where he took skin from my outer thigh to use

152

for a skin graft. That poor skin looked like the surgical team used a cheese grater to remove nearly six inches of skin at its widest point. That skin was transplanted to my ankle where it was used to cover the transplanted thigh muscle. (I can't help but wonder about the terrible situation and desperate patient that prompted this transplant idea in the first place and then allowed the doctors to do it!)

Dad and I were chuckling about my toes when the door opened and my surgeon walked in. He gracefully walked across the room to stand at the foot of my bed. It was about eight o'clock in the evening and I immediately noticed the blood on his scrubs and the circles under his eyes. I wondered what kind of life or limb saving surgeries he had performed on that particular day. I had been told he was in high demand and I was fortunate to have him as my doctor.

I asked him if he was having a good day, but he skimmed over the question to get to business: my foot. "How do you feel this evening?' he asked.

"I'm drowsy from the medication, but worse than that my butt hurts from sitting in this bed and not moving," I explained. "My pain levels are around a five but I think that's thanks to the drugs."

He listened as he walked around my foot and poked at my toes. He and my dad started conversing about how grateful they were the swelling in my toes had subsided.

Next, he pulled out the stethoscope and listened for the pulse in my foot. Until this adventure, I had no idea the stethoscope could be used on a foot, but apparently this was every one of my doctor's favorite medical instruments and my foot was their favorite place to use it. They all wanted to hear my pulse in my foot, which meant I had circulation and that would translate into healing.

As I watched my doctor listen, I saw his enthusiasm as he heard the peaceful beat of my heart pumping blood to my toes. "We have a strong pulse," he said with a smile.

I was grateful my foot was singing to my doctor. It was a nice change to be looking at my surgeon and observe a calm demeanor as I was being examined. I was finally breathing easy.

After his initial assessment, he looked at me and asked if I was ready to have a look.

"You mean unwrap it?" I clarified.

"Yes," he responded as he gently lifted my leg and started loosening the bandages.

Dad came a step closer and the two of us watched anxiously as though he was unwrapping a coveted Christmas present. I felt bad my mom wasn't there to experience the "big reveal", but I was also glad she was taking some time for herself.

As he started unwrapping the yards of gauze and getting closer to my skin, I could see the remains of dried blood. I didn't think much of the blood as I was anxious to see what my "remodel" looked like. I was free of any expectations.

The doctor pulled the last yard of gauze off my leg. All that remained was a perfectly square piece of moist, medicated gauze sitting directly on my skin. He very carefully grabbed an edge of the moist fabric and pulled it off.

Dad was standing on my right with his hand on my shoulder. What we saw next, we were not prepared for.

I stared dumb-founded and speechless. My dad went silent and his face turned white.

We were staring at a large mound of flesh that looked like an epic-fail of a pathetic-joke from a haunted house. It looked as though my doctor had taken a steroidal apple, cut it in half, and welded it to my ankle. Since the apple went through its own trauma during the surgery, it resulted in additional bruising and damages. I had what looked like a large burnt apple attached to my body.

I was horrified, yet my doctor had a look of satisfaction on his face as he genuinely told me it looked "beautiful".

He couldn't have been serious. Was he looking at the same thing I was? Apparently this doctor was in *la-la-land* or forgot to take his reality-pills for the past decade, or both. I know my dad and I were on the same page because we were both stunned into silence.

The doctor kept talking as he rewrapped my repulsion. I could hear him, but I didn't really care what he had to say. I felt mutilated, and worst of all… betrayed. Maybe this was my best option, but I wanted to go back to skinning cats.

I was furious, crushed, distraught, and silently hysterical all at the same time. Not one person, *not one*, prepared me for what they were going to do to my body. Here I was coping with losing a dream, a career, a hobby, a lifestyle, and most importantly my happiness. Now I had a disfigured body and no one even bothered to say "hey by the way, it isn't going to be pretty but this is your last option" or "by the way, we are really sorry about what you are going through" or "by the way, we are going to do our best work so you can keep your foot and walk again" or "by the way, we are going to disfigure you but you'll get over it." Anything would have been better than nothing.

I wanted to curse the very doctors who were helping me. Thankfully, I was shocked into thoughtlessness, which meant I was silent.

When the doctor left, my dad moved his hand from my shoulder to my hand. We held hands and said nothing. Both of us were at a loss for words. We were so baffled and confused neither one of us could speak.

I looked up and *Happy Feet* was still playing. I wanted to run, but I was a prisoner in my hospital bed.

The only thought left in my mind: *those damn penguins suck at dancing.*

**"Keep your head up,
God gives his toughest battles to his strongest soldiers." -unknown**

My x-rays indicated I had trashed my ankle. My exposed tendon had made me a VIP patient at every doctor's office and hospital I was wheeled into. But what would my new "look" make me?

My heart ached because no one knew what to tell me about my future. No one could find anything to give me hope. When I was doing well, I was told it wouldn't last. One doctor even told me I may never walk normal again, while another told me I would opt for an amputation by the time I was fifty, if not before.

The one thing that seemed to be a normal conversation was the unknown. When medical professionals discussed my escalating pain levels they also discussed my pain management options, which meant a life on narcotics. My dreams and goals were quickly turning into a desire to just be able to walk. Dance, and a life on the stage, was fading into the distant background. I just wanted to be able to live on my own and take care of myself. Was that too much to ask?

I was tired. Tired of setbacks. Tired of exhaustion. Tired of crying. Tired of trying. I was the most drained with my daily battle of maintaining a positive attitude. How do you maintain positivity, let alone a constructive attitude, when the world around you is crumbling?

Yes, I had a foot, but was that a good thing? Did the doctors do me a favor by not amputating? With an amputation I could run and hike and ski and walk. I would have long been on my road to recovery by the time I received my free flap. Should they have just gotten it over with so I could move on and start healing? I would have a nub instead

155

of a rotted apple, or mutilated third boob, attached to my ankle. It wasn't a matter of which would be better, it had become which would be worse? Both were deformities.

With an amputation I would have also been on my way to regaining my life instead of constantly navigating the unknown. No, I did not think it was easy to go through life as an amputee, but I did know there were positives to having a bionic leg as well. My real question: which would have provided a pain-lessened lifestyle? I wasn't even asking for pain-free.

All this and they still talked about cutting off my foot. I was starting to ask: *God, are you still there?*

I was never "out of the woods" and everyone made damn sure they kept reminding me of that fact. I lived with a PICC line in my chest. I was losing clumps of hair because of the chemicals they were pumping through my body. The nurses weren't even concerned about my lack of bowel movements or the fact I hadn't showered in over a week. I couldn't have my foot below my heart. They didn't want me to move. They wanted me to lie as still as possible. If my body rejected my flap they would start over. They would continue to mutilate my body until something worked.

It was as though my dreams and my possibilities were intertwined in the rug I had stood on for twenty-four years. And, that rug was pulled out from underneath me and ripped to shreds.

If my path has no obstacles, I have no sense of accomplishment.

My life felt out of control, but I refused to lose control of my self-respect. I may have had to struggle, but I had a positive attitude so positively ingrained within me that if it came naturally once before, I knew I could find it again.

I had a lot to be thankful for – my faith, loving parents, a job offer, an apartment, my personality, my fighting spirit.

I had worked at my attitude so hard that it had become who I was versus who I wanted to be. My dad had trained me well. I thought about our morning routine of looking in the mirror and him asking me "Are you going to have a good day or are you going to have a bad day?" I also thought about all the students across the state of Kansas I had taught about attitude. I told them anything was possible with the right attitude. Attitude is a choice.

"What will you choose?" *I asked them.* "What will you achieve because of your positive attitude? What will you overcome? What will you miss out on because of your negative attitude? Attitude is a choice that only you have control over. Situations and people will try to control it for you, but you are ultimately the deciding factor. Choose wisely."

Crutches or no crutches, wound or no wound, disfigurement or normal, I would fight to get my life back and my positivity. I would reinvent myself if I had to. Whatever my future had in store I would approach it with perseverance. My attitude was my secret weapon that would win the war. My attitude would get me through the obstacle.

I will accept this challenge and go with it – not around it, not over it, but right through it. I will win.

I realized I was living one of my favorite quotes by an unknown person: **"When something goes wrong in your life, yell Plot Twist, and move on."**

Scene Twenty-Nine

The post office, a girl holding a check, an overwhelmed (and a bit terrified) look on her face, July 2006, one month after she relinquished her Miss Kansas crown

(Thirteen months *before* the accident)

"If you do not hope, you will not find what is beyond your hopes."
–St. Clement of Alexandria

I stared at the envelope. Inside was a cashier's check for $1500 made out to a woman I did not know, but who would soon become my roommate. It seemed like a lot of money for a shared studio apartment, but it appeared that was the going rate for the *island Manhattan*.

I had found my soon-to-be roommate, Suzie, on Craigslist and being the innocent trustworthy bright-eyed Kansan I was, I trusted her. All I knew about Suzie was she was a native New Yorker and jazz player looking for someone to split the rent. She had guaranteed me my own space in the studio apartment, which would be furnished with a bed, TV, and single closet. I would have a special divider which would give me private space. I had seen pictures of my so-called room and it looked like a decent size with a twin bed.

It is only short-term and I could do anything temporarily. I told myself. Yet all I could visualize was my bank account that read $9001.31.   I held $1500 in my hand and in addition to the deposit she also had strict instructions my first month's rent was due the day I moved in: another $1500 cash. My nine grand had just depleted to $6000 with one woman holding my hard earned money.

I knew I would blow through my cash, in rent alone, in a handful of months. I was nervous and scared. *Could I really do this? Could I become*

158

the entertainer I had spent the last fifteen years dreaming about? Probably so. *Could I afford to live in the Big Apple?* Probably not.

I knew in my heart it was time to pay my dues once again. To start over. To be a "nobody". There was only one way to find out if I would become a "probably so" or a "probably not."

I had spent the last year of my life sharing my dream with the state of Kansas. I knew it was time to walk-the-walk. I had preached for 365 days that with the right attitude, five minutes a day, and relentless dedication, anything was possible. I told thousands of students "Somebody's gonna do it, so why not you?"

With that thought, I knew now was my time. My preparation had met my opportunity. I was as prepared as I could be. It was time for the next step.

I glanced inside the envelope one last time. There were indeed two zeros behind the "15", and I was about to drop 1/6 of the money to my name in the mailbox.

I licked the seal, took a deep breath, and then gave it a kiss good-bye before I shoved the cashier's check through the slot… "New York here I come," I whispered.

I turned to walk away and couldn't hide the grin I felt stretch from ear to ear. I was scheduled to arrive in New York in thirty days, five hours, and forty-five seconds, but who was counting?

As my thirty days clicked by I began to get nervous about my bank account and the lack of funds it held. I needed a job, pronto.

I began emailing and calling New York business owners left and right, but the answers were all the same "call us when you get to the city". I quickly grew frustrated as I knew my bank account would starve within weeks if I didn't find work.

Lord, please point me in the right direction, I prayed.

One afternoon as I sat at my desk, researching my options on the Internet, my thought process shifted as did my eyes. I glanced over at the books on my shelf and it was my three-inch three-ring blue binder that caught my attention. I pulled the binder off the shelf and stared at the quote on the cover: *As long as you're going to be thinking anyway, think big.*

I had run across that quote during my college years, I believe it was the same summer as Lee (the vocal instructor at "Texas"). The quote resonated with me. After all, it was that summer Lee showed me I

159

needed to think bigger than just wanting to be a dancer. He had shown me I could be a dancer who could also sing.

I had typed the eleven words into a Word document – large enough to take up the entire computer screen – and I printed it.

"As long as you're going to be thinking anyway, *THINK BIG.'* –Donald Trump

Before the ink could dry I had slipped the page behind the clear cover on the front of my binder that housed my sheet music. The quote served as an encouraging reminder that *anything* was possible including learning *how* to read the sheet music, which I held in my hands (and which was housed in the notebook). Somehow the quote, by the famous Donald, lessoned the intimidation of the contents in the binder.

Lee had planted the seed several years prior and I had decided *No, I don't want to simply be a dancer on Broadway, but I want to be a dancer who can sing... And if I'm going to be singing anyway, I might as well be an awesome singer.*

As the quote said, "As long as you're going to be thinking anyway, think big." And a dancer who sings *better know how to read her sheet music.*

I opened the binder and flipped through the sheets of music – *Don't Rain On My Parade – Take Me Or Leave Me – Blame It On A Summer Night – Can't You Do A Friend A Favor.* It was as if all the titles were doing the talking for me... *Come on New York, don't rain on my parade. Can't you do a friend a favor? Take me or leave me, but if you leave me, I will blame it on a summer night.* I giggled at my wittiness, closed the binder and set it off to the side. I turned my attention back to my computer screen.

I typed "restaurants" into the Google search bar. There were thousands of places to choose from. I let out a sigh and sat back in my chair. I looked over at my binder and two words jumped off the page: *Donald Trump.*

I didn't know much about Donald Trump other than he owned several large buildings as well as the Miss Universe Organization. Honestly, I wasn't concerned with *who* The Donald was nor had I really cared. But if I could land a job using my Miss Kansas title, then so be it.

I typed "Donald Trump New York" into my search bar and a web site for Trump Tower on Fifth Avenue was at the top of the screen. I clicked on the link.

The tower had its own web site. There was a restaurant, a store, and contact information. The contact info provided a name *and* an email. I copied the email and composed a message.

I had decided to use my Miss Kansas title (even though I was part of the "America" versus "USA/Universe" organization) to see if I could get anyone's attention. I closed my eyes and I pressed send.

I have nothing to lose, I reassured myself.

The next time I checked my email I had a message from the restaurant manager. He asked that I come to his office as soon as I get to the city.

I sent him a response confirming the date and the time.

I didn't have the job, but I at least had my foot in the door.

Scene Thirty

Fifth Avenue, Trump Tower, New York City, August 2006
(One year *before* the accident)

"Opportunity is missed by most people because it comes dressed in overalls and looks like work." – Thomas Edison

I stepped through the glass doors and into a grand entrance. The building décor was beautifully intimidating. The floors and walls were covered in pink marble and outlined in gold. There was gold everywhere - gold trim, gold elevator doors, gold lettering, gold on the ceiling, gold on the walls, gold, gold, gold, gold everywhere. In some ways it was as if a bank had vomited all over the place. Not really my style, but it was still beautiful.

What *was* my style was the music being pumped through the overhead speaker: Frank Sinatra, Michael Bublé and Harry Connick, Jr. were taking turns serenading Mr. Trump's guests, which included me.

I couldn't pinpoint what made the space so pleasant: was it the soft lighting, the sound of a waterfall, the music, the aroma of good food, or a combination of everything?

I walked past two security guards in front of the gold elevators and continued to the large atrium. I stepped up to the gold railing and glanced over the edge to admire the waterfall cascading down the four-story-tall pink marble wall. The marble tiles were arranged in a mosaic work of art that allowed the water to bounce along the wall as it fell to the ground, creating a pleasant sound. It was definitely not something you would expect to find in the heart of Manhattan.

After I took in the scene, I stepped away from the railing and walked ten feet over to the gold escalator. I stepped aboard and began my decent to the bottom floor, where the restaurant was located. At the bottom of the waterfall was a restaurant that said *The Trump Grill* in gold (what other color?) swirly lettering across a black awning

I studied the people in the restaurant scattered among the tables. Many of the men had on beautiful three piece suits and the women were dressed equally to impress (covered in expensive cashmere and drippy jewelry).

I was also dressed in my best. I had on a black wool pencil skirt with a silk button down light-pink shirt. The buttons on my blouse were made of large diamonds, or rather cubic zirconium, which was more in my budget. I had on layers of drippy silver jewelry mixed with light-pink plastic stones. I finished my look with three-and-a-half inch black leather peak-a-boo stilettos. Definitely *not* the shoes of a working girl.

As I neared the bottom of the escalator an older man sitting at a table caught my attention. I stepped off the moving staircase as I continued to stare at him. He was reading a book and picking at his food. He was acting as though he didn't want to be noticed but kept glancing around to see if anyone was watching, almost willing the crowd to notice him. He was getting exactly what he was after.

It was George Ross, Mr. Trump's executive vice president and senior counsel of the Trump Organization. Although at the time I only knew him from the TV show *The Apprentice*. What I didn't know, was starting that day I would see George at least three days a week. I would also see Eric Trump, Ivanka Trump, Melania Trump, and of course Donald Trump on a regular basis. All of which were always kind and friendly to not only me, but everyone who was in their presence. I must admit, Mr. Trump had arrogance about him when we walked among the public, but I would quickly learn he was a kind and respectful man when in his presence in his private office.

I walked toward the restaurant hostess stand and asked for the manager's office. A woman pointed me down a long hallway that was wrapped in floor to ceiling mirrors *and*, of course gold.

I spun on my heel and proceeded down the gold-mirrored hall. I watched myself as I walked. I had wanted to dance down the hall, but I wasn't the only one in the hallway *and* I was on my way to a job interview. Instead I settled for a model's strut, walking as though I was on the catwalk. I couldn't resist a little 360 degree turn, admiring my modeling talent in the mirrors, as I strutted beside my reflection. I didn't hide my smile.

"If I can make it there I'll make it anywhere," I sang aloud with Frank Sinatra on the loud speaker.

And I'm going to make it here, I told the dreamer in the mirror.

"To begin, begin." –William Wordsworth

When I met the manager it was only a matter of moments, or a first impression, and he asked if I would start that day. "Right now?" I clarified.

"Right now" he had confirmed with raised eyebrows willing me to say yes.

The manager was short staffed and I was in need of a job, which meant I didn't have a choice but to agree. It was my second day in the Big Apple and I had officially landed a role. I wanted to call home and report the good news, but I was formally *on the job* and working.

Mr. Manager rushed me down to the sub-basement where I received a quick introduction to some of Mr. Trump's security guards. I also got my first view of Mr. Trump's fleet of beautifully polished cars.

The friendly old security man, who guarded the fleet, also guarded the time clock. He told me about his years of service with the Trump family and how kind they *all* were. He assured me I would enjoy working with everyone employed at Trump Tower.

As he talked he took digital fingerprints of all ten of my fingers. He explained how to run my fingerprint in the scanner, which was my way of clocking in and out. He also showed me to the back staircase where I could come and go without fighting the crowd on 5th Avenue, "You will see the family using this side entrance," he informed me. It was as though in a matter of minutes I went from tourist/daydreamer to part of the Trump family.

After my quick tutorial, Mr. Security rushed me back up to the restaurant manager and Mr. Manager placed me at the hostess stand in front of *The Trump Grill.* I immediately started showing people to their tables. I was also taking pictures with tourists in front of the hostess stand that of course said "Trump" across the front in large gold lettering. I felt like the stereotypical girl that everyone expected to be working at the front of his restaurant. I was okay with it, but only because I was officially making money.

"**People underestimate me and that's fine.**
I prefer going into negotiations being underestimated." –**Ivanka Trump**

In a matter of weeks I had passed the security inspection, whatever that meant, and it was time for me to learn a new aspect of my "job": delivering lunch to Mr. Trump himself in his personal office that overlooked Central Park. I was up for the task.

Another manager in the building approached the hostess stand where I was standing. He had a plate of macaroni and cheese covered with cling wrap in his hand, "You ready?" he asked.

"Yes." I responded respectfully.

You would have thought we were on our way to the war room to declare an invasion by the seriousness in his tone which indicated the life-altering mission we were about to embark upon. I was headed to ground zero and he knew I would never be the same.

I followed the second manager across the large atrium and over to the escalator. We ascended up the staircase and walked over to the security guards standing in front of the gold elevators. Mr. Manager #2 introduced me to the two large burly men who no one dared to even look at the wrong way. Their looks were intimidating, but their personalities proved them to be nothing more than tame teddy bears working in the heart of New York. With an introduction came large smiles on both of their faces.

"Adrienne, it is so nice to meet you," one of the security guards said before he introduced me to his counterpart.

I extended my hand to shake both of theirs. Their hands were twice the size of my own and their handshakes were strong. I immediately knew that teddy bear had muscle you didn't dare inflame.

They held the elevator door open and the manager and I stepped inside. We ascended at lightning speed up to Mr. Trump's floor.

Ding.

When we stepped off the elevator and into the reception area, I was introduced to Mr. Trump's secretaries who were stunningly gorgeous (of course). I immediately noticed I would never be hired to work with them. Why? Because I was over five feet three inches tall and I weighed more than one hundred pounds. But to their credit, they were as happy and friendly as everyone else I had encountered in the Trump work-family. They simply had the genetics that got them the job.

We walked into another area of the office and I could hear Mr. Trump on the phone. "That is his office," Mr. Manager #2 said as he gestured in the direction the voice was coming from.

We detoured to the kitchen to put the finishing touches on the bossman's meal. Mr. Trump's lunch of the day: macaroni and cheese. I was shown how to remove the cling wrap and wipe the edges of the plate clean to perfection. I was also instructed I could enter the room even if Mr. Trump was on the phone. I was to serve his meal, along with utensils wrapped in a cloth napkin, and then excuse myself. It was implied I could speak, but only when spoken to.

"Today I will actually introduce you so you aren't a stranger in his office." Mr. Manager #2 informed me.

We walked across the hall and stepped inside The Donald's office. We waited quietly until he finished his phone call. I glanced around at the floor to ceiling walls of pictures. Some pictures were stacked along the wall waiting to be hung, but where I didn't know. There wasn't any more wall space.

Mr. Trump hung up the phone and introductions were made. In true Kansas fashion I walked across the room and shook The Donald's hand. I noticed the funny look he gave me, but he was still polite.

Scene Thirty-One

A barren apartment, a girl and her crutches trying to get ready for her new
job, but not her dream job, November 2007
(Three months *after* the accident)

"If you want to make God laugh, tell him your plans." - *Woody Allen*

Okay, so my situation was a slight catastrophe, but God promised
he wouldn't give me more than I could handle, which meant He
believed I could handle this. I realized He had more faith in me than I
had in myself.

I had a new job as the Marketing Director of the musical "Texas".
Bill had offered me the job while I was lying in the trauma ward of the
hospital. Since I had nothing else on my agenda and he needed a
marketing person to promote the show, I took the job. The only
marketing experience I had was in college with *Relay for Life* and my
senior project where I helped create a new marketing campaign for the
sandwich shop *Blimpie*. Sandwiches... *Relays*... theatre... sure, why
not? I knew the show inside and out, all I had to do was go out and
promote it, advertise it, and fill the seats with people. Or, as Bill and I
referred to it "put butts in seats." One-thousand-seven-hundred butts
six nights a week to be exact.

Bill told me I could start whenever my doctors gave me clearance to
go to work. Once I had reached the "okay" to have my foot below my
heart in thirty minute increments, I decided to start my new job.
Besides, I needed something for my rotting mind to do.

Bill graciously allowed me to start with a four hour work day and
build my stamina as the weeks and months progressed. He arranged for
me to have the office closest to the front door, with handicap parking

right outside that door. He volunteered to carry any belongings I needed, including my pillow for my desk.

The pillow sat on my desk next to my computer screen. It was the cushion for my foot. I could only have my foot below my heart for thirty minutes (three times every eight hours), remember? Yes, I propped my foot on the desk in order to have my limb above my heart while I worked on the computer. To extenuate my elevation, I lowered my office chair to its lowest setting, which meant I was practically sitting on the floor.

It was time to start my career and my new life. I was determined to do the best I could with what I had. It was time for me to learn how to make money while sitting on my posterior.

"Write it on your heart that every day is the best day in the year."
–Ralph Waldo Emerson

When my alarm went off in the mornings, I would roll over and retrieve my "socks" and my gloves from the floor. After I put on my green plastic gloves, that looked like rubber gloves to wash the toilet with Clorox (but were a whole lot more expensive), I would prepare my "sock" the same way a woman prepares a pair of pantyhose to slide over her legs. But I needed gloves because the socks were compression stockings and they were that tight! My $80 stockings put Spanx to shame. And you didn't need a prescription to buy Spanx.

The stockings applied pressure to my leg in order to keep the swelling out of my foot and help the size of my gargantuan fat ankle to shrink. I wasn't allowed to get out of bed without the stocking on my leg. So no matter how full my bladder, I had to wrestle the thick lycra onto my foot and up to my knee before I ventured to the bathroom.

After my bathroom stop I would crutch to the kitchen and start a pot of coffee. It was my first morning before my new job that was the most memorable. My "normal" pre-accident morning routine was to drink coffee while I was putting on make-up and fixing my hair, but I couldn't quite figure out how I was going to get my coffee cup from the kitchen, through the living room, and into the bathroom.

I had hopped from one kitchen cabinet to the next looking for a travel mug I could somehow tie around my neck. I had no such mug. How I was going to get my coffee cup, full of coffee, to the bathroom?

By the time I had used the bathroom, and my coffee had brewed, I only had twenty minutes left before my foot had to go back above my heart. And in those twenty minutes I also had to get dressed and get out to the car.

I stood and thought, with my right foot propped on the kitchen counter of course (my new *barre*).

I could crawl and scoot it as I go, I thought. I liked that idea. *But then I'll be on the other side of the apartment without my crutches. Hmmm.*

A light bulb turned on.

I filled my cup and set it at the far end of my kitchen counter that opened into the living room. I took one long stride on my crutches which placed me one foot into my living room. I reached behind me and grabbed my cup. I turned around, faced forward, and proceeded to set my cup on the end-table next to the sofa. I crutched past the coffee and stopped. I turned around and grabbed the coffee and moved it to the coffee table (which I realized for the first time why it was called a "coffee table"). I crutched past the coffee table, stopped, and turned around to grab my cup. I turned around and set the cup on the chair outside the bathroom. I had about four feet to go. I slithered down to my hands and knees and tossed my crutches into the bathroom. I knew I could get the rest of the way crawling and pushing my coffee cup across the floor, which is exactly what I did.

When I had arrived in front of my floor-length-mirror, I rearranged myself so I was sitting on my tush. My left foot was curled in a cross legged position while my right foot was stretched out, propped on a stool. So yes, my foot was above my heart.

I picked up my coffee and watched myself in the mirror as I took a sip. It was exhausting, but I did it. I had a champion's grin on my face. I looked at myself in the mirror and said out loud to the only girl listening, "You're a champ. And yes, today is going to be a great day."

Scene Thirty-Two

A girl getting to know NYC, August 2006

(One year *before* the accident)

"Why not go out on a limb? That's where all the fruit is." –Will Rogers

New York has the energy to harvest dreams, but it also has the ability to instill insecurities as tall as its skyscrapers. But each insecurity has its own valuable lesson attached to it. Life's lessons are not learned unless you apply those lessons to your life. Those who silence the insecurities and fertilize their dreams are the game-changers.

I had been out sightseeing and familiarizing myself with the grid of the city streets and the underground world of the subway system. A couple days prior I had joined my friend, Diana (AKA: Miss Connecticut 2005), for an after hour's musical showcase. We were also celebrating my new job at Trump Tower. After that night *out* I decided I needed to learn my way around in daylight hours.

Diana was more familiar with the city as she had moved to the Big Apple a couple months prior to me. I had taken a detour between my reign as Miss Kansas and my move to New York to attend *Broadway Theatre Project* in Tampa, Florida.

Broadway Theatre Project, or *BTP*, is an intensive three week Broadway training program where I had the opportunity to work with some of the "greats" of Broadway and film as well as some of the leading casting directors from New York City. It was the ideal program to attend for someone who was trying to break into the theatre scene in New York City or Los Angeles. And yes, my Miss Kansas title helped secure my spot for the limited enrollment space. Miss Kansas' Outstanding Teen 2004 had attended the same program and helped me navigate the politics of getting into the audition (it's worth noting the beautiful and talented Haley Hannah is now performing on Broadway).

When I finally joined the rat race of New York City, Diana wanted to show me a positive first impression. She was excited to introduce me to the *inner* beauty of the talented people the city had to offer. Translation: her friend was playing in a three-person musical showcase in a sketchy area of the city.

I didn't know my way around so she had given me subway instructions, a street corner, and a time to meet.

As I skipped up the subway stairs to meet *my* Miss Connecticut, whom I hadn't seen since our time at Miss America, I had to dodge a homeless man peeing in the stairwell, obviously intoxicated.

I met my friend at the designated corner and we walked together in the dark. As we walked past another homeless man I realized he was a little crazier than the last. The nameless man chased me down the street as he was barking like a dog. My natural reaction was to "meow" at him *and run.* Diana grabbed my arm and we fled the scene. When we stepped inside the safe haven of our destination we doubled over laughing at the twilight zone outside.

Diana showed me to a staircase in the back of the bar and I followed her to the second floor. The area was small. It seated twenty people (at most) around a white baby grand piano. It was a tight squeeze for the few of us in attendance, but she wasn't kidding about the place being a diamond in the rough.

We ordered a glass of wine and listened to one of the most talented musicians I had ever heard, in an intimate setting no less. I sat ten feet away from Ben Roseberry as he sang the song "Stay". It was indeed a beautiful introduction to such a talented city with talented people in the strangest of places.

After a couple hours of drinks and music, Diana and I walked back to the subway. It was midnight and I explained to her I had promised my mom I wouldn't take the subway at night (or at least until I familiarized myself with the city). As I started looking for a cab I did some basic math in my head. I quickly calculated the $30 cab ride translated into two and half hours of standing at the Trump Grill hostess stand. That was a long time to stand just to pay for a quick taxi ride.

I changed my mind about the cab and asked Diana for subway instructions. The instructions included a subway line change which sounded easy enough. We hugged, said our good-byes, and went our separate ways into the underground.

I got on my first subway train with no problem, but when I had to switch lines I got on a train headed east instead of west. I didn't know I had made a mistake until my ears began popping from the pressure change. I was under water heading *out of* Manhattan and out to a borough. It went from bad to worse as I had no idea which borough I was headed to.

As my heart started to race I looked around at the other people on the subway. There was a guy at the front of the train car who was slouched over asleep with a trash bag between his feet. He looked as though he hadn't showered in several days. He seemed harmless, but I still kept my distance and my eyes to myself.

At the back of the train was a girl in her late teens. She had jet black hair, thick black eyeliner, black nails, black clothing, and a dark scowl on her face. She bobbed her head to the sound that was coming from her black ear buds stuffed inside her head.

I started to panic. I had promised myself I wouldn't get into a sketchy situation and there I was, not even a week into my new life and I was wondering where the night would end. Exploring a borough in the wee-hours of the morning wasn't exactly on my "to do" list.

When the train stopped I got off, leaving my train-mates, and walked up out of the ground to see where I was. It was dark *and* it had started to rain.

I looked around recognizing nothing. In the distance beyond the water was the Manhattan skyline.

I continued scanning the scene. There were no taxis, but why would there be? It was raining.

I spotted a bus and ran through the rain to get to it. The driver was sitting in the driver's seat reading a newspaper. I knocked on the door. He gestured for me to go away. I knocked again. He ignored me. I started banging until he set his paper down.

He reluctantly opened the door and asked rudely "What do you want?"

"I don't know where I am."

"This is Queens."

"How do I get back to Manhattan?"

"The subway," he said with a roll of his eyes and closed the door leaving me in the torrential down pour.

"Jerk," I said to the glass of the closed door.

I was soaked, confused, and officially scared.

I ran back to the subway and down into the underground. There were a few sketchy-looking people (by Kansas standards) scattered around the platform and I stayed as far away as I could.

I began praying. *God, I'm sorry I didn't listen to my mom. Please get me home safely.*

I waited twenty minutes (praying for those entire twenty minutes) while I also watched the rats play on the tracks. When the subway arrived I got on with the other people waiting on the platform. I was relieved when my ears began popping once again. I was under the water and headed back to Manhattan.

As a result of my adventure, I took a day to familiarize myself with the city *in the daylight!*

"Let New York come to you, don't go to New York."
–Suzie, my New York City roommate

I spent a day in exploration. When I arrived back at my apartment I stepped off the elevator onto floor fifty-seven. My legs were aching and I felt the grime of the city clogged into every pore of my body.

Ten hours earlier I was freshly showered, hair blown to perfection, skin clean, and had on a cute pair of yellow Capri pants. As I had walked the streets, liquid droplets sprinkled down onto my head from the rooftop air-conditioning units scattered across the city. Having spent a day climbing up and down the subway stairs, the soot and pollution had magically found its way under my nails and skin.

By the time I stepped off the elevator I felt greasy and dirty. I had the urine of a homeless man and the dry roasted nuts of the street vendor on the bottom of my shoes.

I inserted my key into my shared studio apartment. I opened the door and stepped inside. I slipped my shoes off and set them next to my closet space, which was actually the front hall closet (and barely big enough to be called *that* as it was more of a cubby-hole).

I walked around the divider wall and saw my roommate sitting on the sofa.

"Hi Suzie."

"Hi."

"Did you have a nice day?" I asked in my friendliest tone.

173

"Yes." Suzie said shortly, not taking her eyes off the book she was reading.

Suzie wasn't exactly the friendliest roommate, but what she was about to teach me made it worth the sour attitude and steep rent.

"I actually saw you today," she said not looking up from her page.

"Really? Why didn't you say hi?"

"Because I was watching you."

My heart sank as my defenses in my stomach churned. "Excuse me?"

"On the subway."

"I was all over the subway today, where did you see me?"

"That's the problem." Suzie finished what she was reading before she closed her book and looked at me. "Adrienne, you need to open your eyes."

"What do you mean?"

"You stick out like a sore thumb. That isn't a compliment in this city. You need to watch your back honey. You're not in Kansas anymore."

There was silence between the two of us and she could tell she was scaring me.

"Listen," she said. "Let New York come to you. You're too excited and it's going to get you in trouble," she paused. "You need to sit on a bench and watch the people of this city. Sit there for a while. Watch the heartbeat. The tick of the city. The flow. Learn people's actions and learn to blend in. You are going to New York, let New York come to you."

I sat down on the adjacent sofa, thinking about what she was telling me. I tried to release the creepy energy she was forcing into the room.

"Where did you see me?" I asked softly and directly.

"On the subway." She opened her book once again, continuing her lesson as she found the place she had left off. "You were standing. Holding the bar. Ear buds in your ears. Not paying attention."

"You can observe a lot by just watching." –Yogi Berra

The next morning I found the closest clothing store and walked inside. I pulled a brown shirt, a black shirt, and black pants off the rack. I changed into the black shirt in the dressing room, pulled the tag off, and walked up to the register to pay for my *new* New York City wardrobe. I took the bag with my old clothes and walked to the entrance of Central Park. I found a bench and sat there for the next two hours people watching.

As much as I hated it, Suzie was right. I looked and acted like a foreigner. As a young single girl in a big city that was a recipe for disaster.

"The thing about paying your dues is you're not the one who sets the price." –Alan Robert Neal

------

Along with navigating the city and delivering Mr. Trump's lunch, I was also auditioning my butt off. It was my first audition that set the tone for the deep-end-of-the-pool I had jumped into.

I had arrived to the open-casting-call early in order to sign in and get a good place in line. But I had to wait my turn. So I waited, and waited. And waited. And waited. And waited some more. I was waiting to audition for an equity (or union) show as I wanted to start gaining equity points. I wanted to become an equity member as soon as possible (as an equity member you have more laws that protect you as a performer). The only way to become an equity member is to gain equity points, and to gain enough points you have to be cast in the right amount of equity shows. It was a Catch-22: the same idea of *you can't get the job without experience, but you can't gain experience without getting the job.*

As a non-equity performer I had to wait my turn. I had to wait until all the equity members had the opportunity to audition first. If you think I was waiting inside some nice building you are completely wrong. As a non-equity performer I wasn't even allowed in the building. I had to wait outside. But don't worry, I wasn't alone. There were hundreds of other performers in line to keep me company.

After the first two hours passed many of us had to use the restroom, but the "equity door guard" wouldn't let us in the building. Hundreds of us were running back and forth to the closest Starbucks to use a public restroom.

Finally, after five hours of waiting, two of the assistants came to get *us,* the non-equity people, in groups of fifty. I had assumed they would take us into a dance studio and teach us a dance combination and then start cutting people. I was wrong! They lined us up in the hallway and allowed us to strip out of our street clothes to reveal our lycra covered bodies.

I had worn a red leotard, tan tights, and three inch tall tan character shoes. It was the perfect look for the musical I was auditioning for: *42ⁿᵈ Street.*

Once we were all in our tights and leotards they started making "cuts". Seriously, the first round of cuts was not based on talent, it was based on height (first), weight (second), and overall looks (third).

I remember standing in a straight line with forty-nine other women (and there were still hundreds waiting outside). The two assistants walked down the line and looked at us from head to toe. Their response was a simple: "yes" or "no thank you". When I got my "no thank you" after less than two seconds of them looking at me, I was expected to exit the building immediately.

I couldn't believe it. I had gone from being *the* featured guest as Miss Kansas to a New York nobody in a New York minute.

Welcome to New York.

Scene Thirty-Three

The "Texas" Musical production office, April 2008
(Eight months *after* the accident)

"If you cannot do great things do small things in a great way."
—Napoleon Hill

My job as the Marketing Director of "Texas" was to find advantageous places to advertise: be it in news publications, online, on billboards, on the radio, and on television. My favorite medium for advertising was TV commercials. Working around cameras and a creative team gave me the "performance" outlet I needed. It meant I got to work alongside the production team of the Amarillo ABC-affiliate station. It was my chance to work creatively in the background with other professionals who also had journalism degrees. You could say I got a glimpse of "theatre" through a different type of lens.

In addition to advertising, I attended tradeshows and gave presentations at area luncheons, mostly for civic organizations such as Rotary, Lions, Kiwanis, and the sort.

I really enjoyed my "job" but always struggled with the fact I was using my "back-up plan" - or "Plan B" - versus what I had set out into the world to conquer. I couldn't see past my ankle and into the future to see I would actually find the stage again. And find it in a more gratifying way. So while I cursed my job, I loved my job at the same time. I continued to learn about marketing and myself. I was developing my character in ways I could have never imagined.

Along with promoting the show, I was asked to be a part of the production team as the "audition director". This job title came with the responsibility of arranging, organizing, and promoting four auditions spread across three states. I booked the theatres and dance studios where the auditions were to be held. I also booked our entire production team's airline tickets, rental cars, and hotel rooms.

I agreed to plan the auditions because 1) I wanted to 2) without great performers it would have been very difficult to "put butts in seats" and 3) there was no one else to do it. The reality was there were only three of us that were classified as full-time employees of "Texas". It was up to us to make the show come to life. It was all hands on deck, all the time! Surprisingly, even with my limited hours and regular doctor's appointments I was one of the three "full-time" employees. I'll have you know that of the three of us only Bill and I were under the age of 75! Our "momma hen" was in charge of grant writing and recruiting major donors. That left Bill and me to manage the operations of the company and the mounting of show. Thankfully we had one part-time college student. Other than that, the rest of the staff were all seasonal employees, including our production staff.

The payoff of organizing the auditions was when I was asked to sit "behind" the audition table to help cast the 150 performers, crew, and staff that would make the show come to life. By the end of our four auditions our production team had seen over 1,000 performers. It was an awesome experience. I learned more, as a performer, running the auditions than I did when I was trying to land a role. Yes, there were times it was hard to watch performers as they put their talents on display, but the constant ache in my ankle kept my reality front and center. Everywhere I went, my production team always made sure I had two chairs: one to sit in and one to prop my foot on. I had learned the more I elevated my foot the lower my pain levels. By low I mean a pain level of "five" (out of ten).

Working for "Texas" with so much being thrown at Bill and me from every direction was a blessing. For starters, I didn't have time to dwell on my situation (when I was at the office). More importantly, I didn't take any of the political drama (being dished-out by our board of directors and one donor) to heart. I saw their silly ploy for power pathetic and superficial. Had I not been in my medical situation I'm sure I would have taken the drama too seriously. I was realizing life was about so much more than the "drama" we create in our own lives. Bill and I dealt with the board politics and went about our jobs. We recruited an outstanding cast, helped mount a beautiful show, and filled the bank account from our ticket sales.

My favorite part of it all: casting. One day the choreographer came by the "Texas" office and asked for my help. The choreographer was the same woman whom I auditioned for when I was in college, *and didn't get cast in the musical.* She walked in my office and said, "Adrienne I need your help."

"What is it?" I asked noticing the bundle of files under her arm.

"I have narrowed down our male dancers into groups," she pulled the files out from under her arm and set them on my desk. "I have them separated into "yes", "no", and "maybe". I have a lot of "maybes". Will you go through them and pick the rest of the male dancers you want to see in the show?"

"Serious?" I asked, my excitement growing.

"Yes, I've looked over each of their resumes several times and I can't seem to narrow them down."

"I would love to go through them! How many definite 'yeses' do you have?" I asked.

"Three. And I know I definitely want those three. I just need help casting the rest." She looked at me in the eyes, "I need a dancer's eye, which is why I'm asking you."

I smiled at her compliment.

"I need male dancers," she continued, "with partnering experience so they can lift the girls. Be sure to keep that in mind while you are making your selections."

"I'm on it," I said. "Have you selected all the ladies?"

"Yes," she said. "I'll come by at the end of the week and we can start calling our male selections."

"You're going to let me offer the jobs?" I asked.

"Yes," she said with a smile. "That is one of the best parts of casting."

The choreographer left her stack of resumes with me. It was my turn to be the person who set a young performer's career on a specified path.

I took the stack of resumes and flipped through them. After I studied the first ten, I gathered my pile and gimped out into the hallway. I sat down on the floor and began rummaging through the "maybe" group in more depth.

I began spreading the resumes and headshots across the carpeted hallway. Bill emerged from his office to see what I was doing. He walked over to where I sat on the floor and stood behind my left

179

shoulder. He knew what I was doing. He stood silently, watching while I organized the performers like a game of solitaire.

"How are you going to pick them?" he asked.

"I'm not sure," I said. "There is a lot of pressure to pick the right person. Not just for the show, but for the person."

Bill didn't respond, because he knew.

I shuffled them around as I started my own "yes", "no", and "maybe" piles. Bill left me to my own thoughts and organization.

After an hour I had narrowed a pile of fifty "maybes" into my own thirty "yeses". I spread the performers down the hallway, headshots staring up at the ceiling. I crawled past my row, looking into the eyes of each performer. I had an idea.

One by one I flipped all the headshots over, making their resumes face-up.

Bill walked out of his office once again to check on me, "Making progress?" he asked.

"Yes," I said matter-of-factly. "I came up with a system."

"Which is?"

"I'm going to narrow my group down by height first, and then I'm going to flip their resumes back over and narrow it down to my final selection based on who I want to look at all summer."

Bill let out a laugh.

I looked at him and snickered, "That's how I got cut at my first New York City audition. Since this is my first show I'm helping cast, well…" I trailed off. "Height first, looks second."

"What is your height limit?" he asked.

"I don't have one," I said. "I'm getting rid of all the shorties and keeping the tall guys." I looked up at Bill. "Do you know how many shows I've been cut from because the men are too short? This is payback."

We both laughed.

Sure enough my top thirty were all over the height of six feet tall. I flipped their resumes back over so their smiles were looking at me and then I selected my top twenty best looking cowboys! I double checked all my guys had dance partnering experience, and the five that had the least were cut from my pile. I was down to my top fifteen.

I gathered up my piles and toted them back to my office.

When the choreographer and I met again, she confirmed my selections, not changing any of them. She selected two as "alternates" and asked me to start calling the rest.

At 3:45 p.m. I gathered my belongings and limped out to my car. I was headed to the pool for my first swim since my "free flap doctor" had released me to water therapy. I planned to swim from 4:15-4:45 p.m. It wasn't long in comparison to copious amounts of exercise I was used to, but I hadn't had any physical activity in over nine months. I wasn't sure I would even survive thirty minutes in the pool. I didn't know how my ankle would even handle the water. I was scared and a little nervous.

I wanted to be home and showered by 6 p.m. in order to eat dinner and go to bed. With my ankle pain I had limited amounts of energy. While I was gaining my stamina at work it usually meant I was in bed asleep by 7:30 at night.

Scene Thirty-Four

Back at Trump Tower, October 2006

(Ten months *before* the accident)

"When everything seems to be going against you, remember an airplane takes off against the wind, not with it." –Henry Ford

I stood at the hostess stand. My feet were aching from the hard tile. I had at least wisened-up and ditched my three inch heels, trading the stilettos for a cute pair of flats.

It was a slow day, even for New York City, and I was doing my best to stay attentive. I had taught myself how to work the espresso machine and threw back a double shot of espresso – no cream, two sugar packets. It was liquid gold. The coffee beans were fantastic and until I had worked at Mr. Trump's restaurant I had never ventured past a mocha. The thought of straight espresso sounded pungent and bitter. But oh was I wrong. It was liquid gold with a supercharged kick of caffeine. The gold matched the Trump décor and the caffeine kept me in pace with the tick of the city.

That morning I had counted out fifteen one-hundred-dollar-bills into the palm of Suzie's hand. It hurt my insides to hand over such a large wad of cash, but I had agreed to at least four months of such steep rent.

I was living in the heart of Manhattan and I was paying a pretty penny for it. I was literally down the "street" from where I worked, which is why my sofa rental was so expensive. I had promised myself I wouldn't move to any "neighborhoods" in the city, or boroughs, until I knew which were safe and which were not. So, $1500 cash is what I pulled from my bank account at the beginning of each month. It wasn't just the rent that was so expensive, city living was proving to be more than I had anticipated too. I needed a new budget *and* a financial plan.

I reached under the podium and pulled out my faux leather purse. I retrieved a notepad and flipped it open to a blank page. I picked up a pen that said "Trump" in gold lettering and scribbled the ink to life. I wrote "Budget" on the top of a clean page. Two lines down I wrote "Income". I had decided to start with the positive.

I was pulling two streams of income and recorded them both:

Trump: $13/hour x 30 hours a week = $1,560/month (This was the monthly total if I only calculated four weeks in a month, but really there are 4.33).

Rental Income: $850/month (Yes, I owned a rental house in Kansas).

Total income: $2410/month.

I reminded myself the $2410 a month was my gross income, meaning I had to pay taxes on that number (I wasn't teaching swimming lessons in Kansas anymore).

Next, I listed out all of my basic necessities and put a price next to each item. I listed everything from dance classes to laundry detergent to a subway pass to toilet paper. I laughed as I wrote *toilet paper*. My native New Yorker roommate had informed me the day I moved in there was no such thing as sharing a roll.

I reviewed my list and felt confident I had included everything. The only extravagant expense was my rent and I knew that was temporary.

I grabbed the calculator on the podium and I started to insert the numbers. When I totaled my calculations I tried not to faint. I was staring at $70,000 a year. I calculated the numbers again. Again I was staring at $70,000. I calculated one more time just to make sure.

I was only scheduled to earn $28,920 per year *before taxes*. If my expenses were indeed going to be $70,000 a year I wouldn't even last a year. I was officially upside down on my finances.

I looked back through my list and started crossing things off:

- one Broadway show a month ($150/month)

- out on the town with friends ($100/month)

- Clothes/shoes ($50/month)

- ~~Cab rides ($50/month)~~

I crossed through several rows of items on my budget and again ran the calculator. Still I was upside down.

I slashed more line items and cut other monthly expenses in half. I had decided if I could lessen the use of my toilet paper, toothpaste, and shampoo I would save money. I could spread those expenses across two months instead of one. If I found ways to cut in my daily expenses, like rationing my body lotion, I could keep my dance classes. It was after all one of the basic "necessities" I needed in order to be successful in New York. But I also started thinking a bit more cleverly: I realized if I attended more auditions I could technically get a dance class for free. So that is what I decided to do, and did.

I went as bare as I could, line item by line item, but when I hit the "=" button on my calculator I was at $50,000 a year. Realization was hitting me between the eyeballs. Even if I reduced my rent and moved to the outer boroughs, $13/hour wasn't enough to survive in the Big Apple, even if I *was* working for *The Donald.*

I closed my notebook and for the first time I could feel New York laughing at the girl from Kansas. I had to make a change, but to what, I wasn't sure.

A man walked up to the hostess stand and I closed my notebook. "Hello. Welcome to the Trump Grill," I said with a smile. It was the man from next door at Tiffany & Co. "It's nice to see you again today."

He said hello as he walked past me and up to the bar. I watched him sit down at his same spot – the same chair he sat in everyday of the work week. He opened his newspaper and the bartender poured him his usual – a glass of chilled white wine.

He sipped on his wine as he read the New York Times. There he sat, nameless to me, in his beautifully tailored three-piece suit. He followed the same routine every day. The only variance was his expensive suit selection.

As I stared at the handsome man sipping his wine, the wheels in my head started turning. Perhaps I needed to use my college education after all, but that would require a fulltime job which would stand in the way of auditions and shows.

I reminded myself "as long as you're going to be thinking anyway, think big." But all I was focused on was dollar signs and the lack of dollars I had.

It didn't take a Rhodes Scholar to realize how fast I was going to run out of money. I knew I could request more hours, but even if I did (and I did), it wouldn't be enough to cover my basic living expenses. Not to mention I wouldn't have the time to truly pursue my performance goals. There wasn't enough time in the day and $13/hour didn't provide enough income.

I flipped my notebook to a new page and began writing ideas for new jobs and new streams of income, but the ideas weren't coming.

"You ready?" A voice asked as I looked up, startled away from my lack of ideas.

I closed my notebook and said, "Yes."

Mr. Manager #2 was standing in front of me with a plate of meatloaf and mashed potatoes under cling wrap. He handed me the plate and the cloth napkin wrapped around the utensils. It was my favorite part of $13/hour.

"I'll cover the hostess stand until you get back," he said as he handed me the plate.

Gladly I left my station and made my way up the escalator and over to the elevator. The security guards pressed the button for me and we waited for the elevator to reach the ground level.

"What is Mr. Trump having for lunch today?" Mr. Security #1 asked.

"It looks like meatloaf," I said with a smile. "Guarantee you it's not as good as my mom's."

We laughed.

"I bet a Kansas mom knows how to make some great meatloaf," Mr. Security #2 said as the elevator door opened.

"You can't beat my mom's meatloaf. It's the best," I said with a smile as I walked past their podium and into the elevator. I turned to face them, "And she bakes it smothered in ketchup. Just the way I like it."

Mr. Security #1 and #2 laughed again as I pressed the button to The Donald's floor.

"You can take the girl out of Kansas, but not the Kansas out of the girl," Security #1 snickered, laughing at his own joke.

A smile spread across my face and I shot my security friends a wink as the door closed.

When I reached The Donald's floor I stepped off the elevator and walked past the beautiful secretaries. I said hello and they responded with happy, pleasant smiles and "hellos" of their own. There appeared to be no life crisis occurring in the Trump office on that cool October afternoon.

I may have worked downstairs and they worked several floors above me, but we were all after the same things. We were all in our twenties hustling work in the Big Apple.

Mr. Trump was in his office and on the phone. I could hear his voice floating down the hall as I stopped in his private kitchen to remove the cling wrap and properly prepare his plate of food for delivery. When the presentation met my satisfaction I walked around the corner and into his office. He was on the phone, obviously discussing a business deal. I tried not to listen.

I approached The Donald sitting behind his desk. The windows behind him framed the perfect view of Central Park. I admired the green trees blended with those that had begun changing to brilliant yellows and reds. From The Donald's view you could see the buildings that lined the northern part of Central Park, better known as Harlem. It was a multi-billion dollar spectacular view.

As I walked around his large desk, Mr. Trump finished his call and placed the phone on the receiver.

"Good afternoon Mr. Trump," I said.

"Good afternoon," he responded kindly.

"Meatloaf is on the menu," I said to my boss as I sat the plate in front of him, "it was specially made for you," I added making up the *specially for you* part.

"Looks good. Thank you," he said as we exchanged glances.

"You are very welcome." I said as I turned to walk out of his office. "Have a nice afternoon."

"I will. You too."

I walked out the door, down the hall, and back past the secretaries.

"Have a great day," I said to all of them as I pressed the down button on the elevator.

When I stepped inside an idea for a larger income came to me.

"Think Epic. Imagine Awesome." – Sunee Ngamkhao

After work I went to the Starbucks in the bottom of the building that housed my rented sofa. I ordered a decaf coffee and connected to the free wifi.

186

I plugged "Miss Universe" into the Google search bar and clicked on the link that took me to the homepage. I needed a name and so I searched. I was looking for the president of the Miss Universe Organization and within a few minutes I had located her. According to what I was reading she was appointed by my boss for whom I delivered lunch.

I opened a Word document on my computer screen and began a cover letter.

I had decided I wanted to work with the Miss Universe Organization. I believed I had the perfect credentials and I had direct access to the head of the organization, Mr. Trump himself.

Once I had my letter and resume perfected, I saved it to my thumb drive, packed up my computer, and headed to the nearest print store. I planned to deliver the items directly to the top dog. I would deliver my cover letter and resume along with Mr. Trump's meatloaf and mac 'n cheese... *personally.*

"There are no failures, just lessons." –Pete the Cat

The next opportunity I had to deliver lunch I indeed delivered my resume.

It was the last time I delivered lunch.

Scene Thirty-Five

The lobby of a high rise apartment building, November 2006
(Nine months *before* the accident)

"Real elegance is everywhere. Especially in the things that don't show."
–Christian Dior

As I stepped off the elevator, I saw Josh standing in the lobby visiting with the doormen. The doormen looked like out of shape garden gnomes next to Josh who was an attractive, trim man standing at a lean six feet five inches. He was the epitome of a retired basketball player: tall, athletic, and handsome. His Italian heritage gave him a natural edge on fashion and a great sex appeal.

I had met Josh the week I moved to New York. On my second night in the Big Apple I was sitting outside our building enjoying the bustle of taxis and the people rushing back and forth. He was standing ten feet from me on his cell phone. I noticed him, but didn't think much of it. When he finished his call he looked up and saw me sitting on a bench and walked over to say hello.

We sat outside for thirty minutes chatting. He was from Massachusetts and I was drawn to his accent that was absent of the "r" in the alphabet. He couldn't get past the fact I was from Kansas. He had never met anyone from Kansas and I think he expected my hair to be in "Dorothy Braids" and a black dog named *Toto* sitting next to me. At the end of our conversation he asked me out for a drink with his friends. I wasn't sure if he wanted to show off his new "find" or if he was just being friendly. Either way I didn't care so I took his invitation. From that point forward we became friends.

A few months later I was headed out on a date with the handsome Josh. Josh was dressed in a tailored navy blue suit, crisp white shirt, and yellow pastel silk tie. To top it off, he had on black polished leather shoes as reflective as black ice after a winter rain. His appearance demanded attention and respect, which meant I didn't mind being his date for the evening. Had he not been a dope-head, I would have considered escalating my status to "girlfriend". I thought about overlooking this highly minor flaw until I learned he got stoned on Sundays (before church). Getting high to go pray wasn't something I could disregard. A bummer, but nonetheless a fact.

As I approached the two doormen and Josh, they all turned to look at me.

"You look beautiful," Josh said as he leaned in to kiss me on the cheek.

He was handsome and polite. *Why be a pothead?* I thought.

"Thank you," I responded, flattered he noticed, but not really surprised.

I was wearing a beautiful black and gray chiffon dress. It was just long enough to be conservative, but short enough to be desirable. The fabric was shear and fitted. The bottom layer fit my body like a glove and the chiffon top was flowing and elegant. The combination of cling and flow gave it the perfect amount of sex appeal. As if to tie a bow around my package, I added a three-inch-wide belt with a huge buckle. Of course I wore my tallest stiletto black heels I owned.

"Thank you again for agreeing to be my date," Josh said.

"Of course," I said. "I'm looking forward to meeting your clients."

Josh had asked me to be his date for a business meeting at some swanky restaurant on Madison Avenue. Since I couldn't afford to eat in that area of town on my own, I didn't hesitate at the opportunity.

Josh was building a mortgage firm and recruiting money to back his business. The dinner meeting was with one of the late Joe DiMaggio's friends and his current girlfriend. Josh had asked me to attend because he needed a "girlfriend" to lighten the mood. In other words he was asking me to play man-on-man defense: *I take care of the girlfriend while he negotiates a deal.* Josh was smart enough to know I could make a positive impression while allowing the two men to talk business. I would also be a good distraction for the *real* girlfriend who was in tow.

Josh and I said our good-byes to the doormen and walked out the door and onto Fifty-Seventh Street. There was a cool breeze in the air announcing fall was on its way. The breeze and the coolness diffused the signature New York City smell of the subway mixed with the sewer mixed with fresh food mixed with trash.

Josh hailed a cab and we climbed inside.

"Seventy-sixth and Madison," Josh instructed the cabby.

When we arrived at our destination, we climbed out of the cab and stepped up on the sidewalk. I could sense Josh's tension so I turned to look at him. I reached out and grabbed his hands, "You will be great," I assured him. "Let's go secure this guy's money."

He looked at me and smiled with appreciation. We dropped hands and walked ten steps before a doorman opened the door to welcome us to his restaurant. As we stepped across the threshold, I was immediately impressed with our destination. Not only was it gorgeous, it smelled heavenly. I was starving and I couldn't wait to try some food that the wealthy dined on regularly.

Josh stepped up to the hostess, "Four for Josh Allegretto."

"Welcome Josh. The other two in your party arrived a few minutes ago. Let me show you to your table."

As we wandered our way through the restaurant, following the hostess, I noticed the men in their expensive suits and the women dressed in elegant attire. Some women were in wool pants and silk blouses while others were in cocktail dresses. No matter the attire, all were dripping in jewels - be it from the ears, the neck, or the wrists. The jewels scattered among the women could have fed a third world country, I was sure. As I was loving the atmosphere, my focus quickly switched to my $30 dress I was showcasing. I was worried I would look out of place in my dress I had pulled off the clearance rack.

I thought about my mom's clothing advice. She had taught me any article of clothing (no matter how inexpensive) can be stunning as long as it is freshly pressed and the girl in it stands tall and walks proud. So that is exactly what I did. Deep down, I also knew no one would know if my earrings were cubic zirconiums or diamonds. I told myself all the people starring at Josh and me as we walked through the restaurant were taken with how tall and stunning we both were. Besides, all that really mattered was what I thought anyway.

When we arrived at our table we were greeted by warm smiles as the couple stood. The man was in his mid-sixties and she was in her early fifties. Both had a friendly, yet well-to-do, aura surrounding them. Their friendliness existed in their smiles.

"Hello John. Evelyn. " Josh said as he gave each a handshake. "I would like to introduce Adrienne."

I reached out my hand to greet the two, "It is a pleasure meeting you both." I said as I shook first his and then her hand.

As we prepared to sit, both men helped their women with their chairs. Stunned by Josh's behavior I realized it was either his manners he suddenly found or the quality of the restaurant which explained Josh's gentlemanly performance. In the four weeks I had known him that was the first time he had treated me like anything other than a little sister. I wanted to give him a hard time, but I knew it was neither the time nor the place. I decided to just be appreciative.

As the basic get-to-know-you conversation began, the gentlemen selected a bottle of wine from the extensive wine list. John and Evelyn were intrigued I was from Kansas. They asked me a hundred questions about my childhood, cornfields, cows, and being Miss Kansas. It was as though every New Yorker was impressed I didn't ride in on a horse, or I didn't have on my best wranglers and a cowgirl hat. Kansas might as well have been Mars by the way people reacted to my presence.

I loved it. I enjoyed being the minority. I also appreciated how people looked at me differently because of where I was born. Believe it or not, it provided an "edge" on all the east coasters. I had learned to embrace our differences and use them to my advantage.

"Enough about me. I want to hear about you two. John, did you really work with the Yankee baseball player? Did you get to meet Marilyn Monroe?"

"As a matter of fact, I did and yes. I even wrote a book about it. "

"Oh?" I questioned.

"I would like to give you a signed copy of my book before we leave."

"Wow. That is so kind of you. I would love a copy," I responded with a smile.

There was something about the people I met in New York. Instead of a business card it was customary to give a new friend, or acquaintance, a copy of an autographed book. In the twenty-three years before I moved to Manhattan I had never met an author. Yet, in my first few months in New York I had received four autographed books directly from the authors. I was beginning to think the people from Mars landed on the east coast, not in Kansas.

As I was giggling to myself about my next autographed book, our wine arrived. Since Josh had ordered the wine, the wine expert stood between the two of us to present the bottle. As he began uncorking the red wine we all watched.

"I would like the lady to taste it," Josh said to the sommelier as he nodded toward me.

Josh was testing me. The first time he took me to dinner he let me taste the wine. It was horrible, but being the polite young lady my parents raised me to be I told them it was fantastic and they poured us both a glass. Josh took one sip, looked at me, and started laughing.

"Adrienne, this is horrible," he had told me through laughter.

I knew it was horrible, but I had never sent a bottle back because I thought it would be viewed as rude. Josh took it upon himself to take me out to dinner once a week and teach the Kansas girl how to taste wine and send it back if we weren't in love with the flavors or the tannins.

That night, in front of the famous Yankee's friend, Josh put me on the spot to see if I would pass the test. The sommelier poured enough wine in my glass for me to have a proper taste. Everyone stared as I swirled the wine and examined the fingers. I stuck my nose in the glass for a deep inhale and then raised the glass to my lips. I took a dainty sip and swirled the wine around my mouth. It had the texture of silk and the flavors of a beautifully aged Carménère. It was magnificent, and a far cry from the *Yellow Tail* I could afford, and only once a week.

I slowly set down my glass. I could feel Josh watching me as I selected my words. "It has a silky texture and deep flavor. It is perfect," I told the gentlemen.

He nodded and began to pour all four of us a glass, beginning with mine. My eyes connected with Josh's and he shot me a smile and a wink. His student had passed his test.

We all raised our glasses as Josh said, "To mortgages."

"And Kansas," John added.

We all smiled and took a sip of our wine.

Josh looked at me and said, "Nice selection Adrienne. This really is a perfect wine."

I smiled.

As Josh and John began discussing business, Evelyn and I started our own conversation.

"So what is the story with you and Josh?" Evelyn asked, skipping over any additional pleasantries.

"What do you mean?" I countered.

"Are you dating?"

"Not exactly."

"Are you sleeping together?"

"Not exactly," I responded, shocked at her blunt question. She waited for me to continue, "Josh is one of the first people I met when I moved here and we simply became friends. In a lot of ways he has taken me under his wing to show me the ropes of a big city. Besides, he treats me like a little sister."

"I see," she said with pursed lips. "Well, if the two of you do decide to date… you simply look stunning together."

I blushed. "Thanks. I think."

"Well, you don't look like a little sister," she said slyly with raised eyebrows "and he doesn't look at you like a little sister either," she paused to take a sip of wine. Not being sure what to say, or do, I mimicked Evelyn's actions and also raised my glass to my lips. "I think you should at least explore the idea of dating," she added.

"Perhaps," I responded and paused. "I guess time will tell."

"Sometimes you have to help time along," she said unapologetically.

We both laughed and took another sip of wine.

As if not to give up on the conversation, Evelyn came at the topic from another angle, "Do you enjoy lingerie?"

"What girl doesn't?" I responded honestly.

"There is a great new boutique that opened, I would love to take you shopping and introduce you to the owner. It is an amazing little place. They do a splendid job of turning a piece of string into the most beautiful piece of *sexy* I have ever seen. Their lace is all handmade and shipped in from France. It really is a splendid boutique. How about it? This weekend?"

"Oh I would love to go shopping with you, but I'm afraid French lace isn't in my budget right now."

"Well, that is too bad," Evelyn paused disappointed, but not giving up, "where do you shop for your lingerie then?"

"Oh… well…" I stammered "I don't really have much in the way of lingerie. I guess I don't have anyone I care to show it to, so I don't buy it."

"Who says lingerie is for anyone other than yourself?" Evelyn said through a laugh as I looked at her with a raised eyebrow. "I love lingerie, but I don't buy it for *that* guy," she said as she rolled her eyes and nodded at John. "I buy it for me. I guess you could say it is my power suit, so to speak. I like to showcase my power on a daily basis."

"I'm listening."

"Oh honey, it is time for you to learn life's most valuable lesson. Hasn't anyone ever taught you the most important article of clothing is that which touches your skin? Especially that which touches your heart and well, your womanly parts?"

"Apparently not," I said as my face turned red.

"Oh most definitely, it is!"

"Why is that?"

"It is important how you treat yourself. How you treat yourself determines how others will treat you in return. We all get dressed every day, right?"

I nodded.

"Do you think powerful confident women wear worn out bras and holes in their panties?"

"Probably not," I responded, very curious in where she was going with the conversation.

"Definitely not! The power in your personality starts with how you, *and only you*, treat yourself. You set the standard that others will follow. Try it. Start wearing powerful lingerie and watch how you carry yourself," she paused to take a sip of her wine. "I guarantee your response will be powerful, which in return will demand the respect of people who come into contact with you. You'll stand taller. You'll be more confident. You'll be more daring. You'll become what you envy in the powerful women you look up to! People, men *and* women, will feel your power which silently demands respect. Women have endless amounts of power and sex appeal. It's a shame so many ladies don't learn how to tap into it, especially when it is so easy."

"But what if I can't afford French lace with matching bras and panties?"

"Who said anything about matching? Have fun with it. My response to French lace... lace smace. Find what works for you. You don't have to break the bank to treat yourself well and portray confidence. With the right effort, your mind will begin to transform a hidden confidence to actual truth."

I thought about what she was telling me. Could confidence, power, and sex appeal really be that easy? Did it really start with what I wore under my clothes?

"Sounds like you need to do some shopping," Evelyn smirked as she swirled her wine. "Well, tell me about your job."

"Right now I'm auditioning when I can, but I recently left my hostess job at Trump Tower to take a job with a catering company. They pay more and have more opportunities to pick up overtime. I work their parties, but I also work in the main restaurant in the Chelsea district. They have a buffet and I stand at the cash register and weigh people's food and collect money. I spend most of my days with food slopped down the front of me. It isn't glamorous by any stretch of the imagination. I guess you could say I'm paying my dues again."

"Everyone has to go through it," she encouraged.

"Yeah, I know. It really isn't that bad. The owners are nice. Until I meet people and build a name for myself it is at least helping pay the bills," I said as I shrugged my shoulders.

"I have auditioned for a spot with the USO Show Troupe. The audition went well and I'm hopeful I will get an offer, but it isn't full time work which means I will still have to weigh food," I said with a sarcastic laugh.

"Well... with your looks and personality you won't be weighing food long."

"Ahh, you are so sweet. Thank you."

We raised our glasses and toasted.

**If you can't enjoy the journey today,
how do you expect to enjoy it tomorrow?**

I slapped the snooze on my alarm and rolled over. I buried my face into the side of the sofa and pulled my pillow over my head, covering my ears.

Fifty-seven stories below me I could hear the buzz of the city with sirens and honking horns. It was another busy day in New York City. I was quickly learning *every day* was a busy day in the Big Apple, which was part of the reason I was attracted to the chaos.

After dinner with Evelyn, I had a new perspective and I was anxious to give *her* outlook on life a try.

I flung my blankets off my body and reached for the alarm – I switched the alarm off and sat up on the sofa. I stood in my little space and picked up the sofa pillows off the floor. I flung them back on the sofa. If I left them on the floor, neatly stacked, they still took up my entire floor space that was my so-called "room".

195

Without taking a step, I reached for the shower curtain that hung from my shelves to the wall (the curtain that doubled as my "door" and fourth wall). I quietly opened the curtain, trying not to let the rings scratch against the metal. I tiptoed down the dark hall and stepped inside the bathroom and closed the door before I switched on the lights.

I went through my bathroom ritual moving from toilet to shower to sink. As I brushed my teeth, I looked at myself in the mirror, toothpaste dripping down my chin, and said to the girl staring back at me "It's going to be a good day."

I leaned over and spit in the sink. I rinsed my mouth with water and when I stood straight again to dry my mouth with a towel, I looked at that girl again and said, "It's going to be a great day."

I set my toothbrush in a cup and reached for my hairbrush. I smoothed my hair neatly. As I began to pull my locks back into a ponytail, something caught my eye. I dropped my hair and reached for a headband in my box of belongings and selected a red elastic band. It was nothing special – plain and simple – it also doubled for the gym. I decided to do something *different* with my hair. No, I wasn't going to the gym, I was going to work. I slid the headband into place, leaving my hair long and beautiful.

When I tiptoed back to my "room" I grabbed my black pants. The same pants I wore every day. The pants had a spot on them that had been there the entire week, but I wasn't concerned as I would be slinging food again that day. I tossed the pants on the sofa before I reached for a black shirt, the same black shirt I wore every day.

As I reached for a bra I stopped, thinking about dinner from the night before. I dug deep into my drawer. From the back I retrieved a red bra, *the exact color of my headband.* I held it up and examined it. I usually matched my undergarments to the color of the clothes going on top, but I decided to change it up on that particular day. *No black sports bra for slinging food today,* I thought.

I hooked my red bra around my waist, twisted it around, and pulled it into position. I pulled my black shirt over my head, careful not to mess up my hair with the red headband, and then I put on my dirty black pants, black socks, and black shoes.

I grabbed my purse and left the apartment. I had just enough time to ride the subway one stop further than I needed and walk *back* to the catering company.

My job was located equal distances between two subway stops and naturally I should have gotten off at the first stop. One day I wasn't paying attention and rode the subway too far. When I got off the train, a stop further and in a panic, I made an unexpected discovery. The extra stop allowed me the opportunity to walk past a fire station. A fire station filled with hunky gorgeous fit men not more than ten years older than I was. With muscles bulging from under their shirts, most mornings the handsome fireman were outside drinking coffee or polishing the fire trucks. Not only were they a sight to drool over, they were also as friendly as they were handsome.

From that serendipitous moment I had determined my new commuting path. I was a happy Kansas girl living in the Big Apple, and my reward for going to work – the New York City *Hot* Firemen.

Within a week of me passing back and forth we had begun to recognize each other and my morning commutes had become the "norm". I felt like I was back in high school planning out my "walking path" from class to class strategizing how to walk past the guy I had a crush on. Once my crush had noticed me I advanced to hours of daydreaming how to say "Hi" (but nonchalantly and unrehearsed, of course).

I was twenty-three years old and doing the same thing as my high school self, except I was headed to work and they were hunky fireman in the capital of the world. *I had officially upped my game.*

I figured it would be another month before I had the courage to stop and actually start a conversation with any of them. Of course, I would have stopped if they started the conversation first.

That morning I was wearing the headband, I decided to try out my new "inner" confidence. When I walked past two of the fireman standing outside, I simply yet confidently said, "Morning."

Both of the men smiled and said "Morning" in return. One even raised his cup as if to say "Cheers". My heart melted, but I tried to look casual. He was gorgeous leaning against the old brick wall with the shiny red fire trucks parked on his right. I let out a sigh and continued walking. I reached my hand up to my headband to make sure it was still in place.

I walked my last two blocks before I stepped inside the catering company. Yes, I worked parties for the company, but to make steady money they hired me to work in their café. The café served a lunch buffet and all the people in the area knew one of our chef's was named the fourth greatest sushi chef in the entire city. So at lunch time we were busy.

My job was to make sure the buffet looked clean and prepared for the lunch rush, but when the rush started I was in charge of the weight machine. In other words, I stood at the cash register and weighed my patron's food and then accepted their payment.

I needed the money so I did it. I struggled with the fact I had just finished a year as a celebrity, being the center of attention at every party and every room I walked into, but in New York no one cared. I was a number. On top of it all, I had a journalism degree yet I was weighing food to pay rent. The job humbled me.

One of the highlights of weighing food: I stood next to the front door where I could see everyone come and go: employees, the owner, hungry New Yorkers, everyone. I took it upon myself to become the "*Walmart*" greeter and within a week I knew everyone that worked at the company. But there was only one I was interested in.

His name was Jason. He was an attractive five feet eleven inches tall (slightly short for my standards), brown hair, brown eyes, a singer, and a working artist. Slowly we went from casual hellos, to sentences, to learning about each other. He was also a performer, but he held down a desk job for the catering company as an event organizer, which meant he wasn't a "starving" artist.

"Good morning Jason," I said when he walked through the door.

"Good morning." He said as he hustled by me and up the stairs, obviously running late.

It wasn't until after the lunch rush that he came back downstairs to continue our conversation.

"How was lunch today?"

"Busy. The same usual people. In a hurry to eat and go back to their cubicles."

"Did you do anything fun last night?" Jason asked.

"Actually I did. Different, but fun."

"And that was…"

"I went on a double date. You know, it was just my date, me… and the late Joe DiMaggio's friend and his girlfriend."

"Serious?"

"Yep. It was interesting."

"And who was your date?"

"A guy from my building."

"Is it serious?"

"Not really. We're just friends."

Jason hesitated but then asked, "So would it be okay for me to ask you out on a date?"

"Does that mean you're asking?"

"Does that mean you're saying yes?"

"Depends."

"On what?"

"I just had dinner with a man that autographed his book and handed it to me over dinner," I leaned across the counter and onto my forearms, "what did you have in mind for a date?"

"Hmmm...." Jason paused as if he was coming up with something crafty, "How about dinner and the theatre tonight after work."

"Hmmm...." I said with my eyebrows raised tall. I dramatically looked toward the ceiling for guidance. "Yes. What time?"

"I'll pick you up at eight? The show is at ten."

"I'll go with you, but you can't pick me up," I said.

"Why not?" Jason asked confused.

"Because I don't know you that well. And rule number one of living in New York City..." I paused.

He leaned in closer so I shifted to a whisper, our mouths only a foot apart. "Don't let strange men know where you live."

Jason leaned back laughing and pulled his hand to his heart, "Oh that hurts."

I laughed.

"How about we meet in Union Square at 7:45." Jason suggested.

"Done," I responded with a smile.

"I better get back to work. See you tonight."

"I'm looking forward to it," I responded.

As Jason turned to walk back across the room and up the stairs he looked over his shoulder and said, "By the way, nice headband, but it doesn't match your outfit."

I smiled, stood a little taller, and said to myself *if you only knew.*

"Most folks are as happy as they make up their minds to be."
—Abraham Lincoln

When I emerged out of the subway station and into Union Square I spotted Jason sitting on a park bench. He was dressed in fitted jeans, a tan sweater, and a hat that reminded me of something Frank Sinatra would wear. He looked better than he did at work and I was pleased to head out on the town with such a hot date.

As I walked toward him, he spotted me and stood.

"Good evening," he said as he leaned in to kiss me on the cheek, his right hand placed gently on my waist.

"Hi," I responded.

"Hungry?"

"As a matter of fact I am," I said slightly flirtatious.

"Great," he said with a smile. "I'm going to take you to this great little Italian restaurant and then we are going to see an off-Broadway show."

"Cool."

"A couple of my friends are staring in it."

"Double cool," I said.

This is where I would love to tell you I remember the name of the musical, but I don't. It was a musical with five guys playing the only five parts. All of them could sing. All of them could act. And all of them could dance. But I remember finding it odd it was only guys. They were all very talented, but something didn't feel quite right about the whole thing.

My handsome date was good friends with *all* of them. *Very* good friends. Such good friends in fact, it was my last date with the handsome Jason.

From that day forward I started matching my headbands to my bra or my underwear or both. I played games of confidence with myself. To my surprise it worked. Even though I spent my days covered in crusted food or beer spilled down the front of my shirt, I always had on a headband that matched one or both of my undergarments. No it wasn't French lace, quite the contrary actually. My most expensive two items were from *Victoria's Secret*, but everything else was from *Target*, *Walmart*, or *Kmart*. My friend was right, it wasn't about it being "Made in France" or "Made in China". There really was something about dressing for *myself* that gave me a deeper sense of self-worth and self-confidence. I had a greater sense of self-confidence knowing no one would even see my colorful, sexy, and beautiful undergarments.

I was learning the only endorsement I needed for self-esteem was, well, my own.

Scene Thirty-Six

The lap pool at West Texas A & M University, five swimmers swimming, a
girl in a blue one-piece Speedo, goggles, a swim cap and a towel, April 2008
(Eight months *after* the accident)

*"If you can't fly then run, if you can't run then walk, if you can't walk then
crawl, but whatever you do you have to keep moving forward."*
–Martin Luther King Jr.

I walked out to the pool taking baby steps across the cold wet tile. I
could feel my anxiety as distinctly as I could feel the dampness under my
feet. I was excited to get in, but I also didn't know what the pool would
feel like. My life for nine months had been a whirlwind of upsets and
setbacks mixed with loss and survival. Would the pool cause more
problems?

I was learning how to walk and reengage in the basic principles of
everyday life. Getting around wasn't exactly easy and I had experienced
more life changing disappointments in a matter of months than I had in
my entire lifetime. And there I was, finally graduating to pool therapy.
Would the pool prove to be yet another disappointment or would it be a
step, figuratively and literally, in a positive direction?

I sat down on a bench and stared out across the water watching the
swimmers as they went back and forth. Everyone looked so peaceful.
Everyone that is, except for the man in the far right lane who appeared
to be half-drowning half-swimming as he splashed around like a
mentally tortured walrus. His lack of gracefulness brought me comfort
as my focus switched to the sight of my gruesome ankle underneath me.

I didn't want anyone to notice my disfigurement. It was
embarrassing and I was ashamed. It looked like the Halloween version
of Rudolph-the-Red-Ankled-Frankenstein-Project. A few people had

201

noticed in the locker room when I was changing, but there wasn't anything I could do to hide my flesh. I was, after all, in a swimsuit. If I went swimming in a sock I was bound to draw more attention to the one area of my body I already despised, and yet, somehow, at the same time was grateful I still had. I still considered the sock.

My ankle looked like a kindergartener's scientific themed art project. Or better yet, it looked like a plastic surgeon came into the operating room, both high on drugs and drunk, cut out a portion of my thigh, slapped it on my ankle and welded the edges to get it to hold in place. Minus the intoxication and drugs it was an accurate description. My free flap had taken to my body physically, and it was serving its purpose, but I was far from finding emotional acceptance of my deformity.

But I liked the thought of being able to swim. I welcomed the freedom of the water. I was also scared. Scared I might have been struck with disappointment. Would a swimmer's kick hurt? Would "*Lucy*" ("*Lucy*" being the new name I had given my ankle because I was tired of saying "my ankle") handle the water, or would it cause more problems? I glanced down at my permanently attached side kick. She was still there. Still red and still extremely large. It had been months since my accident and free flap surgery.

My surgeon assured me that plastic surgery would cosmetically fix "the look" of my ankle, but first I had to give my body time to heal. I liked the idea of surgery, but I knew that option was a long way away. I would have to accept the new repulsion at the bottom of my leg long before that would happen.

But people stared when I had it exposed. Kids would simply ask, but adults were the worst. If they didn't say anything they would stare while trying not to stare. When I was having a good day I would simply strike up a conversation and cure their curiosity. Usually people were amazed by my story of how I came to have my Franken-foot, but other times it amazed me at the lack of filter some people possess.

For example: at a doctor's appointment an x-ray technician asked what disease was growing on my ankle. An acquaintance asked to see my scars and when I showed them to her, her immediate reaction was "Oh my goodness, I think I'm going to get sick." I looked at her with amazement and simply said, "I know, right? Good thing you don't have the same thing on your face. Imagine what people would say then." Little did I know in another few months I would date a guy who would tell me "It's so sad your ankle looks like that. It's even worse you can't wear heels. Heels are what drive the sex appeal of a woman." He didn't last very long.

All of this was my life now. I was learning how to handle the good and the bad. Sometimes I handled it, and sometimes I didn't. Sometimes I cried while other times I made jokes to ease the emotional pain. I suppose I even came up with the name *Lucy* because I enjoyed watching *I Love Lucy* reruns. Lucille Ball had a way of making everything okay by helping an audience laugh at life.

All of this was going through my mind as I finally gathered the courage to take the five steps to the water's edge. I sat down and took a couple of breaths before I swung my feet over the edge and into the pool.

The water felt refreshing and cool on my feet and legs. I could feel the water with my left ankle but not my right, *Lucy* had no feeling.

I could smell the chlorine and I was appreciative for the smell. If anyone in the pool had any sort of fungus growing on their body I knew the chlorine would kill it before it touched my scars. I had been cleared of infection, but I didn't care to revisit that journey in my story... *ever*.

I looked at my feet through the water and I began to gently kick. It felt good. A smile washed across my face. It felt real good. I kicked my feet for several minutes, admiring how far I had come and yet how elementary the simple task was. I giggled at how proud I was of myself. I was sitting on the edge of the pool kicking my feet like a three-year-old. *"If they could see me now"* I sang to myself.

I started thinking about my college days and the benefit swim meets my sorority would host. Our philanthropy was called *Service For Sight* and every year we raised money to aid the blind. Since our sorority mascot was Raggedy Anne and an anchor, we held a university-wide swim meet to raise money for our project. It was always a fun event for a good cause. I hated standing on the sidelines watching so I usually swam in the meet. I typically got suckered into swimming the hard races, most of which included the butterfly stroke, because I was both competitive and strong. I would practically drown myself once-a-year at this swim meet, not because I couldn't swim, but because I couldn't stand to lose. I swam so hard I could hardly pull myself out of the water after the races.

I sat on the water's edge reminiscing, giggling, and singing to myself. I was excited at my simple ability to flutter my feet in the water.

Would I ever be able to do the butterfly stroke again? Honestly, I didn't really care as that was the stroke I was convinced an angry coach invented in order to discipline his swimmers. I found the butterfly stroke about as much fun as running the suicide drills during basketball practice. With my wrecked ankle I would never, and I mean never, have to do *that* again. I was very okay with that.

I did, however, want to swim. I finally slid the bottom half of my body into the shallow-end of the pool. I love that feeling when only half of your suit is wet. You can feel every millimeter of your body as you creep your way into the water.

I immediately felt the lack of gravity on my legs and joints. But the question still persisted, how would swimming feel?

There is no time like the present, I thought.

I backed up against the wall, took a deep breath, and dunked under the water as I pushed off the wall. I slid through the water like a torpedo, my arms stretched out in front and my legs extended behind. It was by far the most freedom, and least amount of pain I had felt in months. I was slippery, like a fish, and *free*.

As I felt my push-off speed slow, I started to flutter kick as I sent my left arm down and around. I was swimming in a freestyle stroke. My right arm followed. I continued to kick. I was doing it. I was swimming. Again, left arm down and around followed by my right. Kick. Kick. Kick. Breathe.

It was the first time in months I felt unrestricted. I was exercising. Again, left arm down and around followed by my right. Kick. Kick. Kick. Breathe. I was living. I was doing something I *wanted* to do. I felt like I was one of my swimming students swimming a stroke properly for the very first time.

I swam to the other side of the pool and as I reached out to grab the edge I couldn't contain my smile. I was swimming! I was really swimming! I was doing something I enjoyed before my accident! Most importantly, I had little pain.

As I swam back to the shallow-end I couldn't wipe the smile off my face and I couldn't quit laughing. I swallowed a lot of chlorine water that day, but I didn't care. For the first time, I knew I would get through *this*.

But *this* still had its moments when I would lose faith. I was smack-dab in the middle of learning life was a series of mountain tops and low valleys. The extremes were a part of the journey. It was the journey between the two peaks where I learned the most about myself *and* my character.

Moments of great faith and moments of great weakness are both a part of a full life and well-lived journey.

Scene Thirty-Seven

A performer's life, November 2006

(Nine months *before* the accident)

"I think the hardest thing to overcome is judging yourself and being your own worst critic so to speak." –Nile Rodgers

I attended more auditions in the nine months I lived in New York than I can even count. Most of the auditions I was cut on the spot while others I was told I wouldn't get a response for up to six months. The biggest challenge was attending an "open call" audition and then receiving a "callback" when the callback time was during a "shift" at one of my various jobs I was holding down. The question became: do I take my chances and go to the audition and get fired from my job or forfeit the audition to wait tables? I did both, which meant I had a lot of different jobs during my time in New York City.

I had auditioned for the USO Show Troupe before Thanksgiving and it had gone so well I received a callback for the week after Thanksgiving. Not only was I excited about the fact I had received *any* callback, but the USO was steeped in our country's history.

The USO was founded in 1941 and stands for the United Service Organizations. It is a non-profit organization and operates solely from donations and volunteers. Honorably, they receive no funding from the government. (The next time you are at a major airport look for the USO, which is located on all the terminal signs. Stop in for a visit. Meet the volunteers and learn first-hand what they do for our amazing servicemen and servicewomen!)

There is no way you can be a Miss America contestant and not be a deep-rooted American patriot *and* not know about the USO. During my year as Miss Kansas I had the opportunity to receive history lessons from World War II Veterans, Korean War Veterans, Vietnam Veterans, and many more. Yes, some of them saw USO shows while serving. But to hear their war-stories in first-person changes you as an individual. Servicemen and women rarely talk about the deaths of their friends they witnessed with their own eyes, but they will tell a young woman who needs to understand history so it doesn't repeat itself. I'll never forget a lunch I had with a WWII Veteran before a parade in Wichita, Kansas on Veterans Day. I was humbled by the descriptive story he told me about his *numerous* jumps onto the beaches of Normandy. As he described his experience I could see the images of *Saving Private Ryan* flashing in my head.

The Miss America contestants used to be entertainers that toured with the USO to visit our troupes! The reality is, the USO is so well-known because of the famous entertainer Bob Hope. Mr. Hope dedicated his life to entertaining our military be it domestically or internationally - in times of war or in times of peace. Mr. Hope understood the value in morale and a positive attitude when fighting for the freedoms you and I enjoy today.

So yes, a callback to follow in the footsteps of the famous Bob Hope was overwhelmingly exciting. I was also humbled by the people I might get to meet if I was to be fortunate enough to land the role.

But first, I was headed home for Thanksgiving break. I had managed four days off from my waitressing jobs, which was unheard of. I could go home with pride as I had a callback waiting for me when I returned *and* numerous jobs that were paying my rent. Finally the stars looked slightly in alignment.

I had tickets to fly in and out of Oklahoma City, where my brother lived, to catch a ride with him and his family to my hometown, a four hour drive each way. The plan was to enjoy the Thanksgiving holiday and then return to Oklahoma City in time to drop me at the airport on a Friday evening to board my flight back to New York. Just enough time to make it back to my job.

On my way back to the airport my whole world shifted.

When we – my brother, sister-in-law, two kids, and me - were halfway between my hometown and Oklahoma City we received a call from my dad. He instructed us to turn around and head back home.

My grandmother and her husband Jay (the two who had so graciously allowed me to conduct a swimming school out of their backyard) had been in a head-on highway car collision going seventy miles an hour. Jay was pronounced dead at the scene and my grandmother was being airlifted to Wichita to fight for her life.

On a lonely country highway my brother turned the car around and headed back to Kansas, we were all stunned into silence and confusion.

We made it to Wichita in time for us to say our good-byes to Grandma, but she never opened her eyes when I was in the room. I was, however, able to hold her hand and tell her I loved her. All five of Grandma's children and all my cousins had made it to the hospital in time to say our good-byes. Within two hours after I last saw my grandma, a panicked "Code Blue" was announced over the hospital PA system. All the nursing staff and doctors raced past where I was standing and into Grandma's ICU room.

Grandma was gone.

The funeral was five days later and since I had a job that barely paid over minimum wage I decided not to fly back to New York for a couple days and then home again for the funeral.

I had three phone calls to make to New York. The first was a call to the restaurant where I was waiting tables. I asked to speak to the manager.

"He's not here. Try sending him a text," the bartender told me.

I composed a text explaining what happened and that I wouldn't be back to New York for another week. The response I received was coldhearted and cruel. It simply said, "Don't bother coming back."

My next call was to the *Les Miserable* Broadway box office. I had purchased a ticket to go see one of my good friends perform. The ticket had set me back $150, which was money I shouldn't have been spending in the first place, but I was supporting a friend so I bought it anyway. I asked the box office if they would exchange my seat for a different night. They didn't believe "my story" and told me "no".

My last call was to the USO office to cancel my callback audition for the USO Show Troupe. I had been invited to the final audition, to sing the *National Anthem* in front of the board of directors. It was scheduled the same week as my grandmother's funeral. I called the USO office and explained my situation. Sadly, the USO knows death all too well. They gave me their condolences and asked me to call the office when I was back in the city as they were happy to reschedule my final audition. I was blown away by their sympathy and compassion.

When I returned to New York, they held true to their word. I was invited into the USO offices in the Port Authority, to sing the *National Anthem* and go through an interview process with the directors.

I sang the *Anthem* with gusto, but I also butchered it. I felt horrible. They had let me reschedule and then I murdered our country's anthem. As a true actress, I stood tall and pretended it was the best rendition I had ever sung.

I answered their questions and then they thanked me for my time and I left. I thought I would never hear from them again. To my surprise, I got the call and they asked if I would represent the USO as Miss USO 2007. I would lead the trio of Andrew's Sisters Singers at all their events.

I was stunned by their offer. I assumed the president of the board was tone death, but I didn't care. With the acceptance of the offer I had my first official performance role in the Big Apple. *And* I got the job by butchering a song – *go figure.*

There would be seven of us that made up the troupe – three ladies, one man, and three understudies. We would be performing in and around New York City *and getting paid.* Our jobs were multifaceted as we would be attending, and performing at military banquets, homecomings and departure ceremonies, parades, major events, and the list went on. The year would culminate with three of us singing in Times Square during the New Year's Eve Celebration.

When I got into the groove of rehearsals I saw the talent surrounding me. I realized there was no way I auditioned as bad as I thought. If I had, I wouldn't have landed the USO opportunity. No one ever told me my performance was bad, I was the only one telling myself.

We are our own worst critics, and if we can learn to silence our negative voices we will open more doors than we can imagine.

Scene Thirty-Eight

A lonely New York City bathroom, a girl, March 2007
(Five months *before* the accident)

"Mountaintops inspire leaders but valleys mature them."
-Winston Churchill

As I put the finishing touches on my make-up, the reflection in the mirror caught my attention. I stopped powdering my forehead and stared back. I began to look past the mascara and deep into the girl's eyes. I slowly sat down the brush without breaking my intense connection with the unfamiliar girl who stared back with the same level of intensity. Who was she?

As I looked deep into her eyes, I could see the rawness of her existence. I saw an innocent girl slowly morphing into a confident woman. She was slowly learning herself and the ways of the world.

I continued to stare as the world stood still in that tiny New York City bathroom. If I moved she moved. I slowly leaned toward her; she leaned toward me, never breaking our eye contact.

I looked deeper into her eyes. I could see her fears sitting next to her dreams. They both inhabited equal parts of her inner being. Both were equal sizes and held equal levels of importance. I could see each had room to grow, shrink, and stretch. It was as if they both existed in a room, but when one became inflamed the other would shrink and when one shrank the other would grow. Both would always exist. The challenge was whether or not they could coexist. They had to choose to build a relationship. They had to choose to work together. Neither could ever leave, or ever die. Neither would ever give up. Each would rest during different parts of her journey, but they would both.always be together. It was as though both her fears and dreams were intertwined in a beautiful dance of infinite confident insecurities. Finding acceptance for their coexistence would be the most challenging and rewarding growth opportunities life had to offer.

I stood and stared the girl into familiarity. That girl was me, and only me. No one else would be me, not in this lifetime nor in another. I was God's unique and original creation, just as we all are.

How would I use my fears and dreams to make a mark on the world? I knew I wanted to leave the world better than I had found it. Just as the seasons change so do the needs of the world and the opportunities to leave a positive and lasting impact.

Accept your fears and dreams. Allow them to dance. Allow them *both* to be a part of your life. Allow them *both* to guide you. There will be times your fears keep you out of danger's path and there will be times your dreams push you through life's greatest adventures.

Accept both. Embrace both. Welcome both into your life, but don't let one or the other dictate your life's journey. It is about finding balance. It's about finding the rhythm in the dance of life. Take turns dancing with both your fears and your dreams.

I knew I had stepped outside my comfort zone and I was finding my place in the world. I was proud of my accomplishments and determined attitude. So much had changed in the past year – my address, my title, my job, my friends. I looked into my eyes searching for the depth of my soul. As I stared, I saw a whole new woman I had failed to notice before. I was looking at the raw me.

Scene Thirty-Nine

A parking lot on the edge of town, Texas, May 2008
(Ten months *after* the accident)

*"For I know the plans I have for you," declares the Lord, "plans to prosper you
and not to harm you, plans to give you hope and a future."
–Jeremiah 29:11*

I pulled to the back of the parking lot, still crying, my eyesight
blurred by my tears. I was on the edge of town. The new cast would be
arriving in a matter of days, which meant a new leading lady would be
waltzing into town to take over the role I didn't get to finish. I didn't
care there was a new leading lady; I just didn't want to watch my loss
play out before me night-after-night for three months.

I stared out across the open, empty field and into the vast
nothingness. Just beyond the horizon, and to my left, was the field
where my life had permanently changed. That was the place my mind
returned time and time again reliving that fateful Sunday evening I was
thrown from that god-forsaken horse. If I could have gone back in
time, would I have made different choices? Would I have thought about
my actions before I made them? What if I had stopped when I said I
was tired?

There was no answer to my hundreds of questions. The reality was:
my fate was sealed. No matter how many "what ifs" I played out in my
mind, I couldn't undo my stupidity.

I sat behind the wheel of my car... staring... crying... wondering...
I could feel the tears sliding off my face and beginning to pool on my
pant legs. I didn't care. Life was miserable. I needed peace. Where
would I find it? It had been months since my accident and without
much effort, I could take myself back to the moment I felt my foot

212

sever. My stomach would once again flip inside-out and upside-down just at the mere thought of how I collided with the ground.

I wanted to run away from my thoughts, but the more I tried to block them from my mind the more vivid they would dance through my head. I wanted to escape my depression that was growing by the day. I was sick of crying, but I was still crying. I couldn't stop. Was I crying because I cared? Or was I crying because I cared I didn't care? What didn't I care about? Life? Career? Purpose? I was desperately searching for answers. I was so completely lost and no one could help me find my way.

I reached for my Atlas in the backseat of my car, and with one hand I swung it in front of me. I opened it to the map of the United States. (For those of you who were born in the smart phone era, an Atlas was a great big book of maps that most people kept in their cars. We didn't have GPS systems built into our phones or our cars so we had to look at a map and study the geography to plan our journeys.)

But where could I go? Where could I start over?

I needed a fresh start, a fresh me. I could go anywhere I wanted. No one was holding me back. I could leave right at that moment. I just had to pick a place.

I scanned the map looking at all the possibilities. I was giving myself a pep talk with my last bit of motivation. I pulled myself together and quit crying. *I get to start over: new career, new friends, new life.*

I considered Austin, Dallas, Chicago, Los Angeles, North Carolina. *Where could I go?* Key West? San Diego? I could have left at that very moment.

I was desperate for a dot to jump out at me and say *"Pick me. Pick me. Pick me."* But all the dots were silent. I scanned north to south, east to west. I was ready to step on the gas. I just needed a destination.

My eyes stopped on the east coast: Manhattan, New York. A piece of me wanted to go back, but my ankle throbbed as I thought about how much walking there was in that big city. I wouldn't, rather I couldn't, last a day walking the streets of the Big Apple. Another tear fell. Besides, what would I do there now that I couldn't dance? Neither my desire nor my will could help me rise above my current situation. It knew my reality. I could barely walk from my car to my apartment. I had no energy. I was exhausted all the time. I hurt all the time. There I was... a girl who once navigated New York City with my eyes closed and now I couldn't even navigate the simple streets of Canyon, Texas.

My tears reappeared as my reality set back in. My tears turned to hysteria as I realized if I ran I would be taking my pain with me. I couldn't outrun my situation, or my pain. I couldn't run away from my problems. I had to live through every breath. I had to live through every tear. I had to live through every set back. I couldn't escape. I could neither speed time up nor slow it down. I had no control. I had to live every moment, every second, every painful step. There was no way out.

With all my might, I hurled my Atlas across the car. It slammed into the passenger side window before it fell between the seat and the door. I doubled over my steering wheel, crying so hard I began to dry heave. I couldn't run and I couldn't hide. I never got a break, not even from myself.

The two thoughts that kept me breathing were 1) with a new day comes new hope and 2) *for I know the plans I have for you.*

Scene Forty

Outside Barnes & Noble, May 2008
(Ten months *after* the accident)

"God allows us to experience the low points of life in order to teach us lessons we could learn in no other way." -C.S. Lewis

I parked my car in the handicap spot, as close to the front door as possible, and slowly walked up to the double doors. I was mindful of my every stride as not to step on a rock or uneven gap in the pavement. I had accepted slowing down and being more mindful of my surroundings. My caution was becoming the new norm. I suppose on many levels that wasn't such a bad thing.

I tugged on one of the big doors and walked inside. I took in the smell and the sight of the bookshelves and tables that were stacked ten books deep with new books. I stood at the front of the huge Barnes & Nobel store and felt my ankle throb at the thought of being on my feet for too long. It was as though just standing there - and looking - made my pain level jump from a three to a seven. But I wanted a good book - I *needed* a good book. I wanted, and needed, an escape.

Besides, I thought, *I can go home to elevate and ice my ankle while I dive into a writer's mind, any mind but my own.*

I pushed my pain out of my thoughts and walked over to the first table. I picked up a book. I opened it and flipped through the pages. I could smell the freshness of the paper. The stiffness of the pages meant I was one of the first few people to examine the freshly printed ink. But that particular book was too thin. I would have finished it in a week. I set the book down and picked up a thicker book.

This one would take me a lot longer to get through, I thought as I flipped it over and read the synopsis:

About three things I was absolutely positive.
First, Edward was a vampire.
Second, there was a part of him- and I didn't know how potent that part might
be – that thirsted for my blood.
And third, I was unconditionally and irrevocably in love with him.

I raised my eyebrows, flipped the book back over and set it back on the table. I made a mental note of the title - *Twilight*. I wasn't about to read something about vampire love. I wasn't into vampires, or zombies, or any of that weird sci-fi stuff. Besides, I was still fighting zombie thoughts and nightmares from a movie my mom and I decided to go see four months prior. It was the new Will Smith movie and we just knew it had to be good because it had Will Smith in it. Neither of us knew what the movie was about and didn't bother to do any research. It was Will Smith for crying out loud. That new movie ended up being *I Am Legend*. Let's just say, I had visions of zombies waiting for me in the shadows for weeks. I didn't need zombies *and* vampires after me. I had my own demons to deal with!

I picked up five more books and read the back, or the inside cover, and nothing seemed to be jumping out at me.

I decided to try another table where I recognized a title – *Eat. Pray. Love*. Again I flipped it over and read the synopsis. This story was about a woman who had everything, or so the world told her, but she felt empty inside. She had experienced divorce and a "crushing" depression (*yep, I knew what that was*). She decided to leave it all and go on a personal journey for a year, spending time in Italy (*Eat.*), India (*Pray.*), and Bali (*Love.*).

I thought about my own situation and the fact I wanted to run away too, but unlike this author I needed my doctors. I wondered if I could find some peace through the writing of Elizabeth Gilbert and her book *Eat. Pray. Love*. I flipped the book back over and studied the cover. I didn't particularly like the cover art, but I liked the words at the top – *A New York Times Bestseller*.

Good enough for me, I thought. Besides, my foot was throbbing and before it got out of control I needed to head home.

As I wound my way through the tables and to the front of the store, I noticed that *Twilight* book again. The one with the apple on the front cover. I made a mental note to buy some garlic the next time I was at the grocery store.

Scene Forty-One

A girl sitting on a bench outside of Starbucks, New York City, April 2007
(Four months *before* the accident)

"You miss 100 percent of the shots you don't take." -*Wayne Gretsky*

I was sitting outside a Starbucks near 72nd and Broadway. I was passing time, taking a break, and waiting for a dance class to start as I enjoyed a creamy yogurt parfait and a mocha.

As I sat on a bench slowly indulging in my snack, I watched the chaos of the city racing around me. I loved New York and I loved my USO gig, but I was tired. I wanted to be a "name" and be noticed when I walked into an audition, or a room. I was a small fish in a big pond. While I loved some aspects of being anonymous, I missed pieces of that "small town" atmosphere and attitude.

In the midst of my thoughts and observations a man walked past me. He was wearing a cowboy hat: a rare sight in New York City. Without effort, it stirred memories. It was spring which meant *"Texas"* was in the midst of auditioning. I knew a fellow cast member (and friend) had become the director of the show.

As I reminisced about my first professional show, my sentimental self decided to send my friend, the director, an email. I wanted to see how everything was shaking out for the 2007 summer season. I had no hidden agendas. The man in the cowboy hat had simply stirred a memory within me and I wanted to say "hi".

I pulled my laptop out of my backpack and composed a short friendly email. When I was done I closed my computer and picked up my yogurt. As I reached the bottom of the cup I scraped it clean with my plastic spoon. I decided to check my email one more time before I dashed off to dance class. To my surprise, I already had a response:

217

Everything is going great. I think we have a great cast this year, but I'm having a hard time finding a great lead actress. Interested?

I was confused. I wasn't looking for a job in Texas or in *"Texas"*. Had my impromptu message landed me a leading role? Could it really be that easy? Was I really being offered a job let alone the lead in a show I hadn't even auditioned for? Had I just arrived?

I felt a pang in my stomach: I *kind of* wanted to get excited. I *kind of* wanted to say yes. I *kind of* yearned for the *big fish small pond* sort of feeling.

Was it my ego or my desire to take a break from the lunch-eating blood-sucking ego-crushing city of New York that was calling me back to Texas? I was being offered an opportunity to be the leading lady in the country's largest outdoor musical... crowds that were as large as 1700 a night... three months of ego stroking...

I sat my empty yogurt container next to me and composed a response.

It is great to hear from you. I would definitely be interested in the role. Are you serious?

A smile swept across my face as I closed my laptop. I stuffed my computer back in my bag, threw away my empty containers and hustled across Broadway for my next dance class.

I practically danced across the crosswalk and skipped onto the elevator, success was the bounce in my step. I was most definitely arriving!

I did indeed accept the offer. In fact, I signed a contract to perform fifty-seven shows over the 2007 summer season.

It was the first time *ever* I was cast as a leading lady in a musical. In *"Texas"* I got to fall in love and get married every night for three months.

The USO graciously gave me a leave of absence. I packed all my belongings into two large boxes and shipped them home. I was headed to Texas to star in the larger-than-life *"Texas"*!

"Two roads diverged in a wood..."

I remembered the first time I set my sights on the musical as one of my goals. It was the early '90s and I was in elementary school when my parents, grandparents, and I went on a road trip (four hours south of my

218

hometown) for an overnight outing. They were taking me to see the grand musical "*Texas*".

The musical, written by Pulitzer Prize-winning playwright Paul Green, was born into existence in 1966. While there have been changes made over the years, it still holds true to its original script. For those who have never seen "*Texas*" I compare it *Oklahoma!* blended with *Seven Brides for Seven Brothers*. Without a doubt "*Texas*" is a classic old-school musical that is family-friendly and the perfect influence for a young girl at the beginning of her dreams.

Together, my family and I enjoyed everything "*Texas*" had to offer including the famous steak dinner, gift shop, and pre-show band before we found our seats among the crowd. The start of the show began when a horse, a lone rider, and a Texas flag appeared at the top of that 600-foot-canyon wall. When the overture started the horse and rider ran the length of the ridgeline until it disappeared out of site. The crowd cheered.

As the sun set and the show unfolded, I remember sitting under the stars and watching the dancers. They were beautiful and extremely talented. I had envied their flair. At one point I had leaned over to my mom and whispered, "I want to be in this someday." My mom smiled and whispered back, "Well, you have your work cut out for you." She paused before leaning back over, "But I know you can do it." A smile swept over my face as I sat in the sea of people *dreaming*.

For the remainder of the show I dreamt about when I would be a part of that beautiful production. I suppose in that hour, when I was ten-years-old, my fate was sealed. I had originally dreamt about being a dancer in the musical and had the honor in 2003. I had never imagined I would be the star of the show in 2007.

God tells us to dream big because He has even bigger plans for us than we can ever dream for ourselves.

Many careers were launched from the Pioneer Amphitheatre stage. That very stage was the launching pad for one individual who went on to star in *Cats* on Broadway while another was a cast member in the hit TV show *Taxi* (he even wore his "*Texas*" t-shirt in the *Taxi* cover art photo). It is my understanding one of the "*Texas*" performers also went on to claim the Miss Kansas crown...

There were dozens of others who went on to have successful careers in the arts: as drama teachers, music directors, show directors, lighting designers, Broadway stage managers, on cruise ships, and so much more. Needless to say, to be the leading lady in such a grand musical, with so much history, was more than an honor. Deep down I knew it was my launching pad.

After I had the grit of New York under my belt I knew what I needed to be successful in the arts. Escaping to Texas for three months allowed me the opportunity to fine-tune my craft before I was scheduled to return to the bustling city and continue my quest toward Broadway (and eventually Hollywood).

That 2007 summer my days started around noon when I arrived at the gym for an hour-long intense and sweaty workout. After my workout I would shower and refuel my body. I spent the afternoon studying vocal musical artists from the past, both their histories and their albums. My favorite was Doris Day. I found her because she was not only a vocal artist but a musical star *and* one of America's sweethearts.

After my studies, I would attend the hour long dance class with the dancers. The dancers were required to attend class to warm up their bodies, while the actors were invited. With my goals always front and center I attended the classes with the same dedication as the dancers.

After class the cast would pile into cars and carpool thirty minutes out to the theatre. We would get in the dinner line with the audience and eat. After a quick bite I would dash to the dressing room where I put curlers in my hair, just in time to make it to our company meeting out on the stage. The auditorium would still be closed to the audience, giving the director, choreographer, and music director adequate time to have the cast run any portion of the show that needed tweaking.

When our company meeting was complete, the cast would head back to the dressing room, but I would stay on the stage. That was the time I had the entire stage to myself. No audience. No cast members. I would put my ear buds in my ears and turn my iPod to my favorite music. I would stuff my iPod into my bra and then I would dance. I would dance *to the music.* No choreography. Just movement. I would typically lose between one to four curlers from my head as I twirled back and forth across the stage dreaming about the performer I was and the one I had yet to become.

Just before the stage manager was ready to open the theatre to the audience I would scoot off the stage and duck into the dressing room with my fellow cast-mates. I was usually dripping in sweat, for the third time in a day, and I would sit in front of a fan as I removed all the curlers from my hair.

The women's dressing room was always lively and fun. The air was filled with laughter as we applied our stage make-up and 1800s-style hairdos. A friend would tie me into my corset and I would put on layers of clothing starting with my bloomers, better known as pantelettes, which were nothing more than cotton Capri pants customary to the era.

Once we were ready for the show, we would meet again for a final company meeting and prayer circle. After our prayers we got into our "places" to await the overture and the lone rider on the top of the cliff.

The night before my injury we had a full house, which meant 1700 people watched my final *"Texas"* performance. The icing on the cake was the standing ovation we received just before the fireworks began. I was excited about my final week of performances, but something about that 52nd performance felt bittersweet. I suppose something inside of me knew my fate...

Scene Forty-Two

A frustrated girl determined to find an outlet, May 2008
(Ten months *after* the accident)

"I have not yet reached my goal, and so I am not perfect.
But Christ has taken hold of me. So I keep on running and struggling to
take hold of the prize." –Philippians 3:12

I picked up my blue tote bag and slung it over my shoulder, car keys in hand. I opened the front door of my apartment and stepped out into the breezeway. I carefully and without speed made my way to the handicap space that was closest to my handicap apartment.

It was a Sunday afternoon and I had nothing to do. It was one of our last few weekends before the new cast arrived for the summer. Those of us working in the office and on the production crew, scattered for the day to enjoy one of our last days off before the chaos of the next several months hit us.

I tossed my bag and my purse in the back seat and I climbed behind the wheel of my car. I put the car in reverse and backed out of my space. I was heading to the canyons. I wanted to stand on that stage before the new leading lady arrived. I never finished what I started the year before and the thought I wouldn't get to was eating at me. I needed closure so I set out to find some.

I put the car in drive and made my way out of the parking lot before I turned west on highway 217. I hit the moon roof button and the window slowly opened. I was fifteen minutes from the canyon entrance and about twenty-five minutes from the theatre. I flipped on the radio and changed it over to my favorite CD, Miranda Lambert's *Crazy Ex-Girlfriend*.

The CD changed over and I immediately began seeking through the songs to my favorite track: track six. When the song started I cranked the volume, put both hands on the wheel, and settled back against my seat.

The song has a great calm beat with an undertone of an out of control tambourine. It sounded how I felt. My blood was bubbling, but not quite to a boil. I was in a feisty mood. Every muscle and ligament in my body felt alive. My pain level had only spiked to a five that day, which meant I was better than good. I needed to release some pent-up energy and emotions. I was tired of crying.

The highway stretched out long and straight. I focused on the lyrics as Miranda reached the chorus:

Desperation - There's danger in frustration

She was singing about a boyfriend, but I knew the emotion behind what made that feeling turn into a song. When people lose boyfriends they usually pour themselves into work as a distraction. What do you pour yourself into when you lose your work? Those lyrics were surely the reason I was drawn to that song on that day when I was on my way to the canyon to do something I shouldn't. No one knew where I was going. I didn't want their opinion. I didn't want anyone's words of caution. I needed to dance and I wanted that whole massive stage to myself.

The song came to an end. I started it again.

In the past I would find an empty studio and dance until I had no more sweat to dance, no more energy to expend on the subject that brought me to the studio in the first place. Given my situation I hadn't danced out my frustrations in *months*. I wasn't enjoying the gym as a place to release energy either. The only downfall to swimming laps was I had no music in my ears.

I liked Miranda's music. She was fierce, defiant, and ridiculously honest. She was willing to say and sing what others were thinking but didn't know how to express. She sings about heart break and she is vivacious when she does.

I pulled up to the entrance of the canyon, turned down my blaring music, and unrolled my window. The guy at the booth recognized my car and then me; I was part of the production staff so I had "anytime" access to the canyon. He waived me through and I said "Good Evening" as I passed by him at 5 mph.

The road switched from painfully straight to nice and winding. I unrolled all my windows and took in the scenery and warm air as I wound my way around the top of the canyon. It was springtime which meant the ground had a green glow to it. The landscape was speckled with green scrubs and wiry looking greenish yellow trees. Any weeds and grass that grew in-between had a nice green tint to them. I knew within a month everything would turn to a burnt brownish red in the hot Texas sun.

I was starting to see glimpses of the red rocks of the canyon walls in the near distance. Some of the canyons sheer cliffs are eight hundred feet tall – that is equivalent to a building that is eighty stories high. The Palo Duro Canyon stretches over one-hundred-twenty miles: that is eighty stories tall and one-hundred-twenty miles long of God's beautiful unique creation.

As I went around the final curve that started my decent into the canyon, I clicked over to my *Watermark* CD and to the song *Captivate Us*. I needed to calm my blood before I walked out on that stage.

The soft plucking of the guitar was the perfect overture to my entrance into such a magnificent place. I concentrated on the lyrics:

> *Your face is beautiful, Ana Your eyes are like the stars*
> *Your gentle hands have healing, There inside the scars*

It was as if I heard those opening lines for the first time. They were so fitting to my situation I wanted to hear them again, so I started the song again.

Again the soft plucking of the guitar introduced the opening lyrics. This time I closed in on the line that caught my attention

> *Your gentle hands have healing, There inside the scars*

My physical scars were healing, but my emotional scars were still gaping wounds.

"Heal me Jesus," I whispered.

As I drove I continued to listen. I took in the beauty of my surroundings and the underscore of the music.

Captivate us Lord Jesus set our eyes on You
Devastate us with your presence falling down

I always felt God's presence among one of His most interesting landscape creations. Every time I went to visit the canyons, it was as if His hand felt closer when I was in His country. I suppose that is one of the many things that drew me to the canyons in the first place.

The canyons that evening were quiet. Not many people had made their way to the Texas Panhandle for camping as it was still early in the season.

I shifted my car into low gear for the long descent as I began reminiscing about my painful cry for help a few months prior. I suppose the drive down into the canyons was similar to my emotional journey.

When my accident occurred I was zeroed-in on survival and healing. The drama of dating, auditions, and the New York City bustle was a distant distraction. Just like the highway that stretched from the town of Canyon to *the* canyon, it was straight and focused - free of distraction. I was surrounded by family and friends helping me with my every emotional and physical need.

When I was set free to begin my new life it was as though I was at the top of the canyon where the beauty started. I could see the rock formations and the possibilities of something great in front of me, but then I started to notice the rattlesnakes, the cacti, the tarantulas, the sheer cliffs. I lost sight of the possibilities when I stepped on a scorpion and backed into a cactus. I turned to run, but instead of catching my breath and gathering my bearings I hurled my inertia forward. I quickly lost my way and my perspective. I started a dangerous decent that could lead to another devastating accident, or worse – death.

When I entered into the decent of my depression it was as if I entered the road to the canyon and instead of shifting down, I sped up. There were curves below and if I didn't get a hold of myself I would go flying over the edge and fall to my destruction. I knew the danger, but I couldn't pull my foot off the gas – it was stuck. I was speeding out of control.

My life had turned into a constant state of tears. I had lost control and if I didn't ask for help I would self-destruct.

When I first started crying, I accepted it as a natural reaction to my situation. I switched from crying out of physical pain to crying out of emotional pain.

As I started spending more and more time alone I was spending that time crying, grieving really, for my situation – my loss of function and my loss of anything I knew as normal. I allowed myself to grieve, but that grief wasn't leading anywhere. I started to cry in every moment I was alone – at home, in the car, in my office, in the pool, *everywhere.* At work, I would walk into a meeting and be perfectly fine – happy, enthusiastic, and somewhat focused. Walking down the hall and back to my private office the silent hysteria would start. My phone would ring and I would pull myself together for the conversation, but when I hung up I was again in an immediate ball of hysteria. Even scarier: I was getting good at hiding it.

What did I do about the pain? I tried to apply the emergency break without taking my foot off the gas. My emergency brake was in the form of chocolate cake.

I had discovered if I was eating chocolate cake, I wasn't crying. If I wasn't crying I was okay, right? So I turned my energy to chocolate cake. I started having chocolate cake for breakfast, for lunch, and again for dinner. The food of champions, I know, but it was working. Or so I thought.

The problem: with the emergency brake on, foot on the gas, and a steep descent, I was wearing through my brakes at a faster rate and there was still a sheer cliff and a sharp turn in front of me.

One night my crying went from bad to worse to dangerous. I crawled (literally on my hands and knees) to my bed and pulled myself up onto the mattress before I curled into the fetal position and cried. I cried until I was dry heaving. That's when the begging began.

I begged God to take my life. I pleaded with Him. I couldn't heal on my own. I couldn't find strength on my own. I couldn't go on *on my own.* I needed Him desperately. In that hour I asked Him to take me home.

In the midst of my hysteria and pleading, calmness washed over me. I could feel His presence.

You see, my journey wasn't over and my worldly mission had not been fulfilled. Instead of taking me, He filled me with His Holy Spirit and calmed my mind. It was in that moment I gave my situation over to Him.

I had more joy in this life He wanted me to experience before I crossed over to be with Him. I couldn't see it, but He could. Don't believe me? There is an entire book that outlines God's grace and love for you and me. If you're curious I encourage you to pick up the number one best seller: *The Bible.*

When I realized I was eating chocolate cake covered in tears, I knew I had a problem that needed to be addressed. Not only was my hinny growing right along with my depression, but I knew if I quit caring about my emotional health I would be doomed.

I needed help snapping out of my frenzy. I knew I had to do something about my situation, but I didn't know how, or who, to go to. I at least knew I needed to get help before I went over the edge.

The next morning, after my slice of cake of course, I went to find one of my favorite nurses. I cried for the entire thirty minute drive to her office. When I walked in, without an appointment, and the receptionist saw my despair behind my red swollen eyes she took me straight to the back and sat me in a private waiting room.

"I need to speak to Angela," I said with a painted smile on my face.

"I'll get her right away," the woman responded.

Within minutes Angela walked around the corner and I started bawling. I was actually crying in front of someone, which was strange.

"Adrienne what's wrong?"

"I'm not okay," I sobbed as she sat down next to me. "This is what my life has turned into. This is what I do." I shrugged my shoulders. "I cry and if I'm tired of crying I eat cake to shut myself up, but now I'm crying and eating cake at the same time." I paused as she reached for my hand. "I need help."

"I'm glad you came to see me," she said quietly. "We'll get you better. Are you ready to try an antidepressant?"

I cried harder.

"Adrienne, being on an antidepressant doesn't mean you are broken. Some people need extra vitamin D because their body is lacking in it, but does that mean they are broken?"

I shook my head "no".

"Exactly. It doesn't. You just need a different kind of vitamin."

I wrapped my arms around Angela and hugged her. I couldn't let go, which meant she couldn't either. She hugged me back. She held me and let me cry until I was done.

I started my antidepressant that day and within two weeks I was crying less. Within a month I wasn't really crying anymore at all. *And* I was craving a salad instead of cake.

My thoughts went back to the road in front of me. I was still in my descent nearing my first turn, and my first cliff if I missed the turn. I slowed from 20 mph to 8 mph. I steered my car around the turn. I continued my descent and turned another corner and another. There was no way I would have made the corner if I was going over 40 mph. I would have tumbled to my death.

I contemplated my cry for help and my gratitude toward Angela as I turned my Jeep into the theatre's parking lot. I drove to the front of the lot and parked my car in the closest space to the theatre entrance. I turned the car off and stepped out into the lonely lot. I was the only one there. The canyons were calm and it would have been silent if it weren't for the birds chirping in the distance.

I opened the door to the back seat and grabbed my blue tote bag before I slammed the door shut. I clicked the lock button on my fob. The car beeped and the sound bounced around the canyon as if the walls were welcoming me to its beautiful place. The birds hushed for a few moments as I made my way through the entrance and under the big iron sign that said *"Texas"*. I could feel the gravel grinding under my tennis shoes as I walked through the courtyard, not really in a hurry, but not doddling either.

The sky was a clear blue and the sun was sitting at an angle which told me I had one hour of sunlight, and another hour of daylight, before the canyons would turn black.

I walked up the handicap ramp and into the back of the theatre. When I reached the top I stared out over the sea of seats and down at the stage. Was that the stage of my last performance... *ever?* I thought about the question but I didn't want to consider the answer. At that moment I didn't really care about the answer. All I cared about was stepping on the stage and *dancing.*

I walked down the flights of stairs, passing the 1700 empty seats (seats I had been working on filling for the past six months) and climbed the five steps up to the stage. I walked over to stage right. I bent at my hips, stretching my hamstrings long, folding my body effortlessly to the ground. I set my bag down and pulled out my *Bose* speaker and then my iPod. I set my iPod on the stage between my bag and the speaker. I was still effortlessly bent at the hips as I rotated my thumb around in a circular motion as I went through my song list. I stopped at a familiar song and set the iPod in the speaker jack. I grabbed the remote control from my bag and stood back up. I walked to the center of the stage and glanced out over the vacant seats before I closed my eyes.

I could hear the chirping of a few birds, but other than that it was quiet and still. It was me and the stage and my imagination. With my eyes closed I started to visualize a crowd of people. They were hushed and waiting in anticipation for the music to begin. On the fifth row was a young girl sitting next to her mom. The girl was attentive and anxiously waiting for the dancer to begin. The mom was watching her daughter's anticipation. Just as I started to notice the facial features of the people sitting behind the mother daughter duo, I opened my eyes.

That wasn't what I wanted. I didn't want a crowd. I didn't want to perform. I wanted the exact opposite and exactly what I had – an empty auditorium. I wanted to be alone in that grand theatre on that grand stage among that grand setting. I wanted to dance for *me* and only me. I was after solace and peace – a sense of closure – definitely not an audience or a standing ovation.

With my eyes open, I planted my feet shoulder width apart. I extended my right arm, pointed the remote at the speaker, and pushed play. I took a deep breath and felt the warm air fill my lungs. The music started slowly. I let the music fill my ears and seep into my soul. I could hear the music, but not the lyrics. I could feel the freedom in the piano and the soft voice of a woman singing. The sound wasn't forced. It was natural and easy.

So I began to dance – natural and easy.

I bent at my waist and swung my upper body from the left and then to the right, letting my arms dangle loosely. I came back to a straight position before I rolled my frame in a circle, never moving my feet. I stood straight again.

Louder – I needed it louder. I pulled my remote from my bra and pointed it at the speaker. I not-so-patiently waited for the volume to increase before I returned the remote to its holder.

I started my movement again. I bent to the right and then to the left in a fluid flowing motion, my arms loosely following my body. I straightened before I rolled my shoulders up and around. As I completed the shoulder roll, I allowed my arms to reach for the sky. I fired my calf muscles and rose to *a relevé*. My muscles stretched and I expanded myself to take up as much space as I could. My entire body was coming to life. There I was – me, the music, and the stage – *my happy place.*

I looked at the sky through my stretched fingertips as I heard the lyrics *"and I stand so tall, just the way I'm supposed to be"*.

I shifted my weight to my left. I could no longer keep my feet in one place. I felt my body lean left as I stretched right - right foot pointed to the best of its mangled ability. I held my position on one leg as I raised my left arm up and over my head in a *combré*. My head dipped to my left - my neck extended and every muscle elongated to its max. I felt myself pause. I took a dancer's breath – an extended pause of beauty - before I took off.

I moved with the music. I glided across the stage to the right and then back across to the left. I tried to be mindful of my ankle, making all my grand movements in my upper body. I couldn't help myself as I started turning on my left leg – single turn – double turn – triple turn. Turn after turn after turn on my left leg. Deep inside I knew if I waivered I would roll my right ankle and possibly reinjure myself. But I couldn't stop. I didn't care. I was in a state of freeing euphoria. I kept moving. I kept turning. I kept dancing. I could taste the drug I had been without for so many months.

I stepped with my left foot and raised my right leg effortlessly into a *battement*. I could feel the air shift as my right leg kicked next to my right ear. My flexibility was incredible. It felt so good in fact, I did it again. I stepped with my left foot and raised my right leg to a grand *battement*. I slowly and in a very controlled fashion lowered my kick in slow motion until my feet were in *fifth* position. I bent my knees, and one good ankle, into a *plié* before I sprung off the stage into a *sissonne*, pushing myself into a jump using all the muscle in my left leg. I spread my legs into a grand split in mid-air. When I came back to the ground I was careful to land on my left foot only. I did it again and again and again until I gently shifted my weight to my right as I took another large step, or *pique*, onto my left foot and raised my right leg behind me, moving my body into a perfect *arabesque*.

I held the *arabesque* as I looked out and over my left finger tips. I pressed my shoulders down and my neck long. I could feel the muscles in my back cramping. I smiled at how wonderful the cramping felt. I began shifting my heel forward which rotated me as if I were on the top of a music box. I maintained my beautiful *arabesque*, not wavering in my movement. When I made a complete 360 degrees I lowered my right leg and found myself back in *fifth* position. I looked out over the seats. I was proud of my efforts.

Again. I thought, and so I did.

I created sequence after dancing sequence. I danced to my strengths and was mindful of my weaknesses. I protected my right ankle all while freeing my mind.

It wasn't flawless, but it was perfect.

I could feel the sweat that had started to build on my temples. It felt good. I continued dancing. The sweat began to drip onto the stage.

I stumbled…

My body went cold as I caught myself on my right foot. My heart skipped a beat as I realized I may have undone my past months of progress. I felt a sharp streak of pain shoot through my heart, not my ankle. I assessed my leg. I didn't hurt anything, but I knew it was time to stop. It was as if God was gently telling me *"Be still."*

I sat down right where I was and retrieved my remote. I pointed it at the speaker and flipped through the music. When I heard the familiar chords of song I once danced to I clicked the volume a little higher. I set the control next to me and I laid back on the warm stage. I stared at the sky as sweat dripped off my temple and onto the cooling ground. My muscles were tired and my mind was relaxed. I let myself soak in the lyrics.

But it's time for me to go home, It's getting late and dark outside
I need to be with myself in center, Clarity, peace, serenity

I laid there in center, clarity, peace, and serenity.

And big girls don't cry, Don't cry, Don't cry, Don't cry

It was a nice change to have sweat versus tears falling from my face.

231

Scene Forty-Three

A July evening in 2008 at the theatre, 1700 people in attendance, 150 cast & crew, Adrienne & Bill at the back of the theatre
(Eleven months *after* the accident)

"If it wasn't hard everyone would do it. It's the hard that makes it great."
–Tom Hanks

I was standing in the back of the theatre looking out over the sea of people when Bill walked up next to me. We stood in silence as we studied the crowd. He could sense my tension and my sadness. It was the crowd that was suffocating my heart.

"You okay?" he asked.

"Yes," I said with a smile, but he knew I was lying.

That night we had ten countries being represented throughout our audience, which also meant we had approximately twenty tour buses sitting in our parking lots. Our first parking lot had overflowed into the second and people were now parking on the road. We were at capacity. Seventeen hundred people had chosen to spend their hard earned money on a seat in order to witness the infamous *"Texas"*. And how did they know about *"Texas"*? Because of the two us standing in the back of the theatre. More importantly, why did they want come to the show? Because of our great marketing. Yes, *"Texas"* really was a rare jewel in the middle of Nowhere, America. It somehow captured the true essence of the West. It was our job to put butts in the seats, so that is what we did. That evening we were sold out.

"It's because of you all these people are here," Bill said.

I looked at him and smiled. "It wasn't just me," I countered. "I would argue we have a pretty good executive director," I said, referring to Bill who was our executive director.

232

"I just manage the bank account," he chuckled. "It takes a great marketing director to fill the seats." He paused. "Someday I think you will find standing in the back more gratifying than being on the stage." Bill turned to look at me. "Don't kid yourself, that standing ovation in a couple of hours is for you too."

Bill turned on his heel and left me alone to process his comments. I understood what he was telling me, but my heart was rejecting it.

There I stood in the back of the theatre success slapping me right between the eyes and a good friend pointing it out, but all I wanted was to be on that stage. We had traveled the country looking for the perfect talent. We had a great cast, crew, and team in the office. I was finding success with my marketing career, which I never thought I would use. But even with all the success it wasn't enough. Something was missing. My heart ached. I wanted to be on the stage. The stage was where I belonged.

As the overture began, the shuffling of program books and children ceased. It was a beautiful, calm, and unusually cool evening for a July performance. The stars hadn't yet started shining. Everyone was excited for the show to begin. I was the only one in the crowd who wasn't.

I needed open air – air away from the warmth of the stage lights and the smell of perspiration from the performers. I turned and walked away.

**"Good things come to those who ~~wait~~
work their asses off and never give up." –Zero Dean**

Our team that summer, of only three full time people, finished the season with our net sales at +254%. And Bill was right. It has taken me time, but today when I walk into a full auditorium I wonder who the brains were behind the operation. I credit the tireless staff as much as the talented performers for a job well done. It takes everyone at their best to pull off a successful performance, but it also takes an office team at their best to get people in the seats to witness the magic.

If you have a job that is behind the scenes, I would venture to say you are the glue that holds the operation together. I've learned that just because you aren't in the spotlight doesn't mean you don't deserve a standing ovation.

If you don't like the path you're on, choose a different path.

233

As I walked toward the cast and crew parking lot I could hear the actors on stage and the applause of the audience. I was headed for my car. I wanted my book and a quiet place to sit and read: a place away from the excitement.

I opened the passenger door of my car and grabbed *Eat, Pray, Love* from the seat. I walked over to the edge of the parking lot and sat down next to a storage building. I leaned my back against the warm brick and stretched my cowboy boots out in front of me. I opened my book to where I last left off. The receipt to my book purchase was my bookmark.

The author had me in the middle of Rome walking the ancient streets and eating delicious food - a far cry from the Texas Panhandle, a steak and baked potato.

I realized the irony in the book and why I related to the author: it was another "average" woman who was on a search for healing.

I needed something to look forward to. I needed some excitement. I closed my book and looked at the cover. At that very moment I should have been in the open waters of the Mediterranean, dancing on a cruise ship. I could have been headed for Rome... not sitting on the hot asphalt in the back of a parking lot in a hole in the ground someone called a "canyon".

Something swept over me: *can I only go to Europe on a performance contract?* I contemplated my question and my situation. I knew I couldn't dance my way around Europe, nor could I backpack my way around, but what about how the author did it? She went to Rome for three months, found a language teacher, and let life take her where it wanted. She was a recovering heart-broken-woman... *so was I.*

Did I want to go to Rome? It sounded nice, but I didn't have any desire to learn Italian. I had studied Spanish in high school and college... *What about Spain?*

I could book a trip to Spain and stay for a couple of months. My ankle couldn't handle a full day of touring, but I thought about a language school. I could sit for half the day and learn the language and the culture, and spend the rest of the day just living.

I knew nothing about Spain other than it was in Europe and they spoke Spanish.

I had $8000 in my savings account. Was that enough? Could I seriously limp my way around Spain? Is there even a language school that offers what I was looking for?

I set my book down next to me and pulled my knees up to my chest. I liked the idea. Could I do it? Could I *physically* do it?

I watched a tarantula walk by in front of me.

Act II

Scene Forty-Four

Madrid, Spain, August 2008
(One year *after* the accident)

"Never forget only dead fish swim with the stream."
–Malcolm Muggeridge

I walked off the plane and into the terminal. I had made it to Madrid - my first international flight and I was completely alone. I was both terrified and proud of my gutsy move. I had a two-hour layover before I boarded my final flight to *Sevilla, España.* —

Why Spain? Because I finally had the nerve to pick a place on the map, throw caution to the wind, and go. Honestly, I had wanted new experiences that would take my mind off my situation and give me new opportunities to re-realize the world was my oyster.

When I booked my ticket I wasn't chasing a job, a dream, or a guy. I was chasing happiness and in many ways searching my soul for what happiness actually looked like. I was looking for a reason to smile. I was also seeking strength in my character.

Up until that flight my ankle had dictated my every move – literally and figuratively – for the past year. Just the idea of being on Spanish soil made me feel as though *I,* not my ankle, was back in control of my destiny.

I walked through the terminal reading the signs. They were in Spanish and I smiled in terror.

I found a coffee shop. Stepped up to the counter and ordered. *"Uno café por favor."* I smiled at the woman behind the counter, proud of my Spanish. She responded in a perfectly beautiful accent, yet I had no idea what she said. I handed her my credit card, not saying anything.

She swiped my card and handed the plastic and the receipt back to me. I looked at the paper, but all I could translate was the international language of numbers. I had no idea how many American dollars I had paid for a single cup of coffee, but I didn't care. I stuffed my card and my receipt back in my wallet. I picked up my coffee and selected a seat where I could comfortably "people watch".

It was nine o'clock in the morning and the terminal was busy. I took a sip of my first Spanish coffee and closed my eyes to savor the dark zesty Spanish flavor. I kept my eyes closed until the weight of my head dipped forward and jerked me back into consciousness. I shook my head from side-to-side trying to rouse myself and took another sip.

I desperately slurped down the rest of the black java before I walked back to the counter and ordered a second cup. The girl behind the counter raised her eyebrows. I responded by handing her my credit card.

I sat in the same seat and took another long sip. Halfway through that second cup I set my elbows on the table and leaned my chin into my hands. I closed my eyes once again. Again I drifted off in seconds. I fell asleep until the weight of my head knocked my arms out of balance. I glanced at my watch. I had an hour before my flight. I picked up my coffee and shuffled my way to my next gate.

When I found the gate, I sat on the floor and leaned my head back against the wall. I slept.

My excitement meant I hadn't slept a wink during the nine hour flight from one continent to the other. On top of the traveling, I hadn't slept the night before I left for my two month adventure. I was too excited and too anxious. I had exactly two months – which translated to eight weeks or sixty days or 1,440 hours or 86,400 minutes – to let life lead me where it wanted.

I awoke to a gate attendant's voice and the movement of people. The sign above the announcer's head was flashing the words "*Sevilla*". I stood and fell in line with the horde of people trying to board the plane, but there was no plane. Instead we shuffled through a sliding glass door and onto a bus. I prayed I was headed in the right direction as the bus took off across the runway. We were headed for a smaller plane parked out on the ramp.

I looked at the gentleman next to me. He was dressed in a beautiful navy blue suit with a pinkish colored shirt and light blue tie. The suit was fully fitted to his thin European frame. The pant legs fit nicely across his posterior and hugged his legs all the way down to his black shiny shoes that were pointed at the toe. The shoes were made of high quality leather, obviously very expensive. I let my eyes follow his physique back up his expensive suit and to his wavy black gelled hair. The shade of his hair was the exact shade of the black leather on his shoes and just as shiny. He had chocolate eyes that were so dark they were almost black. As an entire package he was in the neighborhood of five feet eight inches and maybe 160 lbs – a beautifully perfect Spanish specimen.

He noticed my stare and I smiled at the attention he gave me in return. Not knowing what to say, I verified I was headed to the correct plane, "*¿Sevilla, España?*"

He responded "*Sí*" and gave me a smile.

I was obviously a sleep deprived foreigner with circles under my eyes and greasy unwashed hair that was tied up in a wad – not a pony-tail, not a bun, but a wad on the top of my head. I had on yellow cargo capri pants that were baggy to begin with, but after hours of traveling they were a solid size too big. I also had on a white fitted t-shirt that had a drip of coffee down the front. My compression stockings (on both legs) served as my socks for my bright colored orange tennis shoes. I was far from a stylish former beauty queen and obviously "not from these parts".

I would later learn Europeans didn't understand the American obsession with tennis shoes. Beautiful stylish shoes are a Spanish fascination in which Spaniards take a lot of pride. You can quickly spot a Spaniard from an American by their shoes alone. Well, that and the volume in our loud American opinions.

I quickly learned "the look" of Europeans and tried to adopt their style. I recalled my former New York roommate's lesson on city-living. While I didn't particularly like Suzie, she had taught me a valuable lesson in personal security: "Don't go to New York, let New York come to you." I may not have been in New York, but I was in a foreign country and it was just as important to be aware of my surroundings and watch my back at all times. "Blending in" wasn't a negative thing, especially when traveling alone and in country that doesn't speak your native tongue. I quickly took in the "look" of the Spaniards, letting "Spain come to me, instead of me going to Spain". I had started by taking in the "sites" of the handsome Spaniard.

The bus arrived alongside the plane. It was a big plane, but not as big as the 747 I flew across the ocean. The people on the bus unloaded and the Spaniard gestured *ladies first* insisting I go before him. I said "*gracias*" and batted my eyes. He smiled.

I followed the crowd up the stairs and onto the plane. I found my seat and stuffed my backpack in the overhead bin. I sat in my seat, buckled my seat belt, and laid my head against the window. I was asleep before the plane took off.

"The greatest lesson in life is that you are responsible for your own."
–Oprah Winfrey

When I arrived in *Sevilla* I spotted a man outside of baggage claim holding a sign with my name on it. I was thankful I had paid my language school an extra one-hundred American dollars to have a driver waiting for me upon my arrival. The $100 covered my driver's fee to deliver me to my school-appointed-apartment where they had placed me for the weeks ahead. Given the expense for my ride I was expecting at least a thirty minute drive.

I crawled into the backseat while my driver threw my suitcase in the trunk.

After five minutes he pulled up in front of an apartment building and turned off the car. "*Estamos aqui*," he said. It didn't matter what language you spoke, when someone charges you $100 for a five minute ride you know you are being taken advantage of. I was on the outskirts of *Sevilla* in a lower income area. I wasn't thrilled with the setting, but I decided I wasn't in the right mindset to pass any judgment.

I was so tired I didn't have the energy to argue. I just wanted to find a bed. I knew I could reassess my situation after I got some sleep.

For $100 I let my driver carry my bag up the stairs. He introduced me to my new roommates and handed me a key and a packet of info. I said "*adios*" before I closed my bedroom door and crawled into my new bed fully dressed. I put a pillow under my right foot to elevate it and reduce the swelling. I laid back. My eyes were so heavy I was asleep before my head had time to sink into the mattress.

I was exhausted. I only budged when it was time to shuffle down the hall and use the restroom. I had no lock on my bedroom door and I didn't have the energy to care. At one point, someone barged into my room and started speaking Spanish to me. I had no idea what they were saying and instead of responding I rolled over and went back to sleep. I slept for almost 24 hours.

When I finally awoke, I took a long stretch and opened the blinds on my window. My view was of another apartment building across a concrete courtyard – not much to look at. There was nothing lovely about the area. It felt industrial, cheap, and like I was on the wrong side of the tracks. But, I didn't really care. I was on a new adventure. I was looking for a fresh start and I told myself "if this is where it was going to begin, then so be it."

I walked down the hallway and locked myself in the bathroom, grateful for the lock. I brushed my teeth and studied myself in the mirror. The girl staring back smiled with a mouth full of toothpaste. *"It's going to be a good day,"* I told her as toothpaste dribbled down my chin. I was excited *and* nervous.

I showered and dressed quickly. Class was scheduled to start in an hour and I had no idea how to get to my new school.

I sat on my bed and studied my city map. My school was just off the city center. It was a long walk from my apartment, *too long*, but I saw a bike rental not far from my new apartment – approximately four blocks.

I grabbed my backpack and cautiously walked down the stairs being mindful of my ankle.

Once outside, I inhaled the fresh Mediterranean air as I welcomed the warm sun on my skin. It was 8 a.m. I felt rested and ready to explore my grand city.

When I made it to the bike rental I was thoroughly relieved, as was my already aching ankle. It appeared there were a series of bike rentals around the city with bike routes that crisscrossed throughout. All I had to do was slide my credit card through a machine, punch in a number, and pull the bike out of its slot. It was somewhere in the neighborhood of $2 for the first hour and then fifty cents for every thirty minutes after that. Given my limited walking ability, it was a smoking deal.

I selected my bike, pulled it from the machine, and set out in the correct direction. As I pedaled, I took in the sites of my ancient modern city of old buildings blended with new. People were emerging from apartments and cafes freshly dressed for the start of their Spanish work week. The people were tiny compared to my tall frame and most of them had long black hair that nicely outlined their olive skin.

I was happy to be among new people. I loved the idea I was *a nobody* in a city far away from my troubles.

As I pedaled back and forth across the city (making several wrong turns) I finally figured out many alley-ways and sidewalks were also "roads" I was looking for on my map. I had allowed extra time to find my new school and I had needed every second after the multitude of detours I had taken.

When I finally did find the school, I locked my bike (using the lock built into my rental) next to the beautiful and ancient Moroccan-style building. The building was made of white stucco while the arched windows were framed in dark wood and colorful tile. The architecture seemed to have a heavy Arabic influence that mixed nicely with the Spanish cobblestone streets. Inside, the building proved to be just as anciently beautiful. Many of the walls were covered with Indian-influenced tile-work of beautiful mosaics that covered the majority of the walls throughout the fourteen tiny classrooms. But it was the massive amounts of woodwork around the windows that made the building so richly dramatic. In many ways, the building's style reminded me of *The Sultan*, from the Disney movie *Aladdin*.

But it was the Spaniards, inside the building, that made the environment so warm and welcoming. The instant I stepped through the front doors I could feel the excitement in the learning environment. The bustling movement of people in the tiny entryway was contagious. Several students were hustling up the stairs and to their classrooms while I stepped inside the office to check-in and obtain my room assignment.

I was directed to the second floor where I would join eight other students from around the world. I smiled when I learned I was the only American in my class. To add to the fun, my teacher was from heaven: her name was *Cielo* which literally translates to "heaven".

Cielo stood at five feet four inches and had a curvy frame that could have rivaled Jessica Rabbit's. She was gorgeous with long curly black hair, and her personality made her even more exotically beautiful. She was enthusiastic and animated as she taught, making it as much a performance as a Spanish lesson. She would have been a perfect contender for the Miss America Pageant.

She spoke zero English which served me well. I couldn't cheat by asking for clarification of my lessons in English, something I often did in college. I was fully immersed in Spanish from 9 a.m. until 2 p.m. five days a week. I knew I would learn *and I did*.

My ankle problems were disappearing as I couldn't properly explain what had happened, in Spanish anyway, and so I began letting my sob-story disappear into my past. Yes, the pain remained and my ankle reconstruction struck a lot of curiosity, but people didn't dwell on it. My acquaintances didn't really care. So while they didn't spend time judging me on my ankle, I slowly quit judging myself.

I began making friends from around the world, many of whom were also traveling on their own. Several of us teamed up to go on weekend outings to various corners of Spain. Two of us even adventured across the Strait of Gibraltar and over to Morocco.

Morocco proved to be an uncomfortable journey and a subject matter which could lend itself to a whole different book. Why? For starters I was visiting North Africa during Ramadan. It was also during the months leading up to the 2008 U.S. presidential election when worldly controversy was surrounding the candidates of Obama and McCain. Looking out my hotel window and watching the military patrol the beaches with AK-47 rifles didn't put me at ease either. Finally, traveling as a single American woman was a controversial subject for many Moroccan men who were our tour guides.

To add to my discomfort, there was a bomb that exploded somewhere in the country but I didn't know where because all the news stations were in Arabic. When I couldn't get a phone call out of Morocco and over to the U.S. I was ready to leave. Basically, my four-day Moroccan experience was an unfortunate journey as it left me with the lack of desire to ever return to an "eastern" country.

I liked Spain and the warmth of its people. I liked that the workday didn't start until 9 a.m., and even then everyone broke for a late morning coffee or beer (yes, beer) at 11 a.m. Lunch wasn't until 2 p.m. The country spent time dining with friends or family and then retired to a long *siesta*. The workday resumed at 4:30*ish* and went until 8*ish*. Dinner wasn't until 10 p.m.

Spaniards seemed to enjoy the flow of life. There was no such thing as "eating on the run" or getting a coffee "to go" as in America. Anytime you put something in your mouth it was also an excuse to be a member of the community. It was an excuse to slow down and enjoy life versus rushing through it.

But I quickly learned Spanish life wasn't without its crime and threats on my personal security.

My first night "out to dinner" with my new friends was an evening of bar hopping. "Bar hopping" in Spain didn't mean the same thing as "bar hopping" when I was in college. Spanish bar hopping meant we were sampling the cuisine not drinking ourselves into intoxication. We were simply sampling the small plates of food, or *tapas*, each bar claimed as their specialty. It was also a chance for me to get to know my new friends: one from Holland, one from Taiwan, and one from Hungary. That first week we quickly formed a friendship that lasted for the entire duration of my time in Spain. Sadly, I was the only one of our foursome that was learning her second language. My studious friends were learning their third and fourth languages, which is why I was able to form a friendship with them. They all spoke English like it was their native language.

One night after dinner (around 11 p.m.), I said "*chao*" to my friends and pulled a bike out of the rental-rack. I had a fifteen minute ride to the outskirts of the city where I could return my bike to another rental station and walk the four blocks to my apartment. I had been in *Sevilla* for a week and had not ventured anywhere beyond my apartment except in broad daylight. While I knew some Spanish, I didn't know enough. Since I was staying in an area of the city that made me uneasy, I decided to not push my luck. I had allowed myself a week to learn the heartbeat of the city before I started pacing myself with the flow. But I didn't travel to Spain to be a hermit crab, or a wall flower.

Once my bike was locked back into the rental station, I pulled my purple backpack out of the bicycle basket and tossed it over my head allowing it to slide down my back. I secured the straps on my shoulders and I started in the direction of my apartment.

The neighborhood was quiet. No one was on the street (a drastic contrast from the bustling city center). It was dark. The few streetlights cast shadows on the vacant sidewalk, but no lights were near enough to ease my cautious mind.

As I started my brisk five minute walk from the bike rental to the stairs of my apartment, I had an uneasy feeling. I felt like someone was watching me.

I glanced over both of my shoulders seeing no one, but I *knew* someone was there. I could feel their eyes.

The blood in my veins warmed as I broke into a cold sweat. I kept walking. My sixth sense was on full alert.

246

I unhooked my bag from my left shoulder and swung my backpack around to my chest. I unzipped the bag and reached inside. Not stopping my stride, I dug through the contents. I blindly felt around the bottom of my bag. I wanted a weapon.

Just as my fingers felt the plastic of a mechanical pencil, I noticed three men forty paces in front of me: three men trying not to be noticed. Two of them snuck from the shadows of a bus stop to the protection of a dumpster next to the sidewalk. The other man stayed at the bus stop trying to make himself blend into the darkness. I immediately knew they were stalking me.

I pulled the pencil out of my bag and put it in my other hand. I reached my right hand back into the bowels of my backpack and groped for a second weapon. My fingers found a ball point pen and I pulled it out. I zipped my bag and flung it back over my shoulders. I gripped the pencil in one hand and the pen in the other. I clinched my fists tight as I made the conscious decision that if any of them came after me I would jam the writing utensils into their flesh. First, I would go for their eyeballs, then their side, aiming for any fleshy middle area that would lead to a vital organ. I knew where to aim because I was prepared.

I had numerous and continuous conversations with the infamous Mickey DeHook, my Miss Kansas publicist and greatest advocate, who was also a former police officer with a lot of respect for busting one of the biggest drug smuggling rings in the United States. He had taken it upon himself to make sure *his* Miss Kansas knew some basic skills in self-defense.

I tried to keep my breathing calm and my mind focused. I couldn't run fast enough to get away. My gimp slowed me too much. I didn't want to turn and walk the other direction, giving them a chance to storm me from behind. I charged forward, walking with my bitchiest, tallest, New York attitude I could muster through my fear. I threw my shoulders back and put a scowl on my face. I stomped toward them, pushing the insecurity from my mind. My adrenaline was turning my blood to a boil. I was prepared to scream. I would go for the eye sockets, and then the scrotum, *yes a change of plan.*

As they tried to hide, I looked directly at one of them who peered at me from behind the dumpster. Our eyes met. I glared at him and tightened my grip on my weapons. I knew he had seen me see him.

As I got closer I could tell they were all shorter than I was, shorter by at least six inches: an advantage. I decided to make their presence known so I yelled in their direction, using my best Spanish accent. I shouted sternly, "I see you!" They continued to hide so I shouted again, and then again. Still they hid in the shadows of darkness. I finally yelled "I phoned the *policia!*"

Finally, one of them stepped out from behind the dumpster into full view, pretending he didn't know who I was talking to. I stomped past him and made a fierce greeting to the other two.

I had blown their cover. While they still acted as though they wanted to attack, one of them looked down at my synched fists and saw I had "weapons". In the dark it was hard to tell what I held in my hands, but their interest in me and whatever they could take ceased as I stomped past them.

When I was five strides beyond the bus stop I turned to walk backwards, glaring at them as I continued on my way. One man finally threw his hands up in the air as if gesturing "okay okay we get it".

My heart raced as I walked the final block to my apartment. My hands were sweaty and cramping from my vice-grip on my pen and pencil.

When I got inside my apartment I was shaking. I let out a sigh as I tried to slow my racing heart.

As you can imagine, I didn't sleep that night. The next morning, when the sun was in full view, I made my way back to the school. When I arrived, I marched straight into the office demanding to talk to the person in charge.

I explained to the woman what happened the night before and while the men's actions were not her fault I blamed the school for their housing placement. I asked to be moved to a different location. When they told me it would take two weeks I looked at them and said "That's not good enough. Do better."

The nice Spanish ladies realized this New York nasty-diva wasn't going anywhere and was going to cause a daily nightmare until they moved her into a new housing facility... I had a new address by that evening.

If New York taught me anything it was to be tough, to not take "no" for an answer, and always put my safety first! And thanks to Mickey, I knew how to defend myself.

"The greatest gift of life is friendship, and I have received it."
–Hubert Humphrey

248

When I moved into my new housing I not only gained an awesome location adjacent to the city center, but I also gained a "house mom" and four roommates. My house mom, Maria, was nothing more than a Spanish grandma that insisted on cooking, cleaning, and doing our laundry. Every breakfast and every lunch we were expected to be at Maria's dining room table to share a meal and talk about our plans for the day. Maria spoke zero English so she was patient with me as I learned her language, and her city. Despite our forty-year age difference, Maria and I quickly learned our two favorite topics to discuss were *zapatos y hombres*. She and I would giggle as I described my adventures as it related to *shoes and men* in her beautiful city of *Sevilla*. The reality, it was a fun topic for both of us and it gave me the chance to expand my vocabulary.

The one time I tried to carry on a conversation about food proved to be a complete disaster. One of the meals Maria prepared was *tortillas*, and a Spanish *tortilla* is nothing like a Mexican *tortilla*. Instead of a flour or corn *Mexican tortillas,* that are used to wrap around food, a *Spanish tortilla* is very similar to an American omelette. Since Maria had never been to Mexico, or the U.S., I tried to bring the Americas to her by explaining the difference between our country's *tortillas*. She kept looking at me with a puzzled look on her face. It wasn't until I moved on with my travels did I realize I was explaining Mexican *tortillas* are made with flowers instead of flour.

Scene Forty-Five

Seville, Spain, Fall 2008
(Fourteen months *after* the accident)

"Enjoy the little things in life for one day you will look back and realize they were the big things." –Kurt Vonnegut

My typical Spanish day is one I look back on and smile, even envy from time to time. My schedule was undemanding and of my choosing. Yes, I was attending school, but if I decided not to go I didn't. But, I loved my teacher from heaven and my friends from around the world. I also loved stretching my mind. My classes kept my mind active while my afternoons allowed me time to explore life - life in its rawest form.

I often meandered my way around the dozens of cobblestone streets, watching people and admiring the window displays. My favorite displays were a toss-up between the numerous bridal gown boutiques and the boutiques that sold women's hand-fans.

As I studied the hundreds of bridal gowns (from outside) I often found myself wondering what kind of gown I would end up wearing in my lifetime. I realized if I was dreaming of wedding gowns it meant deep inside my heart I knew God had created a man for me that would love me *and my ankle.*

I also loved the hand-fans. Since it was the hot Mediterranean a fan was a necessity. As I explored numerous fan boutique shops I admired the elaborate craftsmanship of the traditional Spanish fans for women. I saw fans that were several hundred euros (approaching thousands) made out of hand-carved wood and hand-painted intricate detailing. I also found plastic fans that cost less than five euros. After I had shopped all the fan boutiques I could find, testing out my own ability to fling the fans open with dramatic flair, I settled on a yellow fan with a hand-painted butterfly across its wooden flesh. It set me back approximately thirty euros. It definitely wasn't the fanciest fan, but one I was proud to carry with me fanning myself in synchronization with the native Spanish women.

Until I had arrived in Spain I assumed a hand-fan was a thing-of-the-past and something only used by performers on stage. In fact, during my year as Miss Kansas my favorite song I ever sang was "I Feel Pretty". I used a hand-fan to add to my dramatic interpretation of the song, but my favorite part was when I made the audience laugh as I sang my closing lyric *"And so pretty Miss America should just resign."*

When I wasn't window shopping and I wanted to work on my Spanish vocabulary, I would weave in and out of grocery stores and small markets to study the produce and the proper words that went with the fruits and vegetables.

When I felt homesick I would find a gelato stand and order a small cup of my favorite flavor, which always had the word "chocolate" in its name. After I finished my gelato at one tiny shop I would find another and then another. I tasted my fair share of gelato as I wondered the streets of *Sevilla.*

To combat the gelato I spent hours riding my rental bike up and down the famous Guadalquivir River as well as back-and-forth over the bridges that connected the city from one side to the other. I also sat along the river's edge and read books or studied my Spanish vocabulary. On days in which my ankle felt exceptionally well I would tour a museum or famous building.

I spent my weekends (when I didn't have class) on board a high-speed train so I could visit the beach and other sister-cities in the Andalucía region. Minus the one night with the three *hombres*, I felt safe in Spain. It was a beautiful country with gracious people, good food, and an enriching culture.

But when my ankle hurt, which it did more often than not, I would belly up to a bar and order a *tinto vino.* As I sat alone, sipping my red wine, the bartenders would keep my glass full and slice me thin slivers of *jamón*, a ham delicacy of the region.

Over time I got lost in my healing and I would venture to say I was in perfect harmony with life as I was finding my way back to happiness.

I was also learning that while I was enjoying the rich culture and beautiful sites I had no one to share it with. Yes, I had my friends, but I knew at the end of my Spanish journey I would say "good-bye" to those friends and then see them only on Facebook.

I still had more lessons to learn and more obstacles to overcome.

Scene Forty-Six

Seville, Spain, October 2008

(Fourteen months *after* the accident)

"The greatest glory in living lies not in never falling but in rising every time we fall." –Nelson Mandela

My ankle was achy and stiff. I desperately needed a pool for some long overdue water therapy. I considered swimming in the river with the locals, but that didn't seem like the brightest of bright ideas. There was still crime in my beautiful new city and I didn't want to be mugged nor did I want to deal with the consequences of someone running off with my purse while I was frolicking in the muddy water.

Giving up on the water therapy idea, I decided to take a city bus tour. The open-air double-decker bus gave me a chance to rest my ankle, but still feel like I was exploring the city.

I climbed the stairs of the bus and selected a row in the middle. A row I could have all to myself. I sat down and gratefully propped my foot on the seat next to me. It felt good to get off my feet. My ankle was swollen and my legs were exhausted.

We snaked our way around the ancient city of *Sevilla*. The warm breeze on my hot skin was refreshing and I was immediately pleased with my decision. I snapped pictures of the beautiful architecture on display, but realizing I would never actually print the pictures I turned the camera around and began snapping selfies. Even before selfies came into vogue I had figured out how to perfectly frame myself in a shot.

I listened to the tour guide as he described his city's history. I enjoyed the sound of his articulate voice and the beauty of the language, but given he was speaking in rapid-fire Spanish I only understood portions of it. I didn't really care. It felt nice to be sitting. I was tired and my ankle was swollen so I surrendered to being an ignorant gringo who was along for a joy ride. I was focused on observing the buildings and the people while I relaxed. I didn't have a care in the world. No appointments. No obligations. I was just *being*. Minus my achy joint it was lovely. I was on a new continent, learning a new language, meeting new people, and immersing in a new culture. I was pleased with myself and my more recent life choices.-

The bus turned onto a long narrow street, barely wide enough to allow for the double-decker mammoth. We were in an older part of *Sevilla* which I had yet to see and which also caught my interest. It was another beautiful street of Spanish and Moroccan culture that had been melted together by centuries of the warm sun beating down on the cultures, blending the two.

I turned my ear to the tour guide and began translating to myself. I was picking out a few Spanish words, enough to make out he was talking about the Mediterranean architecture and history of the area which was heavily impacted by the gypsies. (The word "gypsy" is given to a community of immigrants who are believed to have originated from Egypt, but have a dense population in the Andalucía region. Given that *Sevilla* was the heart of Andalucía, the city was engulfed in gypsy influence and culture.)

I noticed up ahead there was a lot of commotion around one particular building. There were people coming and going. The women had their hair pulled back in tight buns and were carrying bags. As we got closer, I noticed a sign above the door that read *Bailar Flamenco*.

My heart stopped as I registered what was going on inside that building. The bags swung over the Spaniards' shoulders were their *dance* bags which no doubt contained their flamenco shoes.

It was a flamenco dance school and I was in the heart of the gypsy culture, the birthplace of flamenco… *and I couldn't even take a class*. I felt anger bubble in my stomach and tears well my eyes.

My breath shortened as I took small gasps of air. I wanted off the bus. I wanted to run.

But I couldn't move. My legs were as heavy as lead. My soul was trapped inside the shell of my broken body. My carefree bus tour had placed me in the middle of my nightmare and reminded me of what I had lost.

Had I not been so stupid to jump on a horse I would have been traveling the Mediterranean as a performer and not as a wrecked person searching for happiness. Had my performance travels landed me in *Sevilla* that was the very neighborhood where I would have spent all my time. I would have learned the flare of flamenco with the best teachers in the world. I would have been studying Flamenco dance, *not* the Spanish language.

I looked over at my swollen ankle lying on the bench beside me. My ankle couldn't handle the stomping of flamenco nor the high-heels and I knew it.

I allowed myself one tear.

The tour didn't stop, it didn't even pause. The whole universe felt heavy, like I was in quick sand. I felt myself sinking into sadness, but it didn't seem to affect the bus or the world around me. Instead, it continued along its path as I sat silently fighting back anger and confusion, trying to breathe.

Just as the bus continued forward, so did my life...

My life had changed and I was searching for acceptance. But would I ever find it? I ran away to Spain looking for a distraction from my situation, yet in the midst of my search the pain hunted me down and slapped me in the face. I was learning you can't run. You must face whatever it is that is ailing you or it will follow you to the ends of the earth.

I dug deep inside my mind and *made* myself find a silver lining. I told myself: *if not for my injury, I would have never made it to Sevilla. Sevilla* was one of my best decisions I had made for myself. Whether or not that was the truth, it was the truth that I needed to believe.

I tried to turn my attention back to the beautiful city that was spread out before me, but I couldn't focus. I was numbly staring into space, blinded by the tears in my eyes. I felt alone. My mind was dead. I was haunted with sorrow for myself and my situation.

I dug deeper into my willpower. I needed to heal. I *wanted* to heal.

I began counting my blessings. I thought about my family, my new marketing career, and the fact I had two feet. I had a lot to be thankful for.

I desperately needed to move on with my life and I was ready to look my nightmare between the eyes *and beat it.* On that bus I made a pact with myself: I would face my hurt and attend a flamenco performance before I left Spain *and I would enjoy it whether I wanted to or not.*

As I continued swimming through my sorrow of inner dialogue, the bus wound its way back to the city center: my body riding along, but my mind floating in a world of sadness. It wasn't until we cruised by the *Universidad de Sevilla* and *The Alfonso Hotel* did I mentally rejoin the tour.

The tour guide listed off the dozens of celebrities who had stayed within the stone walls of *The Alfonso*. In fact, just weeks before my bus tour Madonna had been a guest.

My mind continued to fight me as my inner voice *said "if not for your accident, you would have been one of those celebrities"*.

I tried to silence my negativity by focusing on the hotel, not the people who walked the halls.

The guide described *The Alfonso*, but it needed no description. It was beautiful. A Spanish gem to be admired. The hotel's grand Mediterranean architecture and water fountain at the entrance was what first caught my eye. I also liked the dozen Spanish bellmen standing around the grounds waiting to help their high-dollar guests. The men were beautiful, *and* Spanish, which meant they were rather fun to admire.

As the bus circled around the back of the hotel I glanced over the stone wall. From my second story vantage point I noticed a beautiful pool. The water was so blue and inviting. I could almost feel its cool refreshment from on top of my bus.

Surrounding the pool were palm trees and umbrellas which shadowed the chaise lounges with white fluffy cushions and blue towels perfectly rolled. The lawn was beautifully manicured and to top it off there was a pool boy delivering drinks to his tanned guests. I was so mesmerized and envious. I wanted to be there. I wanted to lie in my bikini basking in the warm sun. I wanted to sip on a cocktail and go for a swim. What made those celebrities any better than me? I was Miss Kansas for crying out loud.

Suddenly I had an idea. Okay, maybe it was not the best idea, but it was an idea.

I decided the next day I would walk into the hotel as though I was staying there. I would find the pool and take my place next to the other bathing beauties. Those folks didn't have anything on me. Besides, I desperately needed a pool for my physical therapy (my justification).

I told a couple of my classmates about my premeditated afterschool activity of the day. I asked some of them if they wanted to go with me, but apparently my plan was too much of an adrenaline rush for their blood.

"What if you get caught?" several of them asked. Honestly, I wasn't worried about it. I would play it off as though I was a student at the university and my parents were in town for a visit.

So after class I said my good-byes, hopped on my bike, and rode over to *The Alfonso*. All I had to do was find the pool and strip to my bathing suit. No one would ask any questions, I was positive.

I parked my bike around the corner from the hotel and locked it to a fence. I walked up the tree-lined pathway holding my shoulders back and my neck tall. I was channeling Miss Kansas. I was walking with confidence like I owned the place. I walked past Spanish bellman #1 and shot him a smile. He smiled back and gave me a gentleman's nod. As I walked past Spanish bellmen numbers two, three, and four I said "*hola*" and batted my eyes. They greeted me and one held open the door to the grand hotel entrance.

"*Gracias,*" I said with my best accent.

The hotel was even more beautiful on the inside. The tile covering the walls was intricate and stunning while the wood beams were massive and beautiful. I could even see my reflection in the brilliantly polished marble floors.

Wow, this really is a hotel for the royals, I thought to myself.

As I walked through the lobby I took in the people as well as the workers. I nonchalantly sized up my surroundings. There was a large wooden archway I walked under. Straight ahead was a sitting area with a garden. To the right were the restrooms and to the left was a long corridor that led to the bottom level hotel rooms. I went left.

As I walked down the long marble hallway, I took notice of the room numbers. I needed a number just in case someone asked which room I was staying in. I needed a name too, but I wasn't about to go that far.

I continued down the hallway and at the very end I saw a sign on the door: *La Pascina.* I had found the pool. I pushed through the door and stepped into a beautiful garden. The garden was so manicured I guarantee someone had trimmed the grass with a pair of scissors and polished the stones with a toothbrush. I followed the path around the corner and there it was… *la pascina.* The pool was even more stunning in person. It was so blue I knew it made the sky jealous.

"*La pascina es muy bonita.*" I whispered to myself.

I calmly strutted over to one of the lounges, set down my bag, and striped off my shirt. I had on my royal blue bikini. The same bikini I wore when I won the swimsuit competition at Miss Kansas. It was classy and beautiful.

I sat down and took off my tennis shoes before I slid my pants off. I leaned back on my lounge and closed my eyes.

This is the life. Madonna, you have nothing on me (except a room number).

After a couple of deep breaths I came back to reality and told myself the moment may not last long. The pool boy was looking in my direction and I knew it was a matter of minutes before he came over to take my drink order.

I calmly got up and walked to the edge of the pool. I sat down to feel the water temperature, which was perfect. I slid in.

The water felt even more amazing with my whole body immerged. It felt as though the pool water was purified soft water. My skin was smooth and I felt like a slippery fish when I ducked under the water, pushed off the side, and started my swim to the deep end. My body was immediately screaming *thank you Adrienne.*

I got to the other side and pushed off to swim back to the shallow end. The cool water and the flutter kick felt nice on my swollen joint.

As I swam back to my starting point I noticed the pool boy approaching.

When I reached the shallow end I dunked my head under the water and slicked my wet hair back as I offered him a smile.

"May I get you something," he asked in perfect English.

"No, I'm fine thank you."

"Are you a guest here?" he asked.

"Yes." I responded, stunned he would ask such a ridiculous question.

"What room number are you in?"

I gave him my made-up room number.

"Name?"

"Rosel." I didn't have a name, so I gave him my real name.

I continued blabbering on as I do when I'm nervous. I told him my parents were staying at the hotel and I was a student at the university. He listened as I dug my hole deeper. I explained my parents were out site-seeing and I decided to stay behind and enjoy the pool. He turned and walked away.

I watched him walk back to the cabana and pick up a phone. I knew he was checking my room number and guest name.

Now I can panic.

I hustled out of the pool, grabbed my clothes (skipping a towel), and took off the way I came in. I didn't look back to see if he was chasing after me, I could feel him.

I stepped inside the marble hallway soaking wet and hurried my way down the long air-conditioned corridor leaving a wet trail as I went. All I had on was my bikini. I didn't have anything to dry myself off, but I didn't have time to think about it.

I scurried down the hall being mindful not to fall on the wet marble. I noticed a janitor's room on my left. I reached for the door handle and it was unlocked. I slid inside.

I started to strip my wet swimming suit and just as I got my bottoms around my ankles a woman from house-keeping came in. She startled me and I startled her. Just as she was about to scream I looked at her and pleaded with her "shh". Confused, she walked back out of the room until I had my swimsuit bottoms back up and over my hinny. I walked out into the hall and dashed past her as I repeated, "*Lo siento, lo siento, lo siento.*" As I pleaded my "I'm sorry" she was too stunned to say anything. She just stared at me as I took off for the lobby half jogging, half limping.

I limped across the lobby barefoot, in a bikini, and still soaking wet. People stared dumbfounded as I ducked into the ladies' restroom. I needed somewhere to hide while I put on my clothes and gathered my wits.

Inside I was greeted by an attendant who was confused by my wardrobe selection. She gave me a funny look but didn't say anything. I stepped in one of the stalls and pulled my bikini off and my clothes on. I leaned over the toilet and tried to wring pool water out of my hair. Since it sounded like I was peeing, I went ahead and flushed the toilet. When I emerged from the stall I calmly walked over to the sink to wash my hands. I looked at the bathroom attendant, muttered "*gracias*" and stiffed her on a tip.

I power walked across the lobby and out the front door. I finally had clothes and shoes on and at least wasn't leaving puddles of water behind me. A few of the beautiful Spanish bellmen looked confused and as though they wanted to make sure everything was okay, but I just kept walking.

I made it back to my bike before I heard sirens.

My shaking hands released the bike lock and I threw my belongings in my basket, swung my leg over the bike, and peddled away from the hotel. All I could think about was going to Spanish jail, which couldn't have been a pleasant experience.

I crisscrossed through the side streets trying to cover my tracks and disappear. When I got far enough away I slipped into a bar and ordered a drink and *tapas*. I giggled as I washed down my *jamón* with *vino*.

What had possessed me to think I could walk into a five-star hotel and *borrow* their pool? Had I lost my mind?

I was grateful I had gotten away with my escapade, but I also decided to steer clear of *The Alfonso* for the rest of my stay in *Sevilla*.

Next time I go back to The Alfonso I better be a guest. And in my lifetime, *I will*.

Scene Forty-Seven

Seville, Spain, October 2008
(Fourteen months *after* the accident)

"Take pride in how far you've come. Have faith in how far you can go. But don't forget to enjoy the journey." –Michael Josephson

I went back to Maria's to shower, change my clothes, and thank God for keeping me out of jail. I really couldn't believe what I had done. It was as though any existence of my intellectual self had temporarily vanished. I had not grasped the possible consequences for my actions *prior* to my calculated stupidity.

As I had quickly gimped across the lobby of the hotel all the conceivable consequences for my actions had come flooding into my mind, but at that point my only option of escaping punishment was to run. That is what I did. I ran (which was more of a scurried gimp). In hindsight, I was grateful I didn't have to call home begging my parents to get me out of a Spanish jail.

When I walked into Maria's house, Gustovo glanced up from the sofa. "How was your swim?" he asked with curiosity.

Gustovo was the only male living in our house full of females. He was also studying at my language school, but studying his third language. As a Brazilian he spoke perfect Portuguese and had studied English in primary school. His English was as flawless as his Portuguese.

"I'll tell you after my shower. Want to get a beer when I'm cleaned up?"

We agreed to leave in an hour.

Gustavo and I left Maria's and sauntered our way down the cobblestone streets. I couldn't walk any faster than an old lady's stroll and he wasn't in a hurry. We made a good pair.

We were headed toward the city center but had no real destination. Even though walking was painful, I loved navigating the narrow streets. I had learned with enough ibuprofen I could mask the pain and push the throbbing out of my mind. I had, after all, flown halfway around the world to take pleasure in the Spanish culture and I couldn't do that by staring at my bedroom walls. The culture shock was enough of a distraction to give me the desire to push forward in my exploration. When I strolled with friends it was an additional distraction from any spikes in pain.

Slowly I was finding acceptance with my new "normal" and instead of fighting it (which didn't change my situation) I timed my medication to make sure the drugs never left my system. I was learning to manage my pain to the best of my ability. I was able to manage my pain with over-the-counter medications and mental toughness. More importantly, I was also learning to slow down and enjoy the simplicities of life.

As Gustavo and I strolled, I found myself wondering what beautiful love affairs or dramatic scenes had taken place on the very streets we navigated. It was the perfect setting for a great romance novel or chick flick movie: an ideal location for a great love story.

Even the infrastructure of the narrow streets was romantic. Some of the *calles* were so constricted you could extend your arms and touch the buildings on both sides. There was barely enough room for a scooter to pass, let alone for two people to walk side-by-side. The only other place I had been in my lifetime that came close to the narrow-street-charm of *Sevilla* was the Financial District on Wall Street, but even at that the architecture and culture made the comparison preposterous.

Gustavo and I chatted in Spanish *and* English. He was patient as I dug through my Spanish vocabulary for topics other than *shoes and men*. He laughed at my stubbornness to completely immerse myself in the Spanish *language* - the culture: yes, the language: no. He was always trying to talk to me in Spanish and I would converse with him until I got so frustrated I reverted back to English. My Spanish vocabulary simply wasn't as large as my English brain. The result: Spanglish. He never gave me a hard time, he simply transitioned back and forth following my lead.

As we strolled I described my experience as the unwarranted guest at *The Alfonso*. He politely laughed and listened with raised eyebrows. I could tell he was captivated with my boldness and determination to find the fun in life. Most of all, he was impressed no one had caught me especially given my lack of speed and grace.

As we rounded a narrow corner the *Catedral de Sevilla* came into sight. I suggested we find a local bar where we could sit and enjoy the majestic view of the cathedral as the sun set. Besides, my ankle couldn't handle any more walking.

The cathedral was one of *Sevilla's* best treasures both because of the ancient design *and* the people that walked the stone streets. It was also the burial site of Christopher Columbus, a worldly treasure indeed. The cathedral was surrounded with horse drawn carriages clickity-clacking down the rough stone streets as they dodged the tourists and locals alike. There was a refreshing buzz the people of all nationalities (and the animals) brought to the area.

There were always clusters of women desperately fanning themselves with their beautifully hand-painted fans - mostly tapping their breasts to filter air through their overgrown cleavage as they discussed life's most important topic: food. Likewise, the men were scattered about in small groups. Many were at outdoor dining establishments enjoying their beers, coffee, and flamenco music. The men had the more interesting topic of discussion: the world's greatest love-affairs. Or perhaps the men were planning their own affairs with young mistresses of *Sevilla*.

All this unfolded while wedding parties pranced about taking pictures as they documented their own personal love stories.

Spanish romance was indeed alive and well. Tourists blended into the scene as they took pictures of the buildings, wedding parties, and locals. The smell of the citrus trees that lined the walkways and *calles* was a glorious detail that topped off the enchanting scene: a small detail you can't inhale by looking at pictures on the Internet.

We settled at an outdoor table in a bar directly across from the cathedral. Within moments of our first beers arriving, a couple of American acquaintances walked by.

"Liz. Tom." I said as they whirled around.

"Hey Adrienne," Liz said cheerfully as the men exchanged *"holas"* in tandem.

"Want to join us?" I asked the two.

"Absolutely," they said in unison and pulled up a seat.

Tom and Liz were the first friendly faces I met upon arriving in Spain. They were two American attorneys who decided to quit their jobs and head to Europe for a year-long adventure. I admired their adventurous spirit and desire to live life on *their* terms, not society's. There was something about their *carpe diem*, or *seize the day*, attitude that attracted me to the couple.

More beers arrived at the table. The sun set and none of us had an obligation to fulfill. So we sat. We drank. We laughed. And we talked about nothing of worldly importance.

I repeated my story of *The Alfonso* and Liz told us about their recent weekend get-away to *The Alhambra* in the neighboring Spanish city of Granada.

The Alhambra is a palace and fortress originally built in 889 A.D. (and of course added to throughout the centuries). While it has a history of Islamic roots that turned Christian then turned to complete abandonment, the palace was restored in the nineteenth century and is now a major tourist attraction set in the foothills of the Sierra Nevada Mountains. The intricate tile and stone mosaics which cover the walls of the fortress were constructed in geometric patterns that are overwhelmingly stunning in their beauty. In fact, the inspirational construction has influenced artists such as poets (who refer to *The Alhambra* as "*a pearl set in emeralds*") to song writers to movies to ballets. There is even a video game that features *The Alhambra* as well as an asteroid that has been named in its honor! How do I know all this? Because after listening to Liz's description of the magical palace, that naturally glows gold at sunset, I planned my own weekend getaway to the ancient *Alhambra*.

After a few beers and several shared stories, our party of four decided to "go out" on the town (as if we weren't already). We paid our bill and left the bar.

As we wandered around the old-world we eventually stumbled upon a bar that had energy flowing from the inside-out. When we stepped inside I was amazed by the scene. While it was a typical bar with average looking people dressed in nothing special, there was a group of early twenty-somethings gathered in the center of the bar dancing flamenco. I thought flamenco was only for the stage, but I quickly learned the ancient dance was still very much alive in twenty-first century Spanish culture.

While my friends walked up to the bar, I was dumbfounded by the impromptu non-choreographed dance. I slowly approached the group. I was fascinated by their stomping, clapping, and twirling.

I stood off to the side and watched as a girl and guy "tangoed" around each other in a flamenco. I was mesmerized by the way their eyes had zeroed in on one another in a sensual way that screamed *sexo* yet was respectful of each other and the art. It was as though the anticipation was the climax, not the actual act. Several of the bystanders clapped their hands, not only in encouragement but to add sound (in a third dimension) to the flamenco guitar that was being pumped through the sound system. Somehow, just as the actual flamenco dance was sultry, so was the clap of the participants' hands.

As they clapped, they kept their palms tight to each other by sliding one hand all the way down to their fingertips of the other in order to give the clap an additional elongated sound. It was almost a sound of low-grit sandpaper being rubbed slowly down a board, allowing a supplementary musical sound to be made. The "clappers" were taking a quarter music note and extending it to a whole note. I never knew clapping your hands could be so sensual, but I was quickly learning.

I was also learning my sheltered world of dance wasn't very worldly. In fact, my knowledge of dance was very small. While I was an expert in tap, jazz, ballet, and lyrical (or what I called "the basics"), I had no idea what the fundamentals were of not only flamenco but salsa, tango, polka, samba, and so many more styles. There was so much about dance I didn't know, nor did I know I didn't know.

As I watched the flamenco being displayed so effortlessly and passionately before me, I was happy to be where I was. I was happy to be "observing" a new world of dance.

After that night at the bar, I not only went to one flamenco performance, but I went to three. I fell in love with the art of flamenco. I loved that I didn't know the technique. My ignorance in the art allowed me to sit, watch, and enjoy versus judge, critique, and over analyze.

To this day, I believe flamenco, when performed in an intimate setting and danced with passion, is one of the most beautiful forms of dance.

I will never forget my first flamenco performance when I walked down a narrow walk-way and stepped inside a tiny building. There was ivy growing down from the ceiling and the space was dimly light with drippy candles. I had selected a seat on the second row, which was the back row.

There were only two rows of chairs on three sides of a ten-foot by ten-foot stage. It was the most intimate setting I had ever seen for a performance. For an hour I watched the passion unfold before me. I could see every facial feature and emotion as the dancers and musicians stomped their feet and clapped their hands. I also watched the guitarist as he rapidly plucked the strings with his overgrown nails.

As the scene of dancers and musicians blended in perfect harmony a tear escaped from the corner of my eye, not out of pity for my situation, but from emotion being stirred in my soul as I watched the passion being danced before me.

I remember my heart fluttering as I watched the gift of dance unfold. What I didn't grasp at the time: I was feeling the first pangs of gratefulness for my broken journey. I was realizing it was because of my brokenness I was pushing myself to discover new horizons in not only my physical world, but within myself.

Scene Forty-Eight

Canyon, Texas, November 2008
(Fifteen months *after* the accident)

"If you don't know where you're going, any path will get you there."
–Lewis Carroll

After Europe I returned to Texas and my job, but I didn't want to be there. The instant I stepped foot back on Texas soil it was as though the treads of my shoes were weighted down with the red clay mud.

Yes, I was advancing my career as a marketing director and I was having an unprecedented amount of success, but I still felt empty. I had once felt the joy in a job and a job-well-done as a swim teacher, a *Relay for Life* organizer, Miss Kansas, and Miss USO. In Texas I hated sitting in the background as I watched the other performers pursue their dreams. Every day I went to work was a constant reminder of what I had lost and what I could no longer pursue. It was as though every day was a slap-in-the-face.

I needed a fresh start. I needed to find a place that didn't remind me of my ankle or my accident. I desperately needed something new. I began to brainstorm about where I could go. I wanted to move to a place that didn't know me *or my ankle*.

I weighed my options. This time *without an Atlas.*

Most of my family had moved to Denver and since family was my support system I wrote "Denver" on my list of options. I had spent a handful of holidays in the beautiful mile-high city, but other than that I didn't know much about what it had to offer.

I also wrote "California" on my list. Why California? *Why not?* It had the ocean, the cities, and the mountains.

266

Ultimately my decision came down to one question: do I want to spend my money on an airline ticket to 1) visit family or 2) go on vacation? With that, I decided I would move to Denver to be next to family.

I didn't have any dreams or goals other than to find a fresh start.

I picked up the phone and speed-dialed my dad. He picked up after the second ring.

"Dad, I want to move to Denver," I blurted into the phone. "May I stay with you and mom until I find a job and an apartment?"

"Of course!" he said excited. "We would love to have you!"

"Alrighty then. I'm going to give my two weeks' notice at work. When I come for Thanksgiving I'm coming to stay."

My mom joined in on the conversation and the three of us discussed my decision. They were excited. I was ready to move on and with my parents support I knew it was the right choice *for me*.

Before I hung up, I said, "I love you… and thanks."

Scene Forty-Nine

Denver, Colorado, February 2009
(Seventeen months *after* the accident)

"I am not afraid of storms, for I am learning how to sail my ship."
–Louisa May Alcott

Within a month I found a job as the Membership Director at a country club. Within two months I moved into my own apartment which meant I bought an apartment full of furniture. I also replaced my constantly broken-down-car with a new one, and a car payment. I was an adult who had officially joined the rat race.

After the first day at my new job I knew it sucked, but it was the best paying job I had ever claimed. It included full benefits (health insurance, 401k and dental). I was set *by society's standards.* So, I plastered a smile on my face and cried in private. I did my best to adjust my attitude to reflect the positivity I knew I had buried somewhere deep inside of me. My fire for life had gone out, but I knew I could relight it. While I didn't know how, I knew I would figure it out. In the meantime, I at the very least had a job that paid *all* my bills.-

I will get through this damn it. I told myself over and over again. *I will find a new dream and I will overcome this… whatever "this" is. "This" does not define me or my destiny.*

Scene Fifty

Cinco De Mayo 2009, three women, a celebration, *The Rio Grande*, Lone Tree, Colorado

(One year and nine months *after* the accident)

"A good destiny is when two people find each other without even looking." –unknown

Six months into my new life in Colorado it was finally time to celebrate something, *anything*. As if a perfect Colorado evening of no bugs, no wind, and seventy degree temperatures wasn't enough of an excuse to sit outside, drink margaritas, and eat Mexican food, I had a better reason. It was my new friend's (and work colleague's) twenty-fifth birthday.

As long as I had somewhere to sit I decided to make the most of my mid-twenties which consisted of no goals, no dreams, and new beginnings. I wanted (and thought I needed) a margarita or two or three. So in the early evening of *Cinco de Mayo* 2009, Jessica (the birthday girl), Kate, and I loaded into a car and headed to our celebration destination: *The Rio Grande*.

The Rio was known for its margaritas, margaritas, and margaritas. I had even heard a rumor there was a limit on how many margs the restaurant would serve because of the potency in the amounts of tequila per drink. My poor liver crossed my mind, but the pain in my ankle outweighed any thoughts about my overall health. I had come to the realization I was slowly destroying the other joints and ligaments in my body because of my overcompensation and habitual limp. Why not destroy my liver too?

"This is it," I sang out as Kate turned into the parking lot.

"Let's do this," Jessica echoed from the passenger seat.

The three of us giggled. We were three hot women, no men in tow, and on the prowl.

"Alright ladies, here we go," Kate chimed in as she pulled into a parking space and threw the car in park.

I grabbed my clutch and stepped out of the backseat of the suburban. We filed into the restaurant and as we stepped inside my senses were filled with the smell of slowly simmering Mexican food. It was standing room only and I could immediately feel the warmth radiating from the wall-to-wall people. I squeezed my way up to the hostess stand only to be informed the wait was forty-five minutes.

"Let's get a drink," Jessica shouted over the crowd.

Disappointed by our lack of VIP status, but energized by the crowd, we made our way over to the bar.

"You two start a tab and I'll look for a table," I said. Standing around was *not* an option for me.

While the girls squeezed their way up to the bar I scoured the restaurant for an open space. Every seat was taken and every table covered with chips, food, and booze. It was obvious everyone was settling in for a night of Mexican celebration and tequila.

I kept scouring the room willing a seat to magically appear. I turned to walk out to the patio when I spotted two men at a table for five. I strutted over to the gentlemen and introduced myself.

"Excuse me," I said as the two men broke their conversation to look at me. "I'm sorry to interrupt, but my two girlfriends and I are looking for somewhere to sit. May we join you?"

The guys glanced at each other and smiled.

"Sure," guy #1 said.

"Great!" I said as I reached out my hand to shake both of theirs. "I'm Adrienne."

I turned and waved to Jessica and Kate. They waved back, settled their tab at the bar, and then made their way through the crowd with three margaritas between the two of them.

"Have a seat," guy-friend #2 said as I plopped down in a chair next to him.

When Kate and Jessica arrived I made quick introductions and everyone shook hands. By the look on the guys' faces they were happy to have some company of the opposite sex.

I quickly broke the ice by making a toast. I raised my glass and said, "To new friendships. To our Mexican neighbors. And to birthdays. By the way today is Jessica's birthday," I said to the two men.

I raised my glass even higher. As we clanked our beverages guy #1 said, "To Jessica."

"To Jessica," we all echoed and then lowered our glasses to our mouths.

I licked the salty rim and then connected my lips to the frozen glass as I slurped in a big gulp of my frozen concoction of green perfection.

"Well," guy-friend #1 said, "Since it is Jessica's birthday I think it is in order we have a round of tequila shots." He raised his hand to motion over our server.

I giggled as I slurped on my margarita. "Score," I said in a mouthed whisper to Kate and Jessica. They returned my laugh and raised their own margaritas to prompt another toast. The three of us raised our margaritas and as we clanged our thick glasses together for yet another toast. I quickly forgot about my ankle and my sucky job.

Within the hour I had knocked back two margaritas and a shot of tequila. The alcohol had gone straight to my head and given my clear thinking I decided to take it upon myself to expand our little table party to the entire outdoor patio. Before anyone could stop me I was making toasts to anyone who was listening as well as anyone who walked by. I didn't know a stranger when I was sober and given my drunken state my outgoingness was multiplied by ten.

My friendliness must have paid off as drinks kept magically arriving at our table. At one point I took inventory of the plethora of empty margarita glasses, empty shot glasses, and half-full wine glasses.

Somewhere along the way our boss from the country club, who was spun as tight as a top, showed up. His out-of-character arrival for a fun evening prompted the three of us to celebrate his presence by ordering yet another round of margaritas.

Upon the delivery of our final round, our server explained to us that *The Rio* wasn't allowed to serve us anymore alcoholic drinks. We toasted her announcement.

As the night stumbled forward I recall another shot of tequila arriving, but not from our server. The shots were thanks to the group of men at the table next to us. I had quit drinking the free drinks. I was maxed. My veins had turned into a surging river of alcohol, *but* I no longer felt the constant pain in my ankle. I could, however, feel my heart pumping the booze to the beat of the salsa music coming from the second level of the restaurant.

Around the time the sun had dropped behind the mountains salsa music had started thumping its way out onto the patio. It was as though the music was singing my name and inviting me to let loose and enjoy life as though I never had an injury – never had a pieced-together-joint-of-ruin.

The music was calling me like a moth to a flame, like words to a sentence, like aroma to food. Dancing was a part of me. And it had been so long since I had moved to music.

With my prompting, the three of us agreed it was time to dance *and* get away from the unending flow of drinks. We split our bill, threw some money on the table, and said good-bye to our patio full of friends. The patio of people cheered.

When I reached the stairs I looked up to where the music was coming from and I could see couples moving gracefully back and forth in the open space. Women were twirling and men were looking extra *machisimo* as the women's hair whipped around in graceful circles, following their body's movement.

I miss dancing so much.

I grabbed the handrail and started up the stairs.

I just want to dance.

I rounded the corner to the second flight of stairs.

God, please don't let me hurt myself.

That's when I saw him. A tall, striking man leaning against the stair railing on the top platform. He was staring out over the crowd watching the dancers. I studied him. First, I noticed his lean body that stood out under a tan shirt and jeans that made his hind end look like God's greatest creation. His goatee was cleanly manicured and his hair was perfectly combed with a touch of gel that made it lay flawlessly. I noticed his feet. He was wearing black jazz shoes.

Was this dude for real?

I had never seen a guy with ballroom shoes on his feet. Not out in public anyway.

Next I noticed his nationality. He wasn't east coast Anglo Caucasian, he wasn't Spanish, he wasn't Mexican. I couldn't tell what he was. I didn't really care what his nationality was, it was just that I had never seen another man quite like him. As I continued to stare I noticed the most important detail - there was no woman on his arm.

I zeroed in on the mystery man and I walked up the final few steps. Without losing my gaze, I walked straight over to him. He turned to look at me. My heart fluttered. He was even more handsome up close.

I inhaled sharply and presented a question with the best flirtation I could muster while focused on appearing sober. I gestured toward the dance floor, "Do you know how to do this?" I asked, implying *do you know how to dance salsa?*

While most people would have waited for a response, I grabbed his hand and tried to drag him out on the floor. I wasn't taking *no* for an answer. I wanted to dance with *him* and since I had been drinking tequila he didn't have a choice. He was going to dance with me whether he wanted to or not.

He didn't resist my direct question or confident gesture. Instead, he took command of *my* hand and directed *me* to the dance floor.

It had slipped my mind I didn't have the slightest clue what the basic steps were to a salsa. I knew ballet. And tap. And jazz. Not ballroom. And not salsa! I didn't care. He was handsome. He was available. And I wanted to dance.

He stopped on the dance floor and turned to face me. He took my right hand in his left and placed his other hand just below my left shoulder blade. I reached my left hand up to his arm, grabbing his bicep. My gaze met his. He smiled and then gracefully pushed me backward into the first three steps of a salsa. Then he pulled me toward him for the last three steps. I immediately fell into his rhythm and it was as much his hands as it was his hips that guided me to follow his movement.

We rocked back and forth in a basic salsa movement of 1-2-3, 4-5-6. Back and forth we went. He rocked into me and then I rocked into him.

I could feel the warmth of his hands as they connected to me – hand-to-hand and hand-to-back. His smile was welcoming *and perfect.*

He gently directed me to follow his lead. At one point I glanced down at my feet and they were moving! My feet were moving, really moving. I looked up at the mystery man. He smiled and then opened his stance to guide me through a cross-body-lead and into a turn.

Oh, careful, my ankle!

He proceeded to turn me right. Then he turned me left. I was spinning all over the floor. I was giggling and laughing. More importantly *I was dancing.* I was dancing with someone that not only *didn't* know me, but didn't know my story either. I was dancing with someone who didn't know I was broken.

Yes, I was nervous about my ankle and whether it had the stamina to do what I was asking of it. But it didn't hurt so I kept going.

Within minutes I fell into my "dancer" training and I began trying to lead, but he was stronger than I was. He kept forcing me into his movement. He pushed me around the dance floor commanding me to follow his lead, not by his words but by his graceful movement.

He moved with poise and beauty. I followed his lead to the best of my ability. His movement was polished and refined. Mine was drunk and messy. He could move his hips like I had never seen before, for a tall white man anyway. He was strong. He was commanding. He knew how to dance. I was impressed and quickly smitten.

Who is this guy?

As the song came to a close he walked me to the edge of the dance floor. I looked up into his eyes and without a filter asked, "Can I ask you a personal question?"

He looked at me with a smirk on his face and muttered "Sure."

"Are you gay or straight?" I blurted out.

He laughed and said, "I'm straight, but thanks for asking."

"Well, where I come from good lookin' straight men don't dance like that."

He laughed again. "Thanks," he said. "I think."

"You're welcome. Dance with me again then," I said as more of a command than a request. I didn't let him respond before I drug him back out on the dance floor. I wasn't about to let go of the tall, handsome, hip-movin', salsa-dancin', good-lookin', fine-specimen of a *straight* man... he didn't seem disappointed by his dance partner either.

We danced another song. Well, he danced while I sloshed.

When the second song came to an end, again he walked me to the edge of the dance floor. We were both a bit winded from the hustle around the floor and he offered me a drink.

"Water?" he asked.

"That would be great," I said as he turned to walk over to the bar.

As he put distance between the two of us I heard Jessica over my shoulder, "Who's the hottie?"

"I have no idea, but holy cow can he dance," I paused to look at her "and he's straight," I said with raised eyebrows.

"No way."

"Yep," I confirmed stone cold.

"What's his name?" she asked.

In that instant I realized, "I have no idea."

"You don't know his name?"

"Nope," I said. "Nor do I really care. He is hot, he can dance, and he is available," I responded with a smirk as she laughed.

He returned with my water.

"Mr. Salsa. This is Jessica," I said introducing my friend to the mystery man.

He reached out his hand to shake hers, "Jessica. It's nice to meet you."

"And what is your name?" Jessica asked as she held his hand in a casual handshake.

"Apparently it's Mr. Salsa," he said with a laugh as he released his hand from hers and we all joined in on the chuckle.

"Well, Mr. Salsa, today is Jessica's birthday," I added.

He turned to look at Jessica, "And how old are you today?"

"Twenty-five," she said.

"Happy Birthday," Mr. Salsa said in response.

"Thanks," Jessica said before she turned to leave.

I took a sip of my water as I turned to watch the dancers on the floor. I felt like I was in the twilight zone. I had never seen so many ballroom dancers in one place (out in the public and not in a formal studio).

"Where did these people come from?" I asked Mr. Salsa as we stood shoulder to shoulder watching the dancers.

"There is a huge dance community in Denver," he responded. "The community moves around the city."

"Seriously?" I asked.

"Yep," he paused. "This is actually the first time they have brought dancing to *The Rio* and I wanted to come check it out."

We stood next to each other in silence for a few minutes, or rather a few seconds, before an idea on how I could extend our little meeting came to my mind. "Any chance I can talk you into teaching me?" I asked.

He raised his eyebrows.

"Salsa," I said as I gestured to the floor. "Formally," I added.

"Perhaps, but I don't really think you need me as a teacher," he explained. "You just show up. You can salsa seven nights a week around Denver if you want."

He wasn't taking the bait.

"In fact," he continued, "when I first started dancing I had two left feet, but I just kept at it and eventually it started to click."

"That's cool," I chimed in. "But I still need a teacher."

"It's a really great community of people too. *And* it's not always in a bar setting like this."

I took another sip of my water, wishing myself to sobriety and wondering if my signals weren't strong enough.

"So *I* have a personal question for *you*," he said as he leaned in closer to my ear.

I turned to look at him.

"Yes?" I asked.

He hesitated as he leaned close to my ear, "What is your name?" he whispered.

I started laughing. "I'm Adrienne," I said as I extended my hand for an official handshake. "And you are?"

"Mr. Salsa."

"No seriously, what is your name?" I asked.

"Mr. Salsa!" he said laughing. "Let's dance again."

Without hesitation I let him lead me back onto the floor. We danced another six-minute salsa before he went back to the bar to refill our waters.

When he returned, he handed me my water and excused himself, "I'm going to let you hang out with your friends."

"Did I scare you off?" I asked playfully.

"No, I want to get some fresh air. I'm hot."

Yes, you are. "No problem," I responded. "I want to sit down anyway." At that we both turned and went our separate ways.

I walked over to a bar stool and sat down. I could tell my ankle was going to be screaming by morning, not to mention my head. I crossed my right ankle over my left knee and grabbed my big swollen graft. I gently massaged it in a circular motion. I was surprised everything was intact considering the way I was flinging myself around the dance floor, but all seemed to be okay.

As I rubbed my thumb across my sock I could feel my scars protruding through the thin knee high black stocking I had over my compression stocking. Both the stockings were serving as a cover for my embarrassing deformity.

As I rubbed my lump and looked out over the crowd, I thought of the guy I dated in Texas and how he told me I had lost my sex appeal… which apparently was based on my ankle.

Screw him, I thought.

I reached for my purse and started digging through the innards of my handbag. I was looking for my wallet and when I found it, I pulled it out and onto my lap. I opened my wallet and started flipping through the contents – receipts, a $2 bill (for good luck), a twenty, a single, and a stack of business cards – half of which were mine. I pulled one of my own cards out, set my wallet on my lap, and studied my card. I had my headshot, my name, phone number, and email on the card. That was it. I liked the mystery in the lack of detail.

"Hey," Mr. Salsa said, startling me out of my trance. "Your friends are leaving you."

"What?" I asked confused.

"Yes! Go! Someone came to pick them up. They're loading into a car and pulling out of the parking lot."

"What?!" I asked irritatedly yelling.

"I told them to wait for you and they said to hurry."

"Here," I said, thrusting my card into his hand. "Call me!" I added as I rushed past him. "I need a teacher!"

I hustled over to the stairs, stumbled down the two flights, and out the door.

"Jessica!" I yelled as I flung the door open.

There was a suburban waiting at the curb - Kate in the passenger window and Jessica in the back.

"Are you leaving me?" I asked in hysteria.

"Yes!" Kate said.

"But only because you found a hottie-pa-tottie!" Jessica laughed, "Get inside and get that!"

I paused, a little confused as I digested their advice.

"Adrienne!" A voice yelled from behind me.

I turned around and it was Mr. Salsa. Jessica and Kate started woo-hoo-ing at the sight of the mystery man.

"You forgot your wallet," he said as he reached out to hand it to me.

"She's not going with us," Jessica said.

"I'm not?"

"Nope. You're staying here." Kate chimed in.

And with that their designated driver pulled out of the parking lot.

"Have fun!" the girls screamed out the window as they turned out of the parking lot and onto the main road.

I turned around and looked at Mr. Salsa. "I guess I lost my ride," I said with shrugged shoulders.

"Umm... do you want me to call you cab?"

"No. I don't live very far," I said.

He raised his eyebrows.

"Seriously. It's *maybe* a five minute walk. Ten at the most."

"I'll walk you," he said.

"No you won't," I said boldly with my nose curled.

"I won't?"

"No!" I said. "Number one I don't know you and number two you have on dance shoes," I paused. "You'll ruin your leather soles."

"One more dance then?" he asked.

"Sure," I said as I took his arm and walked back inside and up the stairs.

Scene Fifty-One

A girl's one-bedroom apartment, the morning after
(One year and nine months *after* the accident)

"You cannot tailor-make the situations in life, but you can tailor-make the attitudes to fit those situations." -unknown

When my alarm went off I sat up, threw my blankets to the side, stood, and walked across the room to switch the blaring music *off*. Not snooze, but *off*.

My head was pounding, but it didn't stop the smile spreading across my face. Was I giddy because I had danced? Or was I giddy because of a nameless guy's phone number I had stored in my own phone as "Mr. Salsa"?

As I walked into the bathroom I picked up the glass of water I had left on the counter the night before and chugged the remaining contents. I was dehydrated and my head was throbbing.

I opened the bathroom drawer and reached for a bottle of ibuprofen. I had bottles of that candy stashed all over my apartment and in every hand bag I owned. But I wasn't about to knock back a couple of pills of relief because of my ankle, it was because of my head.

I looked at myself in the mirror. My hair was *sort-of* in a pony-tail. I had as much hair pointing in every direction as was tied back. I had rings of black mascara under my eyes and the remnants of leftover red lip liner. "If they could see me now," I said to the girl in the mirror, referring to all the people that pictured a flawless Miss Kansas.

I laughed and hiccupped at my own joke in my lonely bathroom, tasting tequila.

I grabbed my toothbrush and the tube of paste, marrying the two, before I lifted the stick to my mouth. I started a good foam that was a welcomed wintery-fresh contrast to the nasty tequila leftovers. Just as I started to foam into suds I pulled my toothbrush out of my mouth, pointed my brush at the girl in the mirror and said, "It's going to be a good day."

I smiled a wide foamy white smile before I leaned over and spit into the sink.

I couldn't wait to call my best friend and tell her about the handsome man I had met the night before… *and the way I met him.* I didn't care about the headache. The dancing was a defining moment.

Scene Fifty-Two

An office at a country club, May 6, 2009
(One year and nine months *after* the accident)

" What if one opportunity could change your life?" –Marie Forleo

My phone buzzed, interrupting me from my Facebook stalking, which I wasn't supposed to be doing at work anyway. I glanced in the direction of the *buzz*, skimming the surface of my desk. No phone. I dug through piles of files scattered across my desk; my green slider phone nowhere to be found.

As I frantically patted at my stacks of papers, I was grateful the ringer was on silent, instead of screaming *I'm ringing! I'm ringing! I'm ringing!* It would have been painful with my headache status. Thankfully, my phone was frantically *buzzing* in hushed tones of *answer me, answer me, over here, ANSWER ME!*

As I patted the far left edge of my desk I felt the vibrating papers. I lifted the files and there was my phone with the name *Mr. Salsa* flashing across the caller I.D.

"Jessica!" I yelled in a whisper. "It's him!" I hissed.

As I finished my frantic announcement she was instantaneously standing in my doorway with a huge smile spread across her face. I smiled back at her as I took a deep breath and slid the phone open and very calmly answered, "Hello."

"Hi," a deep voice said.

I danced a silent happy dance (which was a combined version of the 1986 running man and an over-excited kid receiving her most coveted present Christmas morning).

"How are you feeling today?" he asked as I paused and calmly fidgeted with my hair, turning to look out the window.

281

"I'm okay," I said nonchalantly, trying to hide my excitement. "I have a slight headache but nothing ibuprofen can't handle."

"Well, that's good."

"Yes," I said.

There was a moment of silence before I returned the question, "How are you today?"

"I'm good," he responded. "I'm actually calling to let you know about a place to go salsa dancing this Thursday."

"Oh?"

"Yes. It's called *La Rumba*. Downtown. Good place. Another bar setting, but if you go early they teach a lesson and then its open dancing 'til 2 a.m."

"That sounds fun," I said, confused if he was inviting me, asking me out on a date, or simply relaying the information. "Will you be there?" I asked.

"I don't know yet. I might. Might not," he said.

Well, make up your mind. I thought.

"I just wanted to let you know because you said you wanted some formal instruction."

He had missed my point so I tried again, "But I won't know anyone there," I said.

"That's not a problem."

Duhh, I thought. *Dude, I lived in New York where I knew no one. I'm not afraid to go to a salsa lesson. I'm trying to ask if you are going to be there!*

"It's a great community of people and everyone is really friendly," he continued as I turned to look at Jessica to make a confused and irritated face.

"Hmmm. Well, I might go, I suppose."

"Okay, well I just wanted to let you know."

"That was kind of you," I said.

With that we said "good-bye" and hung up the phone.

I slid my phone closed and looked at Jessica.

"That was weird," I said.

"What did he say?" she asked.

"Well, he told me about a place to go dancing this Thursday but didn't say if he was going. He didn't ask me out nor did he offer to meet me there. But," I paused, "he did call the day after I met him, which isn't standard protocol for dating." I threw my hands up in the air, "What is that supposed to mean? Either he is clueless or he isn't interested."

"Are you going to go?"

"I don't know. I really do want to learn the proper technique. I'd also like to see him again. But I don't want to seem desperate either."

"You should go," she encouraged. "Maybe he'll show."

"I hope so," I said and then let out a big dramatic sigh. "He seemed too good to be true. Handsome. Talented. *Straight.* Single." I paused before I continued. "*But...*" I looked Jessica in the eyes and grimaced as I said, "He did say he has kids."

"Uh oh," Jessica said. "You didn't tell me that!"

"Yeah, I know," I let out a big sigh. "To add to it, he claims they are almost my age."

"*They?*" She asked with raised eyebrows. "How many *they* are there?"

"I don't know," I said sheepishly.

"He didn't look old enough to have a kid our age let alone multiple kids," she said appalled.

"Right? He can't be more than ten years older than me," I said, agreeing with her astonishment.

"Who cares anyway?" Jessica chimed in on my thoughts. "You should go on Thursday," she said. "If he shows, great. If not, who cares?"

"You're right! It's not like I'm going to marry the man," I continued. "I just want to learn salsa and have some fun."

I went silent so I could think for a moment before I made up my mind, "I'll go... Hey! You should come with me?"

"No," Jessica said laughing. "Dancing isn't my thing. Besides I have dinner plans with David."

"Fine! Be that way," I said joking. "Will you at least be my friend that knows where I am in case I disappear?"

"Sure," she said with a smile before she rolled her eyes and continued with, "But you're not going to disappear."

"Don't forget your brain when you follow your heart." –Bianca Olthoff
----

I did go dancing at *La Rumba* that Thursday night. But, before I drove downtown I went through three rolls of athletic tape in order to wrap my ankle the way I did when I was playing high school basketball. Three rolls was a little extreme but I figured the more tape the more protected my ankle. As if my ankle wasn't compressed enough with the tape, I carefully pulled a compression stocking over my work of art.

I was terrified I would roll my poor ankle so after I bandaged myself up I found the most realistic flat dancing shoes I could dig out of my closet. I shoved my fat foot into the shoe before I rolled my pant leg over my lump. My jeans were just long enough that they touched the floor, disguising my ankle.

No one could see the tape, which was good, but I was the only woman in the class that had on flat shoes. As a trained dancer this meant I was back in the amateur category, which I desperately despised.

The class proved to be boring, but informative. The most important part: I didn't hurt myself - no rolled ankles and no protruding bones. I was proud of my joint, but I also realized the tape was a little excessive.

The instructor dismissed the class and the DJ immediately took over. With the magical talents of the DJ came the influx of people flowing through the front door. I quickly realized that being American, with English as my native tongue, made me a minority.

I was uncomfortable with my surroundings, not to mention I was in downtown Denver in a Mexican bar and the only person that knew where I was, was Jessica.

I told myself I had to stay for the duration it took me to drink a single beer. I started to make my way over to the bar, but I was detoured by a guy asking me to dance.

"*¿Quieres bailar?*" a man, five inches shorter than me, asked with a welcoming smile spread across his face.

"*Sí,*" I responded as I took his hand and walked out onto the dance floor.

"*¿Como te llamas?*"

"*Adriana.*" I responded "*¿Y tú?*"

"*Jose.*"

"*Mucho gusto Jose,*" I said, grateful for my time in Spain.

"*Tu es muy bonita,*" he responded.

"*Gracias,*" I said simply and we began to salsa.

As we danced I couldn't help but notice the size of the crucifix around Jose's neck. It had to have weighed more than my jewelry, shoes, jeans, and purse (which was heaped full) combined. He was friendly and welcoming, but as I glanced around the room I realized I was the only English speaking American. I was officially counting down the seconds until I walked out the door. I didn't know enough Spanish to be in the setting where I, and Mr. Salsa, had stupidly placed myself.

When the song was done I thanked Jose for the dance and walked over to the edge of the floor. I scanned the room looking for Mr. Salsa. I didn't see him with my first scan and I wasn't staying for a second. I grabbed my purse and bolted for the door.

When I got outside of the building it was dark and I realized I had the wrong skin color to be in that particular area of town by myself. I hurriedly gimped my way to my car, got in, locked the doors, started the ignition, and threw the car into drive.

Scene Fifty-Three

Back at the country club, a girl in her office on her phone, May 9, 2009
(One year and nine months *after* the accident)

"Everything you've ever wanted is one step outside your comfort zone."
—unknown

"Hello," I answered.

"Hi," a deep voice answered back.

"Oh hey, what's up?" I responded nonchalantly acting like I had just realized it was Mr. Salsa on the other end (as though I hadn't looked at the caller I.D. before I answered).

"I was calling to see if you enjoyed *La Rumba* last night," he responded.

"How do you know if I went?" I asked.

"Because I saw you there," he said laughing.

"You weren't there."

"Yes," he laughed again. "I was. As a matter of fact I saw you dancing with Jose."

"Oh? I didn't see you."

"I tried to get across the room to say hello but you disappeared."

I didn't know what to say.

"Did you have a good time?" he asked again.

"Yes, it was okay. A little crowded *and* I was a little tall and a little too white."

He laughed, "Is that why you left so early?"

"I was there for almost two hours."

"I suppose that's true if you include the lesson," Mr. Salsa said, "I tell you what. I know another place that might be more suited for you. It's quieter and nicer."

"I'm listening," I responded.

"Well… I'd officially like to take you out for dinner and dancing," Mr. Salsa said. "What do you think?"

"When?"

"Tonight."

"What time?" I asked.

"I'm not sure yet. I've got some work to finish. Will you call me when you get off work?"

"I get off at five," I said, not playing games.

"Okay, well, can I pick you up at six?" He asked.

"Nope."

"No?" he asked in confused laughter.

"No. I don't even know your name! The last thing I'm going to do is let you see where I live," I paused. "But I'll meet you somewhere."

"Fine. We'll meet then. Let's talk when you get off work."

"Okay. Deal."

"Talk to you later."

"Bye," I said and hung up the phone.

My heart was pounding and my hands were shaking, but somehow my voice was steady. I repeated the conversation to Jessica and again she agreed to be my "friend in the know".

Anything worthwhile is worth the while.

We had plans to meet downtown. As I pulled off the Interstate my anxiety escalated. I wasn't sure I remembered what Mr. Salsa looked like. Yes, I remembered he was handsome and taller than I was, but I really couldn't remember his features and I wondered if I would recognize him when I walked into the restaurant.

We had agreed to meet at a place called *The Opal*, which also doubled as a dance venue on certain nights of the week. Their menu was filled with sushi (one of my favorites) and I figured at the very least I would get a great meal and free dance lesson. That is, if I recognized my date.

When I located the restaurant I made two loops around the block. My first loop was to scope out the area and my second was to verify I wanted to indeed get out of my car. I couldn't find an excuse to turn around so I found the closest parking spot and paralleled my car into an open space.

After I shifted into park, I leaned over to check my lipstick and hair (which I had been fidgeting with) in the rearview mirror. I took a deep breath and shrugged my shoulders as I said to myself *"What do I have to lose?"* I opened the door and stepped out into the cool evening breeze.

I began my walk to the restaurant. Little did I know I was walking a defining "catwalk" down the streets of Denver. Was I was walking in the direction of my destiny?

I could see a figure walking toward me. A guy. Tall. Fit. *Is that him?* I wondered.

As he got closer I was ninety percent sure it was Mr. Salsa, but the ten percent kept me playing it cool.

"Adrienne?" the figure said as I got closer.

"Mr. Salsa?" I responded and he laughed.

"Yes," he assured me as we greeted.

He leaned in to give me a kiss on the cheek – more of a standard European greeting, than anything romantic – which I gratefully accepted.

"Were you not sure you remembered what I looked like?" I asked dramatically astounded.

"Were you?" he jabbed back.

"Was I what?" I asked acting confused.

"Sure it was me?"

I laughed and said, *"No."*

"Well, now that you don't have on tequila goggles, do I meet your expectations?"

"Visually, yes. We'll see how dinner goes. But first I want to know your name."

"We'll see how dinner goes," he responded with a smile.

I liked his playfulness and the fact he was willing to dish back my sarcasm.

Yes, I found it strange I didn't know his name, but I decided to go with it. Besides, it had quickly become more of a joke than a secret. I was enjoying our little game of flirtation. I could tell he was as interested in me as I was in him. We turned and walked side-by-side to the restaurant. When we reached the front door he stepped in front of me to open the door.

"Ladies first," he said with a butler's nod.

I gratefully accepted his gesture.

I liked his chivalry (from what I had seen). In the limited amount of time I had spent with him he was opening doors (sadly I had been on far too many dates where the guys were clueless to this small gesture that spoke volumes). I wasn't just impressed with the opening-of-doors. At *The Rio* he had offered to walk me home and was gracious when I refused his escort due to the fact I didn't know him, he even refused to kiss me that first night (which was less impressive given I was willing).

He *seemed* to be a good guy, but I was still skeptical. If I made another friend out of the date – *awesome* – if not, well, it was an adventure.

I suppose that was my typical approach to most dates I had been on, not because I was clueless, but because for years I had been focused on my career. A career as an entertainer didn't exactly lend itself to relationships. I had been committed to my dream and knew the dedication it required. With the level of success I was pushing myself toward I knew I would be moving around the country *and the world*. It was a recipe for disaster when it came to long term relationships. Not only did I know the recipe, I had tasted the meal. A broken relationship due to a career, and in my case a dream, went something like this: it felt like having my heart ripped out of my chest, stomped on it until it was on the verge of nothingness, then drug through the mud, thrown off a mountain, and just as it was about to completely give out someone stuffed it back in my chest and said, "Okay, there you go." I started to build calluses around my heart and sadly, I was okay with that. I had gradually shifted my focus from the value of relationships to achieving my goals.

Things had changed with my injury. First, I wasn't in the entertainment industry any longer. Second, my injury had taught me one of life's most valuable lessons: when shit hits the fan, it isn't your career waiting for you on the other side... it is those you have built relationships with. During my recovery I promised myself, and my Maker, I would never put my career before people *ever* again. Sadly, in the years following my injury I saw people, more often than not, hold their careers and their jobs on a higher pedestal than the precious moments spent with loved ones – moments they will never get back.

But please don't misinterpret this life lesson: dedication toward your dreams will require great sacrifices, and those great sacrifices will be worth it. The complication comes when deciphering sacrifices based on *things* versus *people*. This is your reminder that no matter how amazing your dream, always keep your relationships at the top of your priority list. When you make it to your destination those are the exact people who will make the accomplishment so much more fun to celebrate. Remember: lone celebrations are, well… lonely.

With the lesson about putting people above careers, I was trying to learn how to be open to relationships – be it friendships, romantic relationships, or time spent with family. And that is exactly how I approached Mr. Salsa – nonchalant, noncommittal, but completely in the moment and open to where the moment led.

As he pulled out my chair for me to take a seat, he received another brownie point.

"Thanks," I said and he looked at me as if to say *this is what a guy is supposed to do, no "thanks" necessary.*

He sat down across from me, giving me the chance to study his face. He had a slightly rounded shape to his head, which was framed nicely by his brown hair - hair that covered his entire head. He had gelled his long crew-cut ever so slightly giving his look a "put together" feel, but not so much it made me feel like I should have spent more time on my own look. He seemed to have a little cowlick of hair on the left side of his forehead giving him a subtle curl that reminded me a bit of Superman. He had finished his look with a cleanly manicured brown goatee.

As we made small talk, I continued to study him, his features, and his mannerisms. I liked the way he talked with his eyebrows as much as he did with his hands. His hands were big and his fingers long. As he told me what it was he did for a living (he was a woodworker) I remember being impressed he still had all ten of his long fingers.

As our conversation of small talk pressed forward, we bantered back and forth learning the basics about one another. He was born in Arizona. Me: Kansas. He was the youngest of seven. I was the third of four. His parents had always been married. So had mine. I loved to travel, while he wanted to do more. I skimmed over Spain and New York. And when the ball was back in his court he told me about his three kids: ages fourteen, nineteen, and twenty-two. I got stuck on the fact not only did the handsome man have three *old* kids, but one of them was not far from my age!

"You don't look old enough to have three kids," I said with raised eyebrows. I cocked my head sideways and squinted my eyes to ask, "How old are you?"

"Old enough, but not too old," he said, matching my stare.

"And how old is that?"

"Forty-one," he said and then paused to study my reaction.

Honestly, he was about four years older than I anticipated, but I wasn't *that concerned* about his age. After all, I had quasi-dated a guy five years older than *him* when I was living in New York (an Army Ranger and TV correspondent I had met in the Rainbow Room of Rockefeller Center when I was co-hosting a USO event with Tom Brokaw).

"And since you asked," he said, "I get to ask: how old are you?"

"Twenty-six," I said without hesitation.

He laughed and muttered, "Oh boy."

"How old were you when you had your first kid?" I asked, not concerned about our age difference but more concerned about how close in age I was to his oldest.

"I was nineteen."

"Wait a second," I paused to do the math. "I was born in '83, you graduated in '86 and had your first kid in '87?"

"That sounds about right."

Uh oh.

I took a long sip of wine, buying time to remind myself I was just getting to know this guy and nothing more. As I sat my glass down he picked up his Crown and Sprite to take a long drink.

I started laughing and so did he.

"Well…" I said with a loss for words. "At least we can be friends."

He laughed and raised his glass to a toast and we clinked our glasses together.

"Shall we dance?" he asked as he stood and extended his hand.

Without hesitation, I took his hand and followed him to the dance floor. It was, after all, the reason we were enjoying the evening out.

I knew I should have been freaking out about our age difference and at the very least about the fact he had three kids, one of which was born in my same decade. But, I reminded myself I didn't care. He was nice. Friendly. Honest. And I wasn't looking for anything more than a good time and possible new friendship with someone that shared the same love for dance. *Or was I?*

We stopped in the center of the dance floor. I turned to face him and he gave me a few pointers on how to properly follow his lead. I was grateful for the direction. He moved into his starting stance.

He moved me into a basic salsa. We rocked back and forth several times before he moved me through a cross-body-lead. His movement was graceful, masculine, and affirmative - giving me the natural ability to follow his lead.

He felt me follow and almost immediately opened me into some turns: I twirled left and then right before he moved into a repeat of the basic salsa step.

"You are a natural," he said.

"Thanks."

"Remember though," he said as we continued in a basic step, "As the floor gets crowded you have to pull your movements in."

He was referring to my natural ability to "take up space" – a result of my training to fill an entire stage in grand theatres, and in many cases, theatres that were outdoors. The bigger the movement the better. Naturally I expected people to not only notice me, but to get out of my way. On a crowded salsa floor, however, that was a formula for making immediate enemies.

He pulled me closer and continued to guide me through the basic steps. As we rocked back and forth I studied his eyes, which were a beautiful light brown that faded into a steal blue. Behind the color was warmth, goodness, and honesty.

He transitioned me into elegant turns, testing my ability. I gratefully and gracefully kept up with his lead. As I came out of a series of turns, that only a true dancer could handle, he caught me behind my low back and dipped me into a deep backbend. I released my head backward, allowing all my energy to move into a deep dip. My right leg naturally kicked up into the air in the same way a girl's foot pops when she receives a storybook kiss.

When he guided me back up to face him, he pulled me closer. I remember the smell of his breath mixed with the scent of his soap. Our dancing shifted from a salsa to a close body sway. As we slowed to study each other in a more intimate way, my eyes naturally closed as he leaned in for a kiss, a gentle kiss that was well received.

"If music be the food of love, play on!" –William Shakespeare

------

As the evening progressed I told him about my ankle, and my brokenness. To my surprise, he wasn't fazed, but rather impressed with my perseverance and resilient spirit. I felt pangs of being proud of my scars and what I had overcome.

"I would have never guessed you had an injury by the way you can move," he complimented. The best part of his compliment: his sincerity.

"Well," I said and shrugged my shoulders, "it is what it is."

The mystery man was accepting me for who I was – not my former career, not my former title, not my injury – he was accepting me for the girl I was. Nothing more, nothing less. I wasn't sure I had felt that kind of acceptance from anyone, besides my family, in a long long time.

Our evening moved forward and we rotated from eating to dancing to drinking to dancing. When we got too hot from all the exercise, we took a break and walked outside for fresh air.

I remember the sky was misting that night and the freshness to the wet air was welcomed. It was a fairytale setting to our dancing date. I leaned against a railing to relieve my weight from my joint and my date leaned on the railing next to me. We leaned shoulder-to-shoulder.

I was completely satisfied with where I was in the world, what I was doing, and who I was with. I didn't want the evening to end and I wasn't sure I had ever had that feeling when out on a date.

I felt my mystery man reach his left hand over my right hand, pulling me back to his presence and away from my thoughts. His palms were dry despite the top of my hand moist from the mist. He turned to look at me. I smiled at him and he accepted the invitation.

He turned to face me. He reached out his other hand to grab my free hand. When both our hands were connected he slowly leaned his body into mine. He stretched his arms long to pull my hands behind him. Our bodies connected: first our hips, then our chests, then our lips.

His kiss was soft yet definitive. He kissed me on purpose, but with respect. His mouth was closed and I held my breath as I felt the electricity shoot through my chest. With the surge of energy I melted into him. He dropped my hands and reached around my waist, pulling me in for a deeper, more romantic wet kiss. We tasted each other, mist turning to rain. I didn't care about the rain or anything in the world except the man I was connected to. I wrapped my arms around him and held on for the last first kiss I would ever experience.

Scene Fifty-Four

The suburbs of Denver, Mr. Salsa's house, July 2009
(One year and eleven months *after* the accident)

"You must know yourself, love yourself, and accept yourself before you can expect anyone else to do so." –R. Bulinski

Without realizing it, in a matter of weeks I had quit dating or even looking at anyone else. I was spending all my free time with the mysterious Mr. Salsa. A guy who on paper wasn't exactly the perfect fit, but for whom I was perfectly falling in love.

As if Mr. Salsa wasn't impressive enough on the dance floor, he was also an expert mountain biker. With my strength, stamina, stubbornness, and dedication to impress him, he taught me how to navigate miles of single track trails in the colorful Colorado Rockies. Surprisingly I could bike for miles with no pain in my ankle. The low impact sport allowed me to become a true, fierce athlete once again – and the term "fierce athlete" being a description I had written off with my injury.

Our first summer together we spent hours in the wilderness – at times, me on the bike and Mr. Salsa holding my seat-post running behind me down the mountain, coaching me on my technique. By the end of that summer together, I could navigate almost any intermediate single track trail Colorado had to offer. I had found my athleticism, something I thought I had lost.

In the midst of biking I also became an expert *novice* at Salsa dancing.

To top it off, all the exercise allowed me to eat pints of ice cream (all while knocking off pounds from the chocolate cake) as I sat next to Mr. Salsa watching movie after movie, night after night, month after month. I had no cravings for cake and there were no tears in my pints of ice cream. I was finding my genuine smile and I had someone to share it with.

Mr. Salsa and I spent copious amounts of time together biking, dancing, cooking, watching movies, and exchanging wet kisses amongst it all. As we grew deeper into our relationship our conversations grew more intimate as well.

"Do you know why a lot of relationships fail?" he asked me one evening as we sat cross-legged with our own bowls of ice cream heaped full – mine with *Extreme Chocolate Moose Tracks*, his with *Cookies 'N Cream.*

"Why?" I asked, curious where he was going.

"Because people don't define love and forgiveness the same," he said simply, yet matter of fact.

"What do you mean?" I asked.

"Well," he paused to formulate his words and lowered his bowl, placing it on his lap. "If I show you love in a way that *I* want to be loved, but it isn't in a way in which *you* express love, then my loving actions will go unnoticed and you will become frustrated I don't show you affection in a way *you* think you should receive it, or simply understand it."

He paused again to take a bite and let me digest his lesson before he continued, "You see, we can both be expressing love to one another but if we don't do it in each other's appropriate love languages then that love is lost: not because we didn't love one another, but because we didn't express our love in a way the other person could comprehend."

I sat quietly thinking about this lesson, realizing in twenty-six years no one had ever taught me such a valuable lesson about love.

"It's the same for forgiveness you know," he added as he took another large bite of his *Cookies 'N Cream* ice cream dripping in chocolate and caramel sauces.

"Oh?" I encouraged him to continue, holding my own bowl of the frozen concoction cupped in both of my hands, waiting for him to swallow his indulgence.

"If I forgive you the way I want to be forgiven, but it isn't the same way you define forgiveness, then the forgiveness is never received. Not out of spite, but out of a language barrier."

After a long moment of silence and another bite of ice cream I asked, "How do you define love?"

He laughed. "No no. You're not ready for that yet."

"*Why?*"

"Because I don't believe you have defined it for yourself."

"So! I'm asking you for *your* definition," I countered.

"Nope. I won't tell you," he said and then took another bite before he continued with a mouthful. "I don't want to give you a guideline to follow," he swallowed. "The definition of love and forgiveness, for you, can only be defined by you."

I sat quietly eating my ice cream before I asked, "Have you actually written down your definitions?"

"Why do you think I brought this up?" he asked with raised eyebrows. "I want you to think about it," he continued. "It's something that takes time to formulate. You can't hear the concept and come up with the definition all in the same setting," he laughed again. "This is something that takes time to define."

More silence filled the room as we scraped the bottoms of our bowls. I would later learn *The Five Love Languages* in greater detail when Mr. Salsa loaned me the book written by Gary Chapman.

Mr. Salsa continued gently, "You must truly know yourself to know how *you* define love and forgiveness… Do you know yourself?" he asked.

"I think so," I said.

"*I think so* isn't an answer. You must know yourself, love yourself, and accept yourself before you can expect anyone else to do so… and to do so in a language that you understand."

I raised my eyebrows and nodded as if to say "Point taken."

I sat quietly with a man that fell somewhere between the definition of "friend" and "boyfriend". His wisdom was attractive yet frightening, and his lesson was wise yet direct.

I had never been asked to define love or forgiveness. But what stumped me most was: did I truly know myself? Did I know myself in a way I could properly define two of the most important words (love and forgiveness) that make the world go round? First I had to know me, and know me better than anyone else on the planet.

Mr. Salsa was patient with my immaturity in years, but respectful of my maturity from the valuable life lessons I had learned the hard way. He knew I was still healing and he was respectfully patient as he watched me continue my healing process.

Through the course of dating Mr. Salsa, he reminded me several times I could not find the right relationship until I became right with myself.

On my drive home that night, I had thirty-five miles between our houses to think about our evening's conversation. Do I actually know myself? Do we, as a human race, actually know ourselves as individuals? The definitions could hold the key components to tolerance and peace among all people. And if we *don't* know ourselves how can we understand love and forgiveness?

How many times had I been looking for myself in other people? How many times had I tried to pin my happiness on a person, or an event, or a job?

I had spent so many years defining myself as a dancer, an entertainer, a singer - all of which felt empty and lost. The lesson Mr. Salsa was teaching made me realize those definitions where nothing more than *careers*, not a definition of *who* I was. My lost career, and those careers I had yet to discover, make up a piece of me, but not the whole me.

In the midst of my injury, and in the time frame of this valuable lesson of love and forgiveness, I found myself with a loss of identity. With my identity gone I had vanished into a world of negative energy. I had attached my entire self to something that was objectified, something that couldn't last.

In my new reality I had transformed into a nucleus of negative energy.

Despite the fun I was having with Mr. Salsa, I felt pangs of being broken and dreamless. I was lost and trying to find a place to bury my negativity.

I struggled because the only place I knew to go for clarity was a dance studio. Before my accident, I would dance out my frustration, my confusion, my happiness, my excitement. I would dance my every emotion. Dance was what I knew, but *that* freedom of expression had evaporated with my decision to jump on a horse.

The few times I managed to sneak into a dance studio, and stumble around the room, became time spent in anger toward my ankle instead of the dance for clarity. Because I couldn't move like I wanted to in a formal dance studio, I repeatedly rehearsed the curse of my loss and I eventually quit exposing myself to the instantaneous tears. But, the constant anger toward the two women who were with me in the field on that fateful day remained prevalent for years. I didn't know the definition of forgiveness nor could I seem to find anything that resembled it.

I made up every reason I could muster in order to place the blame on *them*. Sadly, it would take me years to realize *I* own my decisions, nobody else, and I must therefore own the results – both positive and negative – of those decisions.

Over time I would learn I couldn't bury it – the "it" being my injury that changed my life's direction. I had to accept "it", I had to own "it", I had to make "it" a part of me and then find an avenue to turn "it" into a positive in my life. I would eventually have to learn to quit placing the blame for *my* actions on anyone but who was really responsible – the responsibility lies with me. Accepting responsibility was step number one. Step number two: learning to forgive *myself*.

To begin my healing, I more or less began dating myself. I needed to discover who I was at the core. How could I forgive myself if I didn't know who I was?

I got involved in my church by becoming a singer with the praise band, something I had always (secretly) wanted to do. I sought out counseling. I began to exercise. I began to paint. I adopted a kitten from a homeless shelter. I auditioned for shows. I was even cast in a few musicals. Yes, I sang, danced, and acted professionally *again*. I applied for jobs. I even volunteered to work for companies in industries I was interested in exploring for a career.

By dating myself I started to more clearly define *who I was*, what life meant to me, what I wanted out of life, and the kind of people with whom I wanted to spend my limited time on earth. I knew better than anyone that life could change in an instant.

I began to compose my own definitions of love and forgiveness.

And yes, I eventually wrote those definitions on paper. As much as I would like to share them with you, I won't. You must write your own definitions. I cannot give you a guideline because if I do then it is not authentically yours. But remember, first you must know yourself and love yourself. If you don't know who *you* are, it's time to go on a date.

"A relationship should be between two people and not the world."
–unknown

Two and a half years later I married the mysterious Mr. Salsa. But our marriage, at least for this book, is not for publishing. It is *our* beautiful story. God gave us each other so we may face the world *together*, and through our intimate relationship we have developed the appropriate armor to take on the world.

Scene Fifty-Five

A girl conveying a message

"The two most powerful warriors are patience and time." –Leo Tolstoy

Life marched forward as did the progression in my pain. Yes, I had many nights of tossing and turning, combating my inability to sleep with armed forces of ibuprofen and tears. The restless nights caused days of pure exhaustion and at times the cycle felt like it would never end.

But, I did get better.

Slowly I moved from days with pain levels bouncing around eight to ten, to days with levels around six to eight, to days of four to six, and on rare occasions I would get through a whole day with pain levels bouncing around the twos and threes. I could have counted, on one hand, the days my pain gave me the glory of a level one.

Eventually my pain tolerance had trained my brain to accept levels from one to three as completely "normal", which translated to pain-free statements of "I'm great!"

My best shield was a good night's sleep, my antidepressant, and making jokes about my situation. Not jokes out of spite, but laughter to help me cope and move forward with life. In the midst of it all, my husband has never left my side. He has spent hours rubbing my ankle, and leg, and hip, and back, and neck as the pain progressed up my body.

As you can imagine, I began losing functionality in not only my ankle, but throughout other areas of my body. While my pain was once all about my ankle, the pain was taking over my whole self.

My doctors – yes, plural – all encouraged me to keep my weight down and muscles strong, "The less weight you have on your joint the less it will hurt and the further down the road you will get." One doctor even told me, "Hang on as long as you can." This was the first doctor that gave me hope there might be an alternative to a fusion or an amputation. I learned to compensate to the best of my ability, but I never compromised my faith.

I slowly found joy in my "who" versus "what" I was. Yes, I tried out a few different careers and I found greatness in each of them, but I found my true joy when I had the opportunities to help others realize their own dreams. I was also gaining a better perspective of life from my new vantage point.

I knew I had the Almighty on my side. I turned to God for direction and He continued to open new doors of opportunities for both my emotional and physical health. On the days my pain levels spiked, and I wanted to have an anxiety attack based around the phrase "I can't do this for the rest of my life", I reminded myself I only had to survive the next hour. When I survived the hour I focused on the next hour and then the next hour and the next.

My mom often reminded me I only had to get through the day, and with a new day brings new hope. With exhausting effort, I steered myself away from my "wits' end" and focused on surviving the present. If I looked too far into the future it was overwhelming.

I learned to appreciate the smaller things in life: like stepping off a curb; biking with no pain; swimming for therapy; never having to run another mile in my life! But I had to know the difference in order to gain the appreciation.

While I would never have the joint that allowed me to practice the beautiful art of ballet, I was grateful for the years I did get to practice it. In fact, I was grateful for the levels of dancing expertise I reached, which I never dreamt I would have in the first place. I wasn't ready for it to come to an end, but it did. Strangely, I was left surrounded with blessings as a result of my love for dance.

Through my accident I opened myself to new experiences, new cities, and new people. My love for dance also brought me to the ultimate dance floor where I met my husband. Mr. Salsa introduced me to a whole new world of dance. A world that was less a performance and more about enjoying the freedom of dance and embracing the fun it brought. It wasn't about a job, it was about enjoying life.

Over the course of our first year dancing together, he broke me of choreographed routines. He re-trained me to leave my "training" behind. I had to learn to move *with* the music and to allow the music to direct *my* movement. In many ways you could compare the lessons to life. Have you ever heard the Woody Allen quote "If you want to make God laugh, tell him your plans."? Breaking me of "choreography" was teaching me to live my life rather than direct it.

When I married Mr. Salsa, our first dance as husband and wife was a dancing masterpiece. Our guests wanted to know how many weeks we had been rehearsing it. The truth was, it was the first time I had even heard the music as my husband selected the piece as a wedding gift to me. We danced with our hearts *not choreography*. A dance from the heart is not something that can be choreographed and rehearsed.

When I combined my obsession of dance with a joint that was bone-on-bone, and with my enthusiasm to learn partner dancing, I had to find a new way to compensate for pain in order to enjoy my new sport. First I tried wrapping my ankle in athletic tape and when that didn't make a difference I switched to ace bandages. Eventually I left it all behind except for my compression stockings. The stockings kept my swelling to a minimum, but not my pain.

The one thing that bothered me most was superficial, still it bothered me nevertheless. I hated the fact I was always in flat shoes and the serious dancers were in the sexiest pair of heels they could afford. Perhaps this chewed at my confidence because of that shallow boyfriend's words "It's sad you can't wear heels. That's a woman's sex appeal." I knew it was a stupid comment and I didn't agree with it, but it ate at me.

I reasoned with myself I could at least give the "sexy" shoes a try. I couldn't have damaged my ankle any more than I already had. So one evening before a class, I slipped a pair of heels on my feet and walked out onto the floor.

I remember feeling the muscles in my calves flex as energy shot up my hamstrings and into my hinny. I looked at myself in the mirror to study my feet (but ignored the bulge on my ankle). All my energy was focused on the extra two inches made out of wood. How could something so small, and so superficial, make me feel so much more confident? For the first time I truly realized why there was so much controversy over the 1994 Miss America contestants walking the stage barefoot versus in stilettos.

I remember feeling beautiful as I studied my feet and tenderly salsa-ed from side-to-side, swaying my hips with more movement than I had in years. I turned in a few circles and smiled. I felt tall and gorgeous, which meant I stood more erect and naturally stuck my chest out like a confident woman.

It was that night I discovered a heel allowed me more mileage out of my ankle, and more confidence for my psyche. A heel opened my joint space, which meant I wasn't grinding my bones together. My pain levels decreased simply because of the two inches. It was a welcomed relief and a beautiful surprise. With my discovery I instantly switched from flat shoes to heels *permanently*. I even put heel-lifts in my tennis shoes and mountain biked with the two inch lifts. It seemed crazy, but what would have been crazier would have been ignoring the discovery of pain relief (not 100% relief, but relief nonetheless).

I slowly got rid of all my flats, donating them to *Goodwill*.

Scene Fifty-Six

Back at the country club, August 2009
(Two years *after* the accident)

"Hope changes everything" *–unknown*

I needed fresh air and a break from my stale office. I pushed my chair back from my desk, stood, and picked up my phone, sliding it into my back pocket. I walked past Jessica and out into the main area of the clubhouse. It was late morning and I knew there would be several golf members on the driving range - a great excuse to mingle and still be "doing my job".

I walked in the direction of the pro-shop, saying hello to members as I passed. When I opened the doors to the shop I walked straight to the golf clubs on display. I selected one of the drivers, not asking permission to borrow it, before I walked out the back door, club in hand, and collected a bucket of balls.

I slowly walked the curvy sidewalk in the direction of the driving range, soaking in the warm sunshine and fresh Colorado air. It was apparent that everyone was basking in the sunshine *and* their coveted sport of golf. There was a glorious silence that was only broken by the sporty metronome of sound as the metal connected with the rubber and plastic in the balls.

I stepped into a vacant spot and set my bucket off to the side. I selected a single ball from the top and placed it on the stationary tee; I stood horizontal and took my stance. I focused on the placement of my hands, trying to mimic what the club's golf-pro had taught me. After a couple practice swings I smacked my first ball one hundred yards. I smiled and looked around to see if anyone noticed. I was sadly disappointed.

As I placed my second ball on the tee, I wiggled my bum into its proper position. I took a harder swing at the ball and it sloppily bounced along the ground not going very far, nor in the direction I wanted. When I relaxed and hit the ball peacefully it flew beautifully, but when I tried to hit the ball like an angry athlete it would detour to the left, skipping across the ground, confirming my amateur status.

I worked my way through my bucket before I turned and saw one of the members waiting to talk to me.

"It's Dan, right?"

"Yes," he confirmed as he reached out his hand to shake mine.

"I'm Adrienne," I said. "The Membership Director."

"Yes, I know," he said smiling. "But I appreciate the reminder."

"Are you just finishing or are you headed out?" I asked referring to his eighteen holes he played on a regular basis.

"Just finishing."

"Well?" I raised my eyebrows and my voice. "How was it?"

"Pretty good."

"What can I help you with?" I asked, slightly confused why he was initiating the conversation.

"Well," he said, and I could feel his hesitation. "I don't know if you know this, but a few years ago I thought I had lost my ability to enjoy a round of golf," he said calmly as he looked out over the acres of rolling green.

"Seriously?" I asked, surprised as Dan was one of the regulars, even if only for a few holes in the evening. "Why is that?"

"I could hardly walk," he said simply.

"That's hard to imagine," I said as I stood shoulder to shoulder with him looking in the same direction as he.

"Thanks," he said with a singular laugh.

"What happened?" I inquired.

"A doctor botched a surgery and practically destroyed my foot. It was really sad because I went from being completely active to being practically immobile." He took a deep breath, "I spent years in pain."–

"But I can't tell there is anything wrong with you," I interjected.

"Exactly," he said. "I found a different doctor." He glanced at me, "A stem cell doctor."

"Okay," I said. "What does that mean?"

"The stem cell doctor took bone marrow from my hip, extracted the stem cells, and grew those stem cells in a Petri dish. When the cells multiplied into millions he re-injected the cells into my joints. The stem cells more-or-less knew what to do to fix my problem. After a handful of treatments… well, I'm a walking example of the new technology called stem cell therapy."

"Where is this doctor?" I asked.

"Broomfield," he said referring to a community a mere forty miles away. "You know, when I first heard about it I thought it would be a long shot, but I had nothing to lose," he continued, "I used to struggle walking to the mailbox and now I can walk eighteen holes on a golf course."

I stood silently.

"I've noticed your limp," he said gently. "Do you mind me asking what your story is?"

There on the driving range I conveyed my horse story to a golf fanatic. A fanatic that understood the pain I endured on a regular basis. At the end of my story, he handed me a business card with the doctor's contact information.

"At least go for a consultation," he encouraged. "What do you have to lose?"

He turned to walk away and almost immediately tears moistened my cheeks, but I wasn't sad. I felt joyful and hopeful. My emotions went into overload. It was the first time I had a sense of "hope" for my future and a sense of "hope" that I could once again know life without pain.

When I got back to my office I closed my door and called my mom. When she answered I became so hysterically overwhelmed I couldn't speak and she immediately thought something was wrong by my crying and gasping for air.

"Adrienne. *Breathe*," she calmly encouraged. "What's wrong?"

When I finally calmed myself, I started laughing, which really confused her.

"Adrienne?"

"Mom," I hiccupped, "I may have found the solution for my ankle."

I regurgitated the conversation I had with Dan and she understood my tears. I knew she understood because I could feel her hopefulness reflect my own, even through the phone.

Scene Fifty-Seven

A stem cell doctor's office, a girl and her parents, August 2009
(Two years *after* the accident)

"But as for me, I will always have hope." –Psalms 71:14

We sat silently in the waiting room: my mom on my left, my dad on my right. We were each hopeful, but kept quiet as we didn't want to "get the cart before the horse".

"Adrienne?" the nurse announced and the three of us stood. I glanced at my parents and they gestured for me to take the lead. We followed the nurse to the exam room, making small talk as we walked. I noticed the walls of signed photographs, patients thanking the doctors for their health.

When we arrived in the room the nurse took my vitals and asked all the same questions I had just filled out on the reams of paperwork in the lobby. I did my best to repeat my story verbally, including every detail I could recall.

After twenty minutes of listening to me ramble, she stood and went to retrieve the doctor.

When the doctor entered the room, we made introductions. Again, I was asked to repeat my narrative for the third time. While I talked, the doctor sat on a stool in front of me. My feet were dangling off the end of the patient table. He glanced from my ankle to my eyes to my ankle.

He reached out to grab my foot and pull my ankle upward for a closer look. He ran his hands across my graft and studied my ankle from all angles.

"You have quite the story," he said. "And you're lucky to have this foot."

"So I've been told," I commented. "More importantly though, can you help me?"

"Maybe," he paused. "You had a very severe injury. Yes, it's possible to help you, but I can't promise anything."

"Let's talk about options," I encouraged. "Dan told me about your clinic and gave me an overview of stem cell therapy, but I would like to hear it from you."

"Yes, Dan called to tell us about you," the doctor smiled. "An explanation of the process sounds like a good place to start. As a-matter-of-fact, we have a few different options we can try. Let's talk about stem cell therapy first."

"Okay," I responded.

"Our stem cell procedures," he began, "are treatment options for people with arthritis, which you obviously have. Stem cells are in all of us and they are the cells that generate healing for injured bone, ligaments, tendons, and tissues. In your case, we would be taking stem cells from the bone marrow in your hip and re-injecting those cells into your ankle. The marrow is rich in Mesenchymal stem cells; those cells are responsible for healing damaged tissues."

"What happens when you put them in my ankle?" I asked.

"They do what they are designed to, generate healing. Your body knows what it needs and your stem cells are a key component, we are just helping the process along."

"Okay," I said, giving him permission to continue.

"When we precisely deliver a high concentration of stem cells into an injured area, or your ankle, we are giving your body the natural ability to heal itself."

"That makes sense," I commented. "How do you get the cells from my hip to my ankle?"

"We will do a bone marrow draw from both of your hips, using a needle. We will also draw blood from a vein in your arm. Then we isolate the stems cells from the marrow. We also isolate the platelets from the blood sample. Next, we place the components in a Petri dish and allow them to multiply. Once they are finished growing we re-inject them into your ankle using a needle."

"How many injections?"

"Well, it depends on you really. Since you are so young, I would anticipate we will get five or six re-injections from one bone marrow draw."

"Do you inject everything all at once?" I asked.

"No. We hold the stem cells in storage and space it out."

"Downtime?"

"Very little, if any."

I looked at my parents, shrugged my shoulders, and said with raised eyebrows, "Why not?"

I redirected my focus at the doctor and said, "How soon can we get started?"

"Do not mock a pain that you haven't endured." -@thecompanyinspire

------

A bone marrow draw is extremely painful: yes, my doctor numbed the areas where he performed the draw, but I quickly learned I would have rather been fully sedated. My doctor used a needle, with the girth of a ballpoint pen, to extract my bone marrow. While that may not sound big, that was the size of the needle he *man-handled* into the inner depths of my bone. Six different times. In six different places. On the end of the needle was a handle, and he had to manually grind the needle back-and-forth to push the needle through my skin and down into the bone. Once the needle was in place he removed the handle and maneuvered a smaller needle through a larger one. The small needle is what extracted my actual bone marrow.

After three of the draws my doctor had to take a short break and catch his breath. I remember looking over my shoulder and seeing beads of sweat pouring down his temples. He was sweating because it was hard work to drive a needle the size of a pen into the hip of a patient. To better demonstrate the amount of force my doctor had to apply, I encourage you to purchase a piece of wood (walnut would be best) and try to drive a ballpoint pen into the wood. It's not easy.

So, I lay on the table grinding my teeth and squeezing my stress ball so hard its contents threatened to break through the skin. From that session my doctor was able to grow my stem cells to the multi-millions, giving me enough stem cells for five re-injections. But, after injection number three the government stripped me of my rights to access my stem cells in storage. Yes, let me say that again, the U.S. government decided I could no longer access the rest of my stem cells which were being held in storage. I don't recall the exact legislation that was passed, but to this day I'm baffled that *my* government thinks they have the right to tell me whether or not I have access to my own body purely because I had pieces of my body in storage. It's simply not right.

Sometime between my injury and the stem cell doctor, I had received an inheritance check thanks to my late grandmother (the one with the pool). It was an unexpected inheritance, but the timing was perfect.

I decided to commit the entire inheritance to treatment alternatives in hopes I would find a solution for my destroyed ankle. I chose several different forms of treatments. In fact, I received the following therapies: Prolotherapy injections, PRP (Platlet Rich Plasma) injections, intramuscular stimulation (AKA: IMS or dry needling), and stem cell injections.

Some of the treatments worked and some didn't. I loved the Prolotherapy and PRP, but hated the intramuscular stimulation (IMS). IMS was a torture session as I lay on the table and cried while they applied the therapy. But the Prolotherapy and PRP did give me days, sometimes weeks of pain relief. In fact, the PRP allowed me to get back on stage and dance once again professionally.

All the treatments were trial and error. My doctor always made sure I understood they may or may not work, before we started *any* treatments. I understood I was in a unique situation due to the severity of my injury. I had surrendered to the idea it was going to take a unique treatment to fix the mess I had created.

God gave me a brain and I was using it. When I elected stem cell therapy I believed, and still do, I was making an educated decision. Thankfully I had the freedom to direct my own healthcare. I had done my research, just as every patient should.

But there is a lot of controversy surrounding stem cell treatments, and the controversy varies. As I became acquaintances, and friends, with several orthopedic surgeons, I received an insider's understanding about the controversy. Most surgeons were frustrated because stem cell therapy was considered "experimental", which meant there wasn't enough scientific data to prove it worked. The lack of data complicated things further as the therapy wasn't backed by the insurance companies. This brought forth the argument that patients were being scammed out of their money. While I respected the objections and opinions, I disagreed with them.

I understood it took people like me, in a unique situation and with an open mind, to trust science. I also understood medicine was a *practice*.

The only way to advance science was to have volunteers such as myself. Doctors don't work for free (nor should they) so I had to foot the bill. I was fortunate to have come into some money, which allowed me the opportunity to pay for my treatments.

Sadly, the stem cell injections did not work for me. Nevertheless, I do believe we will see stem cell therapy as a go-to option in our lifetimes. Once the data proves its value, I anticipate the insurance companies will include it in their coverage. At least that is how I used to feel. Given the new conditions of our healthcare system and the unaffordable Affordable Care Act (ACA), well, I'm not so sure what will happen anymore. While stem cell therapy may prove to be a reliable alternative to surgery, we may have to fly to other countries to receive the treatment. Furthermore, my distrust in the ACA has come from dozens of doctors who have explained that in 2007, if we would have had universal healthcare, it would have been cheaper to amputate my foot than to try and save it.

I may sound rather opinionated, or even negative, but I have the right to be. When I laid on the surgical table, wondering if I would wake up with a foot and then years later, face down, for my bone marrow draw, I earned that right to my opinion.

In the end, I walked away from all the therapies. I had blown through my inheritance and I couldn't maintain the $500-a-pop PHP injections. My alternative treatment option was to dig down into my "grit", suck it up, and learn to block the pain from my mind.

I was sad the stem cell therapy wasn't my miraculous answer, but I was accepting of it. Dan was, *and is*, a walking example of the proof it works. That was all the proof I needed. My case was extreme and I had to accept the facts.

I don't do anything normal, or on a small scale, the break of my ankle was a perfect example.

Scene Fifty-Eight

A girl conveying her story

"Dig the well before you are thirsty." – Chinese proverb

Twice a year I would find new orthopedic surgeons, schedule a consultation, and then ask them how they would proceed with my situation. Most were baffled I had a foot and the standard response was "fusion".

Over time I grew a deeper acceptance for my situation, but I also knew there was still an answer to be found. I kept searching. If one day I did decide to amputate, I held on to the thought *at least I'll be able to run again.*

Finally, in 2011 I found an orthopedic surgeon that knew how to think outside the box. He was the first doctor who presented the option of an ankle replacement. But he was nervous to tell me about it because he wasn't exactly willing to perform the surgery.

"You are a little young, even for our youngest patients," he had said.

"What do you consider 'young' in terms of an ankle replacement?" I asked.

"Fifty-five," he said simply. "Most ankle replacement candidates are at least in their late sixties if not into their seventies."

It wasn't exactly the answer I was looking for, it was *more.* For the first time a doctor had offered a solution other than a fusion or an amputation. While that doctor gave me restored hope, he wasn't the right surgeon for me. He was having a hard time wrapping his own mind around the idea of performing a joint replacement surgery on someone as young as myself. I got the impression that before our meeting he had never considered it nor really thought about it.

I needed a surgeon with more confidence, so I kept researching my options and I kept looking for the right doctor. My new goal was to find someone who was willing to consider my age *and* situation; meanwhile, think outside the box. I knew that surgeon was out there, I just had to find him or her.

In the interim, my job was to learn all I could as it pertained to ankle replacements. With a little effort, I found a front row seat to the action. In 2012, I landed a job as the Marketing Director for a prestigious orthopedic group. My new role gave me immediate access to doctors, research, device reps, and answers to any questions I wanted to ask.

As the Marketing Director, I set up community lectures and wrote news publications featuring the latest technologies for ankle injuries, including ankle replacements. I even interviewed ankle replacement patients under the pretext of writing patient testimonials/success stories. While this may sound selfish, I knew I wasn't the only ankle patient looking for answers. I was a patient helping other patients in their quest for information and navigation of the complexity of the medical industry.

Being a patient searching for answers made me a better medical marketing professional on all fronts. I understood the patient. I understood their fears. Sadly, I understood their tears as I sat next to them, silently, outside the surgery scheduling office, handing them tissues to dry their tears and calm their fears.

But of everything I had access to, it was the device reps who were the most informative. I could ask any question my heart desired. Since they never considered me, at my age, a candidate for the technology they were selling, they talked openly about the pros and cons of the surgery. In fact, they talked openly about *every* nitty-gritty detail I inquired about, both positive and negative.

I dug into my research and the months turned into years. As my ankle function continued to regress, I became more and more obsessed with the positive outcomes surrounding an ankle replacement device known as the *INBONE*.

Without question, when its time you will know.

Despite my pain, I still loved spending evenings outside: be it with my guitar or a walk around the block in a pair of heels (at this point I had regressed so severely I couldn't even stand with my foot at a ninety degree angle). I originally picked up a guitar because of my injury. In 2007, I had smarted-off by saying "if my feet can't dance then my hands will!" I was serious. I had tried to learn the piano and I did (but I'm not very good). I switched to the guitar because I could take it anywhere, including outside. My husband is a fantastic guitar player which means we enjoy music together, be it outside around a fire pit or up in the mountains after a day of mountain biking.

Sadly my evening walks were getting more and more painful and shorter in length. Eventually just walking to the end of the block, maybe a quarter of a mile, I did with a limp. If I hadn't taken ibuprofen before the walk I took it after and immediately elevated my foot while the relief tried to kick into gear.

During my painful downhill journey, there were three particular events that stood out, answering the question "How do I know when it is time (for surgery)?"

Event number one was when I ended up in a baby stroller, with the baby on my lap.

One evening, while my husband and I were babysitting our grandson, we had decided to go for a walk, hoping to exhaust some of the two-year-old's energy. As we reached the halfway point, I simply could not go any further. The two-year-old was fine, but I was not. My pain levels had suddenly escalated to an intensity I couldn't communicate. When I put weight on my joint my entire body wanted to collapse to the ground. My ankle was screaming "no more".

Seeing not only the pain in my furrowed brow, but the over-extenuated limp, my husband offered to carry me. I looked at him with raised eyebrows. As I glanced from him to the baby to the stroller, I knew it wasn't realistic for him to carry me and push the stroller, so I did the only sensible thing I could think of... I sat down in the stroller, letting my husband push me home. The comedic relief came when the two-year-old wanted to ride with me because "grandma" was riding in style.

Event number two came when I offered to host my girlfriend's birthday dinner. The dinner party included: me, my husband, my girlfriend, and her husband.

It took me three days to do the grocery shopping, set the table, and cook dinner. Then it took me three days to do the dishes. It didn't take me six days because our little dinner party was *that* elaborate, it took me six days because I could only spend so much time on my ankle at any given point. I had to space things out or I simply could not do it.

My dinner party prep, and break down, went a little something like this...

Day 1: set the table

Day 2: grocery shopping. It is important to note I timed myself in the grocery store. I had to preserve enough energy to get home, unload the bags, and put the groceries away. Please also note I was always conscious of using the grocery cart as a crutch, it allowed me to get more out of my ankle on days I had to go to the store.

Day 3: cook & enjoy our celebration

Day 4: load the dishwasher

Day 5: clean the kitchen

Day 6: put the dishes away

You may be wondering why my husband didn't help. I wouldn't let him. It was *my* friend and *my* gift to her was a dinner party. I wanted to do it. One of my expressions of love is feeding people, and if Mr. Salsa did all the work then I felt like I was cheated out of expressing my love.

Am I stubborn? *Duh.* Do I really need to answer that question?

Incidentally it was event number three that was the game changer.

In the fall of 2013 I had been at work all day, mostly sitting on my rump, so I was in no way pushing the limits of my ankle. After work I had a Rotary networking event to attend. I walked straight into the event and immediately sat down, doing my mingling from a chair. In fact, I sat for over an hour. My ankle was achy, but nothing out of the ordinary.

It was when I stood to leave, I knew something was very wrong. My pain levels were exceptionally high. I dismissed it as *a weather front must be moving over the mountains.* But it felt bigger than a weather front.

I limped to my car and drove fifteen miles home. At dusk I pulled into the driveway. Exhausted from my day and concerned about the pain that was continuing to grow, I was anxious to get inside, change into sweats, plant myself in front of the television, and elevate my foot (with of course, an ice pack wrapped around my limb).

I opened the door to my car and planted my feet on the ground. I stood and then I collapsed to the concrete. My ankle had simply given out. My body had said "enough is enough".

As I lay on the cool cement driveway, I cried as I stared up at the sky that was turning black. The first stars were beginning to come out to say "hello".

I felt pathetic lying in the driveway so I pushed myself up to all fours and slammed the door to my car with my left hand. I proceeded to crawl my way toward the house and up the flight of stairs to our main level. I pushed myself up to my knees to unlock the front door. I crawled inside.

The house was dark. My husband was still at work and I didn't want to call him and describe my situation. I felt pathetic *and scared*. I needed to mourn. I needed to come to terms with "it is time". Time for an ankle replacement or a fusion or God forbid an amputation. Once inside I crawled through the living room and up another short flight of stairs to our kitchen where I laid on the hardwood floor sobbing for an hour.

About the time I had exhausted myself from hysteria, my husband came home to find me. He said nothing. He knew. Silently he lay down on the hardwood floor next to me, held my hand and whispered, "We are in this together."

We laid quietly on the floor, both of us coming to terms that it was indeed *time*.

I knew I could no longer put off the inevitable medical decision. I wasn't sure which medical decision I would ultimately make, and with which doctor, but I knew it was time.

Scene Fifty-Nine

Another orthopedic doctor's office, September 2013
(Six years and one month *after* the accident)

"If there is hope for the future there is power in the present."
– John Maxwell

I walked down the hall. A limp in my step. My husband held my hand while my parents followed behind us.

I was meeting with a new orthopedic surgeon. My older brother, Eric, had heard about this doctor and he begged me to go see him for a consultation before I made my surgical decision. The only thing at stake was a co-pay so I made an appointment.

I had lost track of the number of orthopedists I consulted with, but they were all the same – slightly cocky (some very), afraid of my age, and not willing to consider anything but the "golden standard" of a fusion. Even with my pain, and the facts staring me in the face, a fusion was an unacceptable answer to me. In laymen's terms, a fusion meant a doctor would join my foot to my leg (at the ankle joint) and make it one continuous bone. He/she would screw long screws in an "X" shape through the center of my joint. It would eliminate my pain, but since an ankle joint is designed to help distribute your weight when you walk, my weight distribution would then be pushed down into the joints in my foot. The joints throughout your foot are not designed to take the weight of your whole body, which meant I would wear through my healthy joints in my foot at a faster rate. Eventually I would have to fuse the joints throughout my foot due to pain. A fusion in a seventy-year-old doesn't raise the same concerns. My decision was complicated because of my young age and my projected life-span.

Each doctor listened to my story, looked at my x-rays, confirmed my age, and either offered the fusion or referred me to a different orthopedic specialist. No one wanted to touch me. Why would they? I was a tough case. I was a possible malpractice lawsuit waiting to happen. I would challenge their skill, and for a seasoned orthopedist he/she didn't need to invite that kind of risk into their practice.

But still, I was looking for a doctor who was willing to think outside the box. And true to Adrienne fashion, I refused to give up. My heart told me there was another option. I was on the hunt to find it.

The medical assistant showed us into a small exam room. I took my designated place on the exam table – the paper crinkling under my weight as I adjusted myself on the table. My husband leaned his bum on the table next to me while my mom and dad sat in the two empty chairs. No one touched the doctor's stool that was stationed under the wall-mounted computer screen.

The assistant quizzed me about my injury. I gave her the *CliffsNotes* version. "I was thrown from a horse and when I hit the ground my foot went one way and I went the other. I had a compound fracture in a horse pasture. Six inches of bone exposed. The doctor removed a cup of dirt, gravel, and manure from my leg before he reattached my foot. He could have amputated, but he didn't. I developed a huge wound and two months later I received my free flap." The assistant stopped typing and looked over at me and then down at my ankle.

"May I see your ankle?" she asked, clearly out of curiosity.

"Sure," I said with a smile and untied my shoe and dropped it to the ground. I pulled my compression stocking off and proudly displayed my badge of honor.

She came closer to see my free flap. She didn't say anything, but I could tell it was the first time for her to see something quite like it.

"Let's keep going," she said and then turned back to her computer and continued to type what I dictated.

"I did okay for a couple of years," I said. "My plate broke around the one-year mark, which means my fibula is non-union. Around the two-year mark I discovered pain relief when wearing high heels. The heel opened my joint space and I wasn't rubbing bone-on-bone, but now I can't get my ankle back to a ninety degree angle. I've been this way for almost three years. Basically I've been walking in heels since 2009. My Achilles has shrunk and I have bone spurs in my foot, which the doctor will see on my x-rays." I paused and she looked at me, "I'm the only woman you will meet with one cankle," I said, referring to my ankle that was the same size as my calf. "Those usually come in pairs!"

I offered her a sarcastic smile as I extended my legs, showing off my two ankles. One ankle normal in size and the other triple. "I vacuum, mow, and bike with two inch heel lifts in my shoes."

"Seriously?" she asked as she looked from me to my husband.

"Every man's dream," my husband laughed.

"Well, I used to. I can't really do anything lately," I said. "Oh," I interrupted my own thought process, "and I brought all my x-rays, MRIs, and CT scans along with my medical records." I glanced at the thick stack of files sitting next to me.

"Ok," she said. "The doctor will be in shortly."

She stood and scooted out of the room.

"I think I overwhelmed her," I said with a laugh.

"You're overwhelming without the ankle story," my husband joked and my parents agreed.

The four of us changed the subject from ankles to weekend plans. It wasn't as though we needed a distraction from the reason we were there. We had just exhausted the subject - beaten that dead horse. My ankle catastrophe was a part of us all. We each knew the story, we knew the options, and we had years to discuss the circumstances. In the time we waited for the doctor we talked about the positive, fun, and exciting things life had to offer. We chatted and laughed for at least ten minutes before the doctor joined us in our overcrowded tiny room.

"Wow," Dr. Conklin said as he walked through the door, surprised at our little party.

"I'm Adrienne," I said and reached out my hand to shake his. "This is my husband and my parents Connie and George.

"Mark Conklin," he said, "It's very nice to meet everyone."

"If I hadn't brought everyone with me," I explained. "I would have to repeat everything you say, so I decided to save myself a step. No pun intended," I laughed.

"Fair enough," he said with a smile. "My assistant briefed me on your story, but I want to hear it from you."

(Soap box side note: to this day I don't understand why all the people who want/need the narrative don't all come in the room *at the same time*... it would be more efficient.)

"Okay," I said. I knew the drill. It was just another performance and I knew my script.

As I talked, Dr. Conklin moved his stool from under the computer to in front of me and sat down. He reached out for my foot and took my mangled body part in his hand, studying it from all angles, as I continued into the depth of my story. When I finished, he looked up at me and our eyes met.

"You aren't the first doctor I've met with," I said bluntly. "I'm here because I want to know what you think I should do. I can hardly function anymore. I collapsed last week because my ankle couldn't handle the weight of my own body. But the worst part," I took a deep breath, "I can't go for bike rides anymore without paying for it afterward. In both my ankle and my hip."

"Oh?" he encouraged.

"Biking is, or was, my outlet. I have been able to bike for years with no pain and I can't anymore. To add to the mess, it's really not just my ankle that hurts. I can't sleep at night because my right hip hurts so badly. I'm starting to have more consistent pain through my back and into my neck. I'm afraid my ankle is causing more joint problems in other areas of my body."

"That's probably true," Dr. Conklin said. "When you overcompensate for so many years it starts to have its effect on the rest of your body. As for your ankle, we have a few options." And he too explained the golden standard for someone my age was a fusion. "But," he said.

And 'but' was all I needed to strengthen my hope.

He went on to talk about ankle replacements as an option. He talked in a way that indicated *him* as the surgeon.

Finally. I thought thankfully.

I explained to him I was interested in the INBONE ankle replacement by Wright Medical. "I read about you before I came for this visit, and it is my understanding you implant several INBONE devices every year."

He confirmed the accuracy in my research. In fact, he confirmed he implants several each month.

"But that isn't the device I would recommend for someone your age," he said. I raised my eyebrows. "There is a new type on the market that is designed for younger, more active patients."

"What is young?" I asked.

"Forty-five."

"I don't have another fifteen years in me," I said, "not in my current condition."

He agreed and began explaining the components of the *newer* ankle replacement. He sent his assistant out into the hall to retrieve the device so I could hold it, touch it, and examine it in my hands.

"Who developed this technology?"

"Zimmer."

"How long has it been on the market," I asked. "I work for another orthopedic group, but I haven't heard about this device. I know we use Zimmer products but I haven't heard about the ankle replacement."

"Probably not," Dr. Conklin said. "Not many surgeons are offering it. To answer your question: it hasn't been on the market very long. Not quite a year," he watched my body language as he waited for my response.

I didn't know how to feel about the product's lack of longevity on the market. I wanted something with a high success rate, but the reality was anyone who actually had received the Zimmer implant was still within the first twelve months post-operative. Everyone, in medicine anyway, knows a joint replacement patient continues to feel improvements for an entire year. Not one person on the face of the planet had the Zimmer ankle implant for an entire year.

The assistant returned and handed me the device. It was very low profile and very light in weight. The components were made out of metal and plastic, the plastic acting as the cartilage. Almost immediately I craved for that plastic to be in my own ankle. I longed for that plastic to act as *my* missing cartilage.

"What happens if I wear through the plastic?" I asked.

"I replace it," Dr. Conklin said.

"Is that complicated?"

"It's designed to be replaced if/when you wear through it," he responded, and I felt it was a bit of a politically correct answer. Politically correct because I felt that while yes, it can be replaced, it 1) has never been done and 2) would be very difficult.

"Why this implant and not the INBONE?" I asked.

"The INBONE requires a lot of bone removal and if the replacement fails we may have to consider a bone graft to fill in the space. The Zimmer requires very little bone removal and it gives us room for options down the road. In fact, we may elect the INBONE down the road."

I stared at the device, turning it over in my hands. I admired the porous metal that would be in direct contact with my bone. The pores would allow my bone to grow into the metal, becoming a part of me. I knew it was a beautiful design, *but*, as in life, there was no guarantee.

I started to cry. I didn't want to be faced with a decision that wasn't going to truly heal me, only put a Band-Aid on my screw-up. I felt overwhelmed with the thought of losing a portion of my body. Even though my natural ankle had failed, it was still a part of me. It was specifically designed for me. God had given it to me. And I had destroyed His gift. I knew this doctor would remove what remained of my joint and replace it with a man-made object: an object that no matter how well it was manufactured, wouldn't last. It couldn't. God made our bodies to heal themselves; man cannot create what only God can. But I needed man's help and God's grace.

My husband reached out and placed his hand on my leg.

"I'm sorry," I said to the doctor. "It's just... I'm not supposed to have to make this kind of decision when I'm thirty years old."

There was a long silence in the room.

"I hate that damn horse," I muttered under my breath.

Everyone sat quietly as I gathered my composure to continue our conversation. I collected strength through my husband's touch. Silently I asked God to join our little party of five, the center of my universe inside those four walls.

I took a deep breath and told my tears to go away. "I understand this won't last forever," I said to everyone in the room. "I simply need a solution to get me from point A to point B."

I looked at Dr. Conklin, "If you can buy me ten years, I know there will be more options for me down the road. But I have another question for you," I said.

He raised his eyebrows, encouraging me to ask whatever was on my mind.

"How many of these implants have you installed?"

I could immediately sense his tension, although he was practiced at hiding it.

"You will be my first," he responded serious and unapologetic.

As his response bounced around in my head, my heart tried to jump out of my chest. I sat calmly on the table as I felt my blood pressure sky rocket. I consciously placed my anxiety in check even as I felt the tension in the room surge. I remember being grateful the air conditioner was so cold.

"Oh," was all I could muster. I knew in my head that you *never* elect to be a doctor's *first* on the operating table.

"I know an orthopedist in Salt Lake City and he has installed around twelve. I'm happy to connect you with him." Dr. Conklin offered. "No hard feelings from me. I want you to be comfortable with your decision no matter what it is or who it is with."

I let out a big sigh. I could feel both my parents' and husband's hearts racing right along with mine.

"The thought of flying back and forth to Salt Lake City for follow-up appointments sounds miserable. How many INBONE replacements have you installed?"

"Sometimes a couple a week," Dr. Conklin responded.

There was something about Dr. Conklin that put me at ease. I could feel his warmth and compassion. I could also feel his wisdom. I liked that he had a hip replacement and was willing to talk to me about the tough decision he felt when he had to surrender to his natural joint failing. I felt like he understood what it was that was so hard to put into words. I also got the distinct feeling I was a "person" to him and not just a case number.

"Well, I'm not going to make a decision today," I said.

"Nor should you," Dr. Conklin agreed. "As a matter of fact, I haven't told you I will operate."

I raised my eyebrows and he sat a little straighter on his round stool.

"A surgery like this on a young woman like yourself will classify us as cowboys, or reckless, and I don't run my practice that way."

"So where does that leave us?" I asked

"We both need to think about it."

I shook my head in agreement, "I like that."

"I have a meeting next week with a group of foot and ankle specialists from around Denver. I want to discuss your case with them. Let's both do some thinking and talk again in a couple of weeks." He paused and looked around the room. "Does anyone have any further questions for now?"

No one had questions so I began working my compression stocking back on my foot. I could put my "show and tell" away for the day.

Scene Sixty

"Whatever happens, do not lose hold of the two main ropes of life:
hope and faith." –unknown

Approximately six weeks after that initial appointment with Dr. Conklin, I did indeed receive a full ankle replacement by Dr. Conklin himself. On November 20, 2013, Dr. Conklin installed the Zimmer Trabecular Metal Total Ankle Replacement. My surgery lasted roughly four hours.

On that fateful day I lay under a spotlight or two or three, and was accompanied by a team of medical professionals from Zimmer, who assisted Dr. Conklin with the surgery. I had a team (AKA: an audience) for one of the biggest performances of my life.

I was so grateful to my medical team and my support group (who waited in the lobby, but never left my side). Everyone on my "team" has had a vision that matched my own: a vision that life is full of possibilities and if we don't push the limits then we will never break barriers.

"You can never cross the ocean until you have the courage to lose sight of the shore." –Christopher Columbus

------

I was told when my surgery was completed, and when I began to wake, I repeatedly told everyone how awesome and fantastic they each were. Considering many people wake-up from surgery upset and irrational, I was an unexpected comedic relief for my medical team.

I laughed when I heard the story. I was proud my positive attitude was so ingrained in me I carried it with me into the operating room and it bubbled over even when I was non-coherently high on drugs. There were times I thought that positive girl had died, but by God's grace she hadn't.

I guess the years of positivity began with my dad asking, "Are you going to have a good day or are you going to have a bad day?" For more than a decade I had started my day by looking at the girl in the mirror and *telling her* she was going to have an *awesome* day.

I had six years, with my bum ankle, to practice my stubbornness and persevering spirit. With prayer at my core, I had built my armor to get me through life's challenging moments, moments which had turned into days and days into months and months into years.

The morning of my surgery, I told *her* (that girl in the mirror) how great the day was going to be. I also received a text from my dad that read, "It's going to be a great day! You know how I know? Because Dr. Conklin called and said he slept at a *Holiday Inn Express* last night."

No one got the joke, but dad and me. We had to remind my husband and mom about the *Holiday Inn* commercial that guaranteed a kick-ass successful day if you slept at a *Holiday Inn Express*. While my dad and I rolled in laughter, my husband and mom rolled their eyes at our immaturity, or their lack of the same.

Challenges do not define us, challenges give us opportunities to define ourselves.

In the few years following my ankle replacement surgery, I have had people from around the world stumble upon my social media feeds. Seeing my success, they have reached across the Internet to ask me about my experience. I never realized how many people, let alone young people, were (and are) in the boat I knew all too well.

When they explain:

"I took my daughter camping two weeks ago and I haven't been able to walk since…. I'm 48 years old."

"I used to love going to the beach, but I can't walk in the sand, so instead I avoid it all cost… I'm 41."

"I loved to golf, but it hurts too bad for me to be on my feet… 38."

"I'm tired of living in pain. I don't sleep and I feel cranky all the time… 45."

"I used to be so active. Now I sit on the sidelines and watch as others have the fun… 39."

"I just want to be able to kick a soccer ball around with my five-year-old son… 42."

I understand. I understand what they are trying to explain, but have a hard time putting into words.

I understand there is an emotionally painful back-story that changed the course of their lives. I understand their anger. Their confusion. Their loneliness. Their grief. Their longing. I understand their pain as they sit on the sidelines watching others, unable to participate. I understand their frustration when their loved ones, while they want to be sympathetic, just don't get it. How could they?

Electing an ankle replacement is a sad place to be at the age of thirty. Electing a procedure that is not the "standard" for a young person, with injuries like ours, is flat-out overwhelming and terrifying.

This is what I communicate with people who are searching for answers: your head, your heart, and your joint must all align in order to move forward with big surgical decisions. It is only when all three align you will know the time is right, *and* be at peace with your decision.

But at some point you have to take the leap of faith. You have to listen with your head *and* your heart. You must lean on our Creator to show you the answers.

Will the answers be crystal clear? *Not always.*

Will it be difficult? *Yes.*

Will you be able to get through it? *Yes.*

Most important, please know this one thing: He will *never* leave your side.

I prayed. My family prayed. My friends prayed. We prayed and prayed and prayed for not just an answer, but a solution. I encourage you to do the same. It is only through prayer that you can honestly connect the head and the heart together in perfect harmony.

God gave me peace in knowing if the surgeries didn't work, I could always fuse… and I could always amputate. An amputation seems less scary when I pictured myself on a long run: something I knew I *could do* with an artificial limb but *could not do* with an artificial joint.

In all the conversations I have had with fellow "ankle" friends, the thing that amazes me the most is their fear of the recovery. Honestly, that is a fear I don't understand. If a patient truly spends years, *literally years*, in pain, then what is six months of recovery?

And a six month recovery is a stretch. At six months I was back on my mountain bike navigating the single track trails of Colorado's most beautiful mountains. At six months I was back at yoga. At six months I went scuba diving. At six months I was able to dance with my husband. At six months I was able to get through day*s without* pain.

Okay, so it took me a year before I could *comfortably* walk a white sandy beach. Okay, so it took me a year before I could go on two or three mile walks in the evenings with my husband. Okay, so it took me a year before I loaded a twenty pound pack on my back and went to Cambodia for fifteen days. Okay, so it took me a year before I climbed a thirty-foot rock wall (on the back of a cruise ship in the middle of the Caribbean). Okay, so it took me a year before I could balance on my ankle replacement during yoga.

If you truly need something, is the recovery really that big of a deal?

Did I have set backs? Yes. In fact, at three months post-op I was feeling so good I was doing *too* much. At one point I thought I had caused a hair-line fracture in my foot. The solution: I simply put my walking-boot back on for a week and the issue went away.

Did I get frustrated? Yes. I recall lying on a table during one of my physical therapy sessions and I couldn't hold back the tears. I didn't know anyone who had chosen what I had and I was scared for my future. I desperately wanted someone to talk to: someone who understood my anxieties and fears. But the only one who could help me was, you guessed it, my Lord and Savior. The awesome part: I could call on Him twenty-four hours a day, seven days a week. He always listened intently to my ramblings and freak outs… *and He loves me anyway.*

When I was faced with anxiety, I refocused my energy to the present. In the present moment I was fine. I *was* healing and I was walking heel to toe, in flat shoes, for the first time in *years.*

Yes, I got sick of talking about my ankle. I still do. But that is nothing compared to how much I got sick of *thinking* about my ankle. For six years my every action had been based on my ankle and the associated pain levels. Whether I had spoken my pains out loud, or internalized them, they were always there. Even in the middle of the night I would hold my bladder as long as possible because it hurt to limp to the toilet.

That pain has slowly slipped into my past. Now, *sometimes* I even forget which ankle had the injury! Not very often, mind you, but I do forget.

People still ask me excitedly, "Are you back at 100%?"

And I ask them, "100% based on what?"

My friends and acquaintances so desperately want to hear "Yes, I'm back at 100%". Am I 100% based on where I was before my injury? No, nor will I ever be. I have accepted that. I've also come to the realization I'm older now, and that mere fact will not let me be the same, physically, as I was when I was twenty-four.

Am I back to 100% based off any given time during the six years from my injury to my replacement? Yes, and that's a solid *yes*.

Do I wish to go back to 100% based off my pre-injury abilities? The answer is simple, and that answer is *no*.

My injury is a part of my story. But it is not, and will not, be the entire book of my life. Strangely, I'm grateful for that messy and tangled chaos I caused in 2007. That mess is a piece of me, and if I unravel it, then it changes who I am and the character I have developed.

In fact, I've had doctors offer to "re-sculpt" my ankle to look "normal", but I don't want normal. I'm proud of what I've been through. I'm proud of my scars. I have, after all, earned them. My "new" ankle is a physical testament to my mental toughness.

But let me be clear, my once mangled ankle (that has been replaced with metal and plastic) is a part of me, *but it does not define me*.

My experiences, all of them together, are what make me a stronger person from the inside out. Each experience has given me opportunities to build my strength physically *and* emotionally. I have become a better person because of the hardships I have endured. It is easy to be successful. It is difficult to rise out of the ashes and keep going when you think you can't.

I am perfectly complex. In fact, if I was a painting, I would have the prettiest and most vibrant array of colors.

Through my challenges I have found new passions. I have found new strengths. I see the world differently and the people of the world differently.

My hardship has given me the platform to grow into a more determined, multi-talented, and more powerful woman.

I have learned it is up to us, as individuals, to use life's hardships positively or negatively. Challenges do not define us, challenges give us opportunities to define ourselves.

Just like the chapters in this book don't make an entire book when they stand alone; neither do the individual chapters of your life make up your life's story. It takes *all* the chapters to tell your story.

I have learned God reveals His plan in phases. First, He is careful not to overload us with blessings, or, I believe, we won't suitably appreciate the blessings, but rather expect them. Second, the "phases" allow us the chance to revel in His gifts and properly express our gratitude for each of His individual blessings. When He reveals His blessings one at a time we have the opportunity to grow in deeper appreciation. Think of it like this… at Christmas, if you are showered in gifts, you feel obligated to pick the "best one" (even if only in your mind), and you focus on the "best" when there really shouldn't be a "best" or a "worst" when it comes to a *gift*. But if those gifts are spread out over the course of a year then you have time to adequately appreciate each gift in its own uniqueness; meanwhile developing a deeper appreciation and a greater sense of gratitude. The hard part of the lesson: we must experience negativity in our lives in order to truly appreciate the positive. If you don't know the difference, then there is no knowledge of gratitude. To put it in another way: to know success you must taste failure.

So I encourage you to accept each chapter of your life for what it has to offer. Learn from it and move on. Some chapters you will want to skip because of dullness while others will cause laughter and yet others will result in tears. A good book has many peaks and valleys. Just as a good book has a diverse landscape, so too does a thoroughly lived life.

So I challenge you: Learn to fail. Learn to get back up. Learn to accept tears. Learn to accept others. Learn to listen to the stories of the wise. Learn to find beauty in the face of despair.

Be confident. Be daring. Be adventurous. Be successful.

Be Known.

Put down your cell phone. Get off the computer. You can even put this book down now! Go for a walk. Be present. Be with the people who mean the most in your life.

Remember, your current situation can change more quickly than you can close this book, or jump on a horse.

Far From The End